NEW DIRECTIONS IN AMERICAN ART

Millennial Desire

and the Apocalyptic Vision
of Washington Allston

David Bjelajac

~

Smithsonian Institution Press   Washington, D.C.   London

Editor
Jeanne M. Sexton
Designer
Lisa Buck

Library of Congress Cataloging in Publication Data

Bjelajac, David.
Millennial desire and the apocalyptic vision of
Washington Allston

(New directions in American art)
Based on author's thesis—
University of North Carolina at Chapel Hill.
Bibliography: p.
Includes index.
1. Allston, Washington, 1779–1843.
Belshazzar's feast.
2. Symbolism in art—United States.
3. Belshazzar—Art.
4. Painting, American.
5. Painting, Modern—19th century—United States.
6. Apocalyptic art.
7. Allston, Washington, 1779–1843—Criticism
and interpretation.
I. Title
ND237.A4A64   1987   759.13   87-26619
ISBN 0-87474-264-1 (alk. paper)

∞ The paper in this book meets the guidelines
for permanence and durability of the
Committee on Production Guidelines for Book
Longevity of the Council on Library Resources

Cover
Washington Allston, *Belshazzar's Feast*, 1817–43,
oil on canvas, 12 ft. 1/8 in. by 16 ft. 1/8 in.
©1987 The Detroit Institute of Arts, Gift of
Allston Trust.

In memory of Ruth Bjelajac,
and for Edward T. Gargan

Contents

Preface

My intention to write a history of Washington Allston's *Belshazzar's Feast* inevitably led me beyond that single ill-fated canvas (pl. I). For more than a quarter century (1817–43), during nearly his entire career, following years of study in England and on the European continent, Allston labored and fretted over his most important history painting. When he wasn't actually working on it in his Boston, then Cambridgeport, studio, repeatedly making changes in the composition, it seemed that he was thinking about it, refusing further large commissions so that he could finally finish this one masterpiece.

Belshazzar's Feast was Allston's great masterpiece not in the sense that the picture is a qualitative, aesthetic triumph, because it clearly is not. The painting is a masterpiece in the sense that it was Allston's summation painting, the summation of a career and a lifetime. Within its framework, the artist wished to distill or summarize those religious, moral, and political values which guided not only his life, but also, ideally, the life of the nation for which he painted. In doing so, he addressed fundamental eschatological issues regarding the final judgment of mankind and the possibility of a future millennium.

If the painting is indeed a failure, it is not because the artist lost interest in the picture or that he was never temperamentally suited to the subject in the first place. It seems, instead, that Allston was too passionate about the work. He identified himself too closely to the life of the painting ever to let it out of his hands. He overloaded the picture with symbolism and layers of meaning. There is an iconographic richness to the painting which is belied by its academic appearance. *Belshazzar's Feast* is anything but impersonal, and, despite its indebtedness to the European grand tradition, it is also a profoundly American history painting.

In writing the book, I have utilized many of the biographical details of Allston's life, but the pages that follow do not constitute a biography. His private relationships with mother, father, and stepfather, the intimate details of his two marriages, and speculation as to his possible homosexuality, interesting as they may be as fields of inquiry, have not concerned me here.[1] Nor do I talk about Allston's less ambitious, though more beautiful, smaller paintings, his landscapes and isolated figures in various states of reverie.

That aspect of Allston's career which interests me the most is his role as America's leading history painter. As a history painter, Allston became an important public spokesman, representing the moral and sociopolitical values of a specific intellectual elite centered in New England. Despite, or because of, his legendary reclusiveness, Allston's stature as an artist-prophet grew yearly upon his return to America in 1818. During this period of moral activism and religious revivalism, the artist's Old Testament pictures of divine intervention imaginatively expressed the aspirations of the so-called New England clerisy.

By narrowing my research to *Belshazzar's Feast* and related biblical works, by focusing upon Allston's cultivated self-image as history painter and national prophet, I have attempted to write a cultural history which describes the struggle for identity and purpose in antebellum America. What follows is the history of a specific *mentalité,* apocalyptic in nature, and a certain set of symbols and images, derived largely from the Bible, which served to mediate reality for many nineteenth-century Americans, permitting the formation of a relatively coherent nationalist ideology. *Belshazzar's Feast* did not merely illustrate or mechanically reflect a preexisting nationalist faith. Rather, it was an integral expression of the culture's semiotic system, materializing "a particular cast of mind."[2] In addition, Allston's highly publicized labors upon this single project attained mythic proportions further contributing to its aura and the oracular nature of its message.

The book's introductory chapter examines the end of the artist's career with critics' reviews of the posthumously exhibited *Belshazzar's Feast* and eulogies upon the artist's stature and accomplishments. By starting at the end, I wish to establish at the outset the importance of the painting for a public whose primary concern was not necessarily aesthetic quality. Even those more schooled viewers, who severely criticized the painting's composition, inadvertently revealed the work's power to fascinate the many others, who felt a sense of self-recognition in the evidence of man's fallible nature.

Allston was seen as a kind of prophet, a Jeremiah, a Daniel, or even a Mosaic figure, attempting to lead the American people to the promised land of moral perfection. His struggle for aesthetic perfection in *Belshazzar's Feast* was a metaphor for striving toward perfection in Christ. Failure to unify and finish the masterpiece held an apocalyptic, suprapersonal meaning suggesting that all men have been "weighed in the balance, and found wanting." Yet as religious and art commentators pointed out, Allston's persistent striving upward toward harmony illuminated the path to a spiritual world beyond the dark, imperfect realm of earthly being.

In chapter two, I turn backward to examine traditional interpretations of Belshazzar's feast, the meaning of the story within the Book of Daniel, its relationship to other biblical texts and the manner in which the story was interpreted typologically throughout Christian history as a prefiguration of the Last Judgment and the millennium. Previous interpretations of the subject, both literary and visual, are considered to determine the historical horizon of meanings and assumptions which would confront Allston at his birth. That Allston's own interpretation of Belshazzar's feast differed significantly from paintings of the past, including that of his mentor Benjamin West, is adumbrated both here and in the introductory chapter.

In chapter three, the history of Allston's youth, I attempt to delineate the nature of his upbringing and education, or the process of acculturation which accounted for the artist's tendency to think in terms of biblical or apocalyptic metaphor. The outlines of Allston's childhood in South Carolina and Newport, Rhode Island, are scrutinized in terms of his special relationship to the birth of the new nation, and its foremost founding father, George Washington. I then show the extent to which post-revolutionary America and New England's Harvard College, where Allston attended school from 1796 until 1800, were captivated by the notion that America was a new Israel subject to the spirit of Old Testament law. I also discuss the conservative political views which Allston acquired while at Harvard, how he expressed them in his early attempts at poetry and art, and how they were reinforced when he made his first trip abroad to London, Paris, and Rome.

Chapter four describes Allston's growing importance within New England's intellectual and artistic elite, his informal affiliation with Boston's Anthology Society. The Anthology Society wished to harness American democracy through religion and art, countering the more radical implications of the nation's political revolution with a moral revolution which would establish the sovereignty of God (and, by implication, that of His clerical, artistic, and intellectual representatives) over and above the sovereignty of the people.

Chapter four concludes with the narrative of a turning point in Allston's life, his conversionary experience of 1815, in which he claimed that he had been spiritually born again in Christ. While this would seem to be a very private event, caused by a sense of personal guilt, I am not really interested in establishing a precise psychological cause. I am far more fascinated by Allston's resolution of the problem, which follows a pattern of Christian conversion with a long and venerated history in Puritan New England. The converted learns to sublimate his or her sense of personal guilt by attributing ultimate responsibility to the fall of Adam and the guilt of all mankind. This publicly proclaimed, suprapersonal sense of guilt not only freed Allston from a debilitating depression but gave him a genuine sense of divine mission to join the apocalyptic struggle, on the side of the crucified Christ, against the forces of Satan and the Antichrist.

Chapter five then describes how Allston's revivified Christianity led him to begin the painting of *Belshazzar's Feast* in 1817 during his last year of study in London. I demonstrate the popularity of the theme among English artists, poets, and writers, who used its imagery to prophesy and celebrate the fall of Napoleon Bonaparte and the collapse of French revolutionary ideals. I discuss various artistic sources for the work, how the large canvas differs from two early sketches, and what key changes Allston made when he resumed the painting in Boston in 1820. I analyze the painting's complex imagery and composition in terms of the artist's apocalyptic mentality, his tendency to interpret reality as a cosmic struggle between the forces of good and evil. I also show how the figure of Daniel personifies the Allstonian hero, a peculiar kind of heroism inspired by the passive being of George Washington.

The final chapters of the book thus demonstrate the importance of Allston's painting for an American audience. Rejecting the notion expressed by many art historians that Allston's true home was in England and that *Belshazzar's Feast* was essentially alien to American culture, I attempt to show how popular and significant the painting's images were for the new republic. They were part and parcel of public discourse, thanks to Americans' habitual tendency to identify their history with that of Old Testament Israel. Chapter six focuses upon conservatives' fears of an American Napoleon and the widespread use of the Belshazzar theme in Boston and elsewhere to characterize that danger. It concludes with Allston's Danielic decision to reject the potential riches and success he may have been able to reap in England. Seeking to cultivate his public image as a latter-day prophet,

Allston chose to return to his people in the relatively isolated American "wilderness."

Chapter seven then analyzes Allston's other Old Testament paintings, their relationship to *Belshazzar's Feast* and to the moral reform movements and the religious revivalism then sweeping the American continent. I show how the paintings contributed to a conservative strain of nationalist ideology, which revitalized the biblical symbol system of Puritan New England. According to this ideological viewpoint, Americans would achieve a proper spirit of national unity only through their traditional identification as God's new chosen people. By insisting upon the governmental relevance of the Hebraic covenant, conservatives trusted that the resulting moral self-discipline and obedience to divine law would mitigate democratic evils and, finally, prepare America to carry out its sacred duty of leading the world to Christ and the long-awaited millennium.

Though it is true that Allston never explicitly discussed the millennium or the apocalypse and America's role in these momentous events, he nevertheless thought and expressed himself within the terms of millennialism and apocalypticism. According to the historian W. H. Oliver:

Millennialism is a way of looking at the world, not a set of conclusions; the conclusions which may be reached are extremely diverse, and though their family relationship is apparent, it is a relationship of style, concept, vocabulary and mood, dependent ultimately upon reference back to a common set of biblical texts and symbols. Millennialism is a mood of expectation, not a doctrine. Millennialism is a cluster of attitudes united by a common core of images; the images may be explicitly explored, as is the case with professional biblical exegetes; they may be casually employed, either as figures of speech or as conveniently recognizable reference points, by writers and preachers adopting and adapting a means of communication.[3]

While Allston was not a biblical exegete who felt able to decode Daniel's apocalypse or the Book of Revelation, his belief in a deadly moral dualism, his obsessive spiritual striving and quest for perfection, his repeated reference to Old and New Testament prophecy, his obvious interest in the history and destiny of the Jewish nation, and his remarkable suggestion of The Three Marys at Christ's Tomb for a panel in the Rotunda of the U.S. Capitol, all seem compelling evidence for his apocalyptic and millennialist frame of mind and his hope that America might play a crucial role in establishing a Christian paradise. It is clear, however, that Allston's essential pessimism regarding the nature of fallen man and the dreaded expansion of American democracy significantly tempered his millennial enthusiasm.

The last chapter explains why Allston never lost interest in *Belshazzar's Feast,* even though he halted work upon it for more than a decade in the 1830s. I demonstrate how various social, political, and religious developments—the rise in Catholic immigration and urban, working-class violence, the disintegration of the revivalist movement and the beginning of the Transcendentalist crisis—motivated Allston's return to his masterpiece in 1839. I develop the painting's close relationship to the ideas expressed in Allston's *Lectures on Art* and show how the *Lectures* are not only a treatise on art theory but on theology as well. Both treatise and painting, in fact, became Allston's means for expressing his profoundly Christian disapproval of Emersonian Transcendental thought. The book concludes with the hypothesis that the elderly Allston, who continued until his death to work on *Belshazzar's Feast,* never seriously cared whether he finished the painting. Its tragic lack of finish, coupled with the divided nature of its composition, vividly testified to the reality of man's divided self, the impossibility of attaining a perfected unity while one is yet a pilgrim on this dark earth, and the cruelty of American democracy, whereby the dull, materialistic common man is allowed to starve the man of genius.

Acknowledgments

This book had its genesis in my dissertation for the University of North Carolina at Chapel Hill. I am grateful to Arthur S. Marks for directing my attention to Allston's biblical paintings and their importance as expressions of American culture. For many years, I have benefited from Dr. Marks' scholarship and good camaraderie.

In 1980–81, my research was facilitated by an assistantship at the Institute for Advanced Study, generously offered to me by Clifford Geertz, upon the recommendation of Joan W. Scott. Dr. Scott, who has since joined the Institute's permanent faculty, has been a valued friend. Without her emotional and intellectual assistance, I may never have found my way out of graduate school. Her encouragement since then has been enormously gratifying. While at Princeton, I had useful conversations with many people, including Dr. Geertz, Emory Elliott, and, later, in summer 1986, with Agnes Sherman of the Princeton University Emblem Project. I would also like to thank the librarians and staffs of the Princeton Index of Christian Art, the Firestone and Marquand libraries, the Princeton Theological Seminary, and, of course, the Institute's library, where I spent many beautiful, productive hours.

In 1981–82, I received a Smithsonian fellowship at the National Museum of American Art. Lois Fink, as curator of research, provided me kind and intelligent counsel and has been a good friend ever since. I am deeply grateful to her. While at the Smithsonian, I enjoyed the companionship of many people, but for their invaluable criticism and bibliographic advice, I must credit, above all, Elizabeth Garrity Ellis, Lillian B. Miller, and Elizabeth Johns.

Elizabeth Johns, in particular, has been instrumental in helping me to realize this book, encouraging me to rewrite, broaden, and clarify my thinking. I have happily incurred a debt of sublime proportions to her kind friendship and constructive criticism.

Others who have personally stimulated aspects of the

text through conversation or written criticism include: David C. Huntington, Allan Wallach, John W. Dixon, Donald M. Scott, Grant Wacker, Olaf Hanson, and Joseph C. Sloane. But Dr. Sloane also has to be singled out for his great personal kindness to me. I shall never forget his generous intellectual and moral support and shall always feel a kinship for his scholarship on nineteenth-century history painting.

In terms of logistics and editorial advice, I want to thank Kathy Kuhtz, acquisitions editor of the Smithsonian Institution Press, Jeanne Sexton, my manuscript editor, and Lisa Buck, the designer of this publication. My thanks also to Sharon Barrett, whose skill and forbearance helped me to make deadlines. While at Corpus Christi State University, I received invaluable secretarial assistance from Marjorie Goetsch, as well as much needed travel money through the Paul and Mary Haas Foundation.

Finally, I wish to thank Lou Dellaguzzo for his friendship and editorial assistance. His intellectual enthusiasm often bolstered my flagging spirit, giving me the energy to persevere in bringing the book to conclusion.

Nevertheless, like Allston's *Belshazzar's Feast*, there can never be a definitive "finish" to any human project. I thus acknowledge that all errors and omissions are entirely the author's responsibility.

CHAPTER 1   *The Assumption of Washington Allston*

Secluded from the hurly burly of Boston's merchant economy, Washington Allston, that city's most beloved artist, had wrestled one more day with his painting of *Belshazzar's Feast*. It was the ninth of July, 1843. At the age of sixty-three, the silver-haired artist was finding it increasingly difficult to climb up and down the ladder, which he had placed in front of the canvas, as he carefully added touches of paint and then, with cigar in hand, examined the effect from the comfortable distance of his chair. No one was permitted to disturb his concentration. At this point, no one was even allowed a glimpse of *Belshazzar's Feast*.

Allston's ivy-covered studio, built in the design of a Greek temple, was hidden away amidst the relative quiet of Cambridgeport, near his beloved alma mater, Harvard College. The great masterpiece, for which he had sacrificed so much of his career, stretched twelve by sixteen feet across almost the entire back wall of the studio. An enormous curtain covered the grand composition whenever the artist rested from his labors, thus preventing curiosity-seekers, close friends included, from spying upon the work before its completion. In once denying his former Harvard schoolmate, Leonard Jarvis, a view of the work, Allston reportedly claimed that "if that picture were seen by any person, I should never finish it. I know . . . that this is a weakness, but I cannot help it."[1]

Thus in 1828, more than a decade after the painting's conception, the landscape painter Alvan Fisher had written his friend Asher B. Durand: "Mr. Alston's [sic] *great work* is still behind the curtain, what it is except in name, we know not. I hope *time* will bring it forth."[2] Fifteen years later, the day of Allston's death, the painting was still behind the curtain. By that time, the artist's secretive painting had assumed the aura of an alchemical philosopher's stone. As one critic recalled several years after Allston's death:

Well do we remember, in the days of our boyhood, the mystery which always hung about [*Belshazzar's Feast*], and the eagerness with which every circumstance, however trifling, that seemed to throw any light upon its progress, was caught up and dwelt upon. To us, Allston was the representative of American art. We never enjoyed the privilege of his acquaintance. We never even saw him. We believed him, nevertheless, to be the greatest genius that our country had produced. We heard of him for years and years, working in his studio . . . upon the canvas that should finally (so we thought) take rank beside the master-pieces of Italy, and bestow an unfading lustre upon the land of his birth.[3]

For a quarter century, year after year, the same question had been asked of Allston: When would he finish his great painting *Belshazzar's Feast?* He had actually begun the work in London in 1817. His return to Boston the following year caused an interruption, and it had not been until 1820 that he resumed the painting. At that point he began to make a series of changes in composition and perspective which he was never able to orchestrate to his own satisfaction. As the aging Gilbert Stuart allegedly said of his younger colleague: "Mr. Allston's mind grows by and beyond his work. What he does in one month, becomes imperfect in the next, by the very growth of his mind. . . ."[4] Stuart thus prophesied that *Belshazzar's Feast* would never be finished, that the artist would forever be making alterations.

In addition to his fastidious work habits, serious illness and persistent financial difficulties hindered Allston's progress, forcing him to mortgage the picture to a group of wealthy Boston businessmen. The painting was to have been the primary attraction for the inaugural exhibition of art at the Boston Athenaeum in 1827. But still unhappy with its imperfect perspective, Allston refused to let the picture out of his hands. The next year he reportedly blotted out a substantial portion of the painting in order to begin the changes all over again.

Blaming the stifling weight of indebtedness, the frustrated artist felt unable to renew work on the alterations for a period of over ten years. However, though out of sight, the painting was not out of mind, as Allston turned down one commission after another in the 1830s, claiming he could accept no further major project until he had finished *Belshazzar's Feast.*

Finally, after friends and patrons organized a retrospective exhibition of his works at Chester Harding's Gallery in 1839, Allston was released from debt and enthusiastically returned to his great painting. Yet, four years later, on the fateful day, July 9, 1843, Allston had still not completed it. In fact, only a day or so before, he had entirely painted over

King Belshazzar, intending to enlarge that figure's proportions. The Chaldean soothsayers on the right side of the canvas were also still fragments waiting for the touch of the artist's brush.

Despite the queries of newspaper journalists, Allston had not been one to heed the clamor of uninformed opinion which failed to appreciate the intellectual labor required for history painting. Yet not all who expressed impatience with Allston's procrastinating work habits were ill-informed journalists. Members of New England's intelligentsia were anxious to encourage religious painting as an instrument for the moral reformation of American society. Allston's obsessive quest for perfection seemed ill-advised in view of the urgent religious and moral needs of the nation (see chapter 7). *Belshazzar's Feast* was to have been a sermon in paint, an expression of the evangelical spirit sweeping antebellum America, admonishing the viewer to repent and reform before the sudden, unexpected arrival of death. Yet its creator stubbornly refused to exhibit until he had fully realized his conception of the subject.

Most men of letters continued to lend their support, chiding Americans' impatience for quick results. As Oliver Wendell Holmes said in Allston's defense only a few years prior to the artist's death:

It remains for the future to decide upon the success of his greatest effort,—*Belshazzar's Feast*—in expectation of which we have been fasting some few years, with only a cabinet picture from time to time to sustain us in endurance. We are disposed to admire the constancy with which Mr. A. has resisted all the busy suggestions of curious and forward people, and waited for his own time and followed his own will.[5]

It was wrong, said Holmes, to compare the work of Allston's creative imagination with that of a bricklayer, a "wood-hewer" or a "water-drawer." He concluded that "factory wheels run day and night, and summer and winter; but there are tranquil waters and silent souls, which an angel visits only 'at a certain season.' "[6]

For Allston, however, on that ninth day of July, the seasons would change no more. As the obliterating black paint over Belshazzar's image continued to dry, the artist sat slumped in his chair, dead from an apparent heart attack. Three days later, Richard Dana, Sr., Allston's brother-in-law, joined by his son, Richard Dana, Jr., and his brother Edmund Trowbridge Dana, entered the deceased artist's studio, as if they were the three Marys entering Christ's tomb. Richard Dana, Jr., recalled:

At 4 P.M. we assembled to enter the painting room and "break the seal" of the great picture. An awe had been upon my mind as though I were about to enter a sacred and mysterious place. I could hardly bring my mind to turn the key. . . . to enter this solemn place, so long and so lately filled with his presence and the home of his glorious thoughts and his painful emotions, the scene of his distresses which no human eye saw, and no human spirits can comprehend![7]

Having mustered the courage to pull aside the curtain, the three then stood aghast at the sight of the unfinished painting, especially the coat of black paint "blotting out" Belshazzar. According to the Danas, this veil of black paint was not only Belshazzar's "shroud" but Allston's as well. The artist had selflessly sacrificed himself for his art.

What happened next, if not unprecedented, was certainly a most unusual event in the history of art. Allston's patrons decided that Belshazzar's shroud should be removed and that the painting, cleansed and varnished, should then be displayed before the public in its unfinished state as a kind of testament to the spiritual striving of the artist. Exhibited first in 1844 at Boston's Corinthian Gallery and then annually at the Boston Athenaeum, the painting's fragmentary condition, biblical subject matter, and disjointed composition proved to be a source of endless fascination and comment (fig. 1).

Critical reaction to the long-awaited painting was decidedly mixed. The artist's Raphaelesque composition, in the tradition of the European grand manner, suited most members of the New England elite, who liked to compare their merchant-based republic with that of Renaissance Florence. *Belshazzar* was praised for its noble, neoclassical style, a style appropriate to the high moral purpose of art.[8] Yet, as we shall see, those who professed admiration tended either to focus upon the moral and religious character of the artist or else the narrative detail of the biblical story itself.

The harshest assessment of the painting came from William Wetmore Story, then a Boston lawyer and an otherwise admiring disciple of Allston's. Story's critique was not grounded upon the unfinished state of the painting, but was an attack upon the artist's conception of the subject, something so fundamental that no further correction or alteration could have improved it. Allston would certainly have found the review unjust, since what Story wanted in a representation of Belshazzar's feast was not at all what he had intended to paint. Their points of view seem to have been completely at odds.

Ironically, for someone who would become a leading neoclassical sculptor, Story was disappointed in the paint-

4

ing's Raphaelesque sense of balance, order, and calm. There was "no overwhelming central interest, and no intensity of action."[9] Having Rembrandt's famous interpretation of the subject in the back of his mind (see fig. 9), he was critical of the fact that:

. . . there is very little opposition and violent contrast of chiaroscuro. The hand-writing is luminous, not dazzling, and a diffused light fills the hall. The idea required violent action, and the light suggests repose and contemplation. . . . Such a scene as the Belshazzar's Feast would have been much more effective with a Rembrandtish light.[10]

Story also may have been mentally comparing Allston's picture with the 1820 painting of the same subject by John Martin (fig. 2). Martin's composition was widely known in America through the sale of engraved prints. The English artist's panoramic view of Belshazzar's palace and the city of Babylon certainly possessed Story's "violent contrast of chiaroscuro," "dazzling" handwriting and "violent action." But as Allston noted in a letter to the *North American Review*, New England's most prestigious literary journal, "the difference between Mr. Martin's work and mine is not of degree, but of *kind*; and things differing in kind (though admitting prefer-

5

Figure 2
John Martin, *Belshazzar's
Feast*, 1821, oil on canvas,
32 × 48 in. Wadsworth
Atheneum, Hartford,
Connecticut; The Ella Gallup
Sumner and Mary Catlin
Sumner Collection.

ence) cannot be compared."[11] In this letter, written three
years prior to his death, Allston said he had long ago rejected
the idea of a brilliant light emanating from the handwriting
on the wall, "because I found that it would very materially
interfere with an important part of my composition."[12] As
Oliver Wendell Holmes said in favor of Allston's more traditional style, "The great points of individual character and
expression" would not be sacrificed "for the sake of impos-
ing effects obtained by theatrical artifice and extravagance."[13]

Allston never intended to overwhelm the viewer with
supernatural terror in the manner suggested by Martin's picture or by Edmund Burke's famous treatise on the sublime.
The Burkean sublime, like Martin's style, was essentially
alien to Allston's temperament. He rejected Burke's empiri-
cist grounding of the sublime in the mere mechanical
response of man's senses to the objects of external nature. As
will be shown more fully in subsequent chapters, Allston
preferred the more ideal theories of the Scottish Common
Sense philosophers or, from his own circle of friends, the aesthetic ideas of William Ellery Channing and Samuel Taylor
Coleridge.

The Scottish philosopher Dugald Stewart thus argued
that the sublime emotion arose from within man, from his
religious sentiments, or an innate moral sense.[14] Coleridge,
meanwhile, in criticizing Burke's ideas, claimed that sublim-

ity was found not in the wildness, disorder, and irregularity of external nature but within the self, or man's internalized "divine ideas . . . which show the attributes of God, or relate to his Worship."[15] Such ideas included the "Law of Conscience" and "Reason."

Allston's vital interest in the moral, rather than the Burkean, sublime led him to interpret Belshazzar's feast in quite a different way from Story's expectations. In doing so he conformed to the demands of his friends and patrons among the New England clerisy who insisted upon unambiguous moral content without superficial pictorial distractions. He thus painted a contemplative political sermon that focused upon the "law of conscience" and the holy majesty of God, thereby appealing to the spectator's highest spiritual faculty, rather than the self-interested fear of bodily pain, which Burke had suggested as the source of sublime terror.

In stark contrast to Story's harsh critique, Henry Greenough, therefore, praised Allston's more subtle and "complicated" harmonies of color, light, and expression, which differed from Martin's "poetical licences taken for effect's sake."[16] Greenough suggested that strong contrasts of hue or chiaroscuro were merely designed "to catch the eye of the multitude." Allston's carefully modulated tonal and chromatic gradations appealed, instead, to the refined, civilized viewer, one who was not taken in by momentary sensations of pain, pleasure, or visual delight. The individual with taste preferred an extended, contemplative experience, in which the total visual effect gradually deepened as his or her gaze passed slowly from detail to detail and the mind reconstructed from the infinite variety, a masterful unity of spiritual content. Greenough likened the experience of viewing Allston's *Belshazzar* to that of listening to a Beethoven symphony. Both needed to be carefully attended to over time and both demanded repeated engagements before their complexities could be fully appreciated.

Story, nonetheless, continued his critique of Allston's painting by noting the lack of spatial unity between the foreground scene of Belshazzar, the Queen, Daniel and the soothsayers and the middle distance of the banqueting table. The table, with its impious revelers, was "almost wholly disconnected" from the main action in the foreground.[17] In addition, the architectural framework of balcony and columns behind the banqueting table "overloads and dwarfs the picture, and shuts up the distances, so that the figures seem to cram the hall."

It would be pointless to dispute the fact that Allston had a problem with perspective and the adjustment of figures to their surrounding space. Faint chalk outlines forming columns and an entablature to the immediate left of the illuminated area for the handwriting on the wall indicate that Allston had still not resolved the picture's architectural space. Since the artist was still adjusting the scale of the figures to the surrounding space, it is difficult to assess precisely what the final result might have been.

Of greater semantic importance is the dissociation between foreground and background referred to by Story. There is, indeed, a startling contrast in scale between the heroic proportions of the foreground figures and the lilliputian dimensions of the figures running along the background flights of steps, a difference that does not seem adequately accounted for by the apparent dimensions of the palace space, which critics, other than Story, confessed lacked the grandeur of Martin's architecture.[18]

In addition, the orthogonals of the palace floor abruptly end in the middle ground at the banqueting table, so that the heavy, oppressive framework of balcony and supporting columns, rising above this area, seems to function more as an imprisoning barrier than a transition. The abrupt change in chiaroscuro between the bright illumination of the banqueting table and the murky darkness of the lower end of the stairway contributes to this sense of disjuncture, as does the contrast between the dark underside of the balcony and the intense light of the chandelier hovering over the idol.

Given the use of so many visual devices to isolate foreground from background, Allston must have intended that the separation convey a significant portion of the picture's meaning. Indeed, one finds the same abrupt juxtaposition of foreground and background space in other of Allston's biblical paintings, including *Jeremiah Dictating His Prophecy of the Destruction of Jerusalem to Baruch the Scribe* (pl. II) and *Miriam the Prophetess* (pl. III), reinforcing the idea that this particular aspect of the *Belshazzar* composition was no accident. As I shall show in chapters four and five, this division between foreground and background space must be seen as an expression of the artist's apocalyptic vision of the universe.[19] *Belshazzar's Feast* symbolized the cosmic moral struggle between the forces of good and evil, the foreground dominated by Daniel's interpretation of the handwriting on the wall, while its moral opposite, a satanic idol, glows triumphantly in the background, isolated by the surrounding gloom and a heavy architectural framework. As Henry Greenough observed, there is a "struggle" between the "supernatural light . . . in the foreground" and "that of the lamps in the distance."[20]

William Wetmore Story concluded his attack upon Allston's unfinished masterpiece with the most common criticism of the work, that the expressions of the foreground figures were stereotyped at best and caricatures at worst. Though Allston had intended to repaint and enlarge the figure of Belshazzar, its critic doubted whether the clichéd attitude of fear would have been improved. The soothsayers, especially, were received with almost universal dismay. Story bluntly characterized them as "grotesque, unnatural and ludicrous."[21]

The modern viewer can scarcely dissent from this harsh judgment, though an appreciation of the artist's intent seems only just. It has thus been argued that Allston's four portraits of Polish Jews, which he painted in 1817, formed "the basic raw material" for the heads of the soothsayers (see chapter 5).[22] Yet if this is true, he certainly altered and exaggerated their facial features for his large painting. The Polish Jews are rendered with a kind of Rembrandtesque sympathy entirely at odds with the beaklike noses, furrowed brows, and angry eyes of the soothsayers (figs. 3 and 4 and pl. IV).

Given the evidence of the warm and spiritual portrait studies, it is clear that Allston could have painted the soothsayers in a more natural, less caricatured manner. However, mimesis or naturalism was not Allston's primary intent. *Belshazzar's Feast* was a moral allegory, and, as such, the *dramatis personae* were simplified or typified for expressive purposes. Allston exaggerated certain traits or features, sometimes to the point of caricature, so that the characters became agents for specific emotional or moral qualities.[23] The painting was to be a biblical *psycomachia*, representing a wide, but codifiable, range of human response to a miraculous, supernatural event. Allston followed the academic rules and conventions laid down by Sir Joshua Reynolds, which, in turn, were based upon the physiognomic studies of Charles Le Brun, Johann Kaspar Lavater, and others.[24] Such studies correlated and standardized facial configurations for nearly every type of passion or human emotion.

Allston was certainly familiar with George Richardson's 1779 edition of Cesare Ripa's *Iconologia* which defended the moral and religious usefulness of allegory. According to Richardson, the artist needed to appeal to the "understanding and judgment of the spectator . . . more than . . . to the external eye."[25] For Richardson and Allston, allegory was a "transparent veil" which dressed one's thoughts and ideas in a poetic visual language. Perhaps as a result of his Harvard education, Allston tended to trust his intellect and the academic tradition more than the direct experience of his eye. He thus classified the visual arts among man's "mental pleasures," arguing that their true origins were intellectual and moral rather than physical.[26] Pigments arranged upon the canvas were no more ends in themselves than were the

9

Figure 3
Washington Allston, *Head of a Jew*, 1817, oil on canvas, 30¼ × 25¼ in. Museum of Fine Arts, Boston; Gift of Henry Copley Greene, 41.291.

Figure 4
Washington Allston, *Sketch of a Polish Jew*, 1817, oil on canvas, 30¼ × 25¼ in. The Corcoran Gallery of Art, Washington, D.C.

objects of nature. All referred upward to the perfect, platonic "Ideas of Beauty, Truth, Holiness."

As Professor David Huntington has shown in his richly suggestive catalogue *Art and the Excited Spirit,* Americans who lived between the War of 1812 and the Civil War perceived the "universe as a vast moral theatre" in which every natural phenomenon including the shape of the human head, seemed to reveal hidden moral content.[27] Thus Allston and his public assumed with the German physiognomist Lavater that "the moral life of man, particularly reveals itself in the lines, marks and transitions of the countenance."[28] According to Lavater, the study of physiognomy can make one aware of the presence of evil which lurks beneath the surface of facial deformities, or in certain unconscious twists of the mouth, or in a particular furrowing of the brow.

For Allston, physiognomic theory was a key ingredient in his visualization of the moral sublime, reinforcing the emblematic division between foreground and background space in *Belshazzar's Feast.* Using spatial metaphors, Lavater had suggested the sublimity of physiognomic studies, referring to the depths of man's depravity and the great distance between his "fiend-like ugliness," when "deformed by sin," and the "perfect beauty" of God, high above, in the heavens.[29] According to Lavater and others, physiognomic contrasts were instrumental for jolting man out of his moral torpor so that he would raise or sublime himself upward, away from his fallen nature toward perfection in God. As physiognomists and phrenologists argued, the active exercise of one's moral faculties would inevitably result in a physical transformation harmonizing with the beauty of God's universe and hastening the advent of the earthly millennium.[30]

Hence, while the eye may wince at the vulturelike soothsayers, Allston clearly hoped that the viewer's conscience would be struck with a moral recognition of sin's correlation with physical deformity. In an equally clear manner, the noble, impassive expression of Daniel, his calm and steady gesture upward toward the handwriting on the wall, conformed to the academic stereotype of the classical orator established by the ancient Roman rhetorician Quintillian.[31] As the Reverend E. L. Magoon, an American contemporary of Allston's, wrote:

The greatest effect ever produced by a consummate orator is achieved by his preserving the aspect and advantage of repose amidst the tempest in which he is involved, showing that he is at the same time master of the elements which agitate others and swell within himself.[32]

11

Story, in fact, thought that Allston did not follow the formula strictly enough in this instance, complaining that the right hand of Daniel ought not to be clenched but relaxed because "the prophet should be the type of calm heroism, to contrast well with the disturbing figure of the King."[33]

Thus, even Allston's harshest critic did not dissent from the principles of physiognomic theory. As Story indicated, the sharp contrast of facial expressions and body language was necessary for allowing viewers to "read" the story easily. The clarity of narrative was of far greater concern for Allston's public than aesthetic perfection or virtuosity. In fact, those who objected to the exhibition of the painting probably did so because they believed that the lack of finish would interfere with the reading of the picture or, at the very least, unnecessarily detract public attention away from the important moral lessons in the story.[34] As it was, only artists and connoisseurs would be able to appreciate the subtleties of the picture and that was really not the purpose for which such an enormous painting was displayed.

The public exhibition of large religious paintings in Boston had been both a popular and morally useful form of entertainment during the 1820s and '30s.[35] Such events corresponded with the religious evangelism of the Second Great Awakening and the various activities of the many Protestant reform societies that held cultural sway throughout New England and America (see chapter 7). The exhibition of Allston's *Belshazzar* in 1844 turned out to be one of the last successful showings of a single history painting in Boston prior to the advent of the moving panorama.

As favorable reviews of *Belshazzar's Feast* indicate, the unfinished state of the painting did not prevent the work from fulfilling its narrative purpose. Allston's stark character contrasts and physiognomic exaggerations encouraged the beholder to imagine the thoughts and moods of each of the players in the psychodrama. The viewer could reconstruct and embellish the original biblical text so as to apply its moral and religious lessons to his or her own personal experience.

Daniel's account of Belshazzar's transgressions cover nearly the entire spectrum of man's fallible nature, from the sins of pride and idolatry to those of luxury and drunken debauchery. While biblical scholars have discredited the veracity of Daniel's "history," no one has denied its exciting dramatic quality nor its power as a vivid lesson in morality and divine providence.

According to Daniel, chapter five, Belshazzar, the king of Babylon, provided a lavish entertainment for the lords of his realm, sacrilegiously using the gold and silver vessels confiscated from the Jewish temple in Jerusalem. However, when a hand suddenly appears, writing a message upon the wall, Belshazzar's revelry abruptly ends, and he begins to tremble with fear.

The Chaldean soothsayers are called upon to interpret the writing. After they admit their failure, the queen suggests that the prophet Daniel be called. Daniel refuses Belshazzar's gifts of gold and a robe of scarlet but agrees to interpret the mysterious words. Before he does, however, he reminds Belshazzar of the story of his "father" Nebuchadnezzar.

Under Nebuchadnezzar, says Daniel, God favored the Babylonian empire with wealth and power, but when the king became "hardened in pride," he lost both his throne and his senses. He became "like the beasts, and his dwelling was with wild asses," until he recognized that "the most high God ruled in the kingdom of men." Daniel accuses Belshazzar of the same pridefulness which nearly ruined his predecessor. But, unlike Nebuchadnezzar, Belshazzar has persisted in ignoring the providence of God.

Daniel then interpreted the damning judgment contained within the strange words, "Mene, Mene, Tekel, Upharsin," which God had written on the wall: "God hath numbered thy kingdom and finished it. Thou art weighed in the balances, and art found wanting. The kingdom is divided, and given to the Medes and the Persians." That night, according to Daniel, Belshazzar was slain and the Babylonian empire fell to Darius the Mede.

However, for Allston and other Christians, there was another, more important moral and historical point to the story, though not stated in Daniel five. That is, with the fall of Babylon, the Jews were to be freed from their captivity and allowed to return to the city of Jerusalem. According to the prophets Jeremiah and Isaiah, God had used the Babylonian Captivity as a means of punishment, but he would soon reward the chosen people for their repentant, humbled acknowledgment of divine providence. Since this aspect of the story is not explicitly referred to in Daniel five, most earlier paintings of Belshazzar's feast do not allude to it (see chapter 2). Yet, it is this particular historico-moral dimension, with its promise of spiritual liberation, which most appealed to Allston's American audience.

Allston's unique inclusion of the captive Jews is the one aspect of the painting for which William Wetmore Story could muster praise. Describing the group of grateful Jews situated between Daniel and the soothsayers, the critic remarked that these few figures were "exceedingly beautiful."[36] Other commentators also singled out the moral and physical beauty of the long-suffering Jews as the single most striking feature of the work.

Writing for the *Christian Examiner,* the Unitarian clergyman William Parsons Lunt went so far as to claim that Allston's painting was not so much about the doom of Belshazzar and the Babylonian empire as it was about the fate and spiritual beauty of the Children of Israel:

The whole picture presents an impressive illustration of a people who had been humbled in every possible way, whose independence had been destroyed, whose city had fallen into the hands of their enemies, who had themselves been carried away captive, and in an idolatrous court were obliged to look on and see the sacred vessels of their religion profaned by Heathen revellers; and who, under these circumstances of degradation, achieved a most remarkable moral triumph by the power of truth. They saw their Prophet respected and consulted, with fear and trembling, by their conscience-stricken oppressors.[37]

Unlike Story, Lunt declined to evaluate the artistic merits of the work. From a clerical point of view, he was satisfied that the picture's narrative and moral content held enduring significance for the American public. He declared that Allston's *Belshazzar* was a monument to the Children of Israel, a pledge "that the acts and experience of that peculiar people shall continue in the memory of all periods of time, to verify the august Providence of God."[38]

As with so many other Americans, Lunt, almost intuitively, interpreted Jewish history as an amazing foreshadowing of American history. Somehow America, in the person of its leading artist-prophet, had been chosen to carry the message of the ancient Israelites, the message of their salvation to those seeking the guidance of providence. As the clergyman breathlessly noted:

And now, eighteen centuries after the time when they finally ceased to be a nation, while the scattered remnants of them survive as wanderers in all lands, there arises, in these ends of the earth, an artist, who, with a master's hand, reproduces one of the most interesting scenes of Jewish story; unites on one canvas, the picture of their wrongs and of their triumph. . . .[39]

Allston's painting appealed to Americans' notion that theirs was the new chosen nation. Henry A. S. Dearborn's review of *Belshazzar's Feast* for the *Knickerbocker* also played upon Americans' identification with Old Testament Israel. As he examined each of the Jewish figures between Daniel and the soothsayers, including the seated turbaned men and the kneeling women, Dearborn imagined the thoughts of the Israelites. Assuming the voice of the captive Jews, he condemned the sins of Belshazzar and praised Daniel as a national hero: "Tremble, thou blasphemous tyrant; for Daniel, our great prophet, the bold, independent, and holy man of our nation, has proclaimed the righteous judgment and swift-coming wrath of God—of the Jew's God. . . .''[40]

The New England audience, quick to identify with the Children of Israel, was also quick to associate Allston's Daniel with their own great orator Daniel Webster. More than a few were apparently disappointed that Allston had not painted his prophet in the likeness of the legendary Webster.[41] Yet, if Allston was at all influenced by the public image of Webster, it was as an ideal orator type rather than as a particular individual. As we shall see in chapter seven, the biblical Daniel was frequently championed as a model for American statesmanship. In his review of Allston's painting, Dearborn furthered this idea, praising Daniel for his selfless, disinterested service to Jehovah, ''his serene aspect and lofty bearing [which] indicate an upright, just and fearless man.''[42]

Meanwhile, Dearborn characterized Belshazzar and the queen in a manner that most members of Allston's New England public would have considered alien and threatening to the American republic. He claimed that the heads of both figures bore a general similarity to the imperious physiognomy of Napoleon Bonaparte.[43] In conformity with physiognomic, as well as phrenological theory, Dearborn was referring to an identity in type, rather than a similarity to Napoleon's specific, individual portrait, and, in this sense, Allston would probably not have disputed the comparison. His original inspiration for the painting had been the fall of the Napoleonic empire and the public celebrations in England and America that followed (chapters 5 and 6). New England conservatives, in particular, had employed the theme of Belshazzar to characterize the fall of the evil French empire, which had so endangered the natural social hierarchy. Indeed, Dearborn was joined by others, including Richard Dana, Jr., who claimed to see a reference to Napoleon in the strong-willed visage of the Babylonian queen.[44] Belshazzar's portrait was, perhaps, in too sketchy a state for Dana to include the king in the analogy as well. Or, perhaps, as Dearborn indicated, the ''haughty'' expression of the queen seemed more imperious than the ''cowering and humiliating condition of Belshazzar.''[45]

Since *Belshazzar's Feast* seemed to possess such significance as a national morality play, it was more than a little disconcerting for his patrons that Allston was never able to complete the picture. Yet, upon the artist's death, friends and patrons alike seemed determined to preserve the unfinished state of the painting, allowing not a single restorer's brush stroke to be added to the master's.[46] When an enterprising copyist by the name of Thomas T. Spear reproduced a ''finished'' version of the painting, ''with a view to carry out the design of the author," he was roundly condemned for his blasphemy, for nothing could compare to the original.[47] Allston's supporters actually assigned a positive value to the fragmentary quality of the painting. According to Nathaniel Hawthorne, the "imperfect beauty" of *Belshazzar's Feast* beneficially demonstrated "that the deeds of the earth, however etherealized by piety or genius, are without value, except as exercises and manifestations of the spirit."[48]

The editor of the *Harbinger*, which published Story's review of the painting, rejected that critic's negative judgment declaring that if the forms were wrong and the painting left unfinished, it was "because of the very greatness of [Allston's] aspiration," the artist's attempt "to burst the bonds of his peculiar nature and compass the Impossible to him."[49] In a similar vein, the Reverend C. A. Bartol based a sermon upon Allston's *Belshazzar* entitled "Perfection." The Unitarian preacher observed that the artist's conception was so exalted and sublime that it never could have been perfected. How is it possible, asked Bartol to "turn the words of the rapt prophet into colors[?] . . . How shall that awful writing of doom be pencilled on the plastered wall? . . . How shall it be done according to the perfect pattern shown in . . . God's word?"[50]

Bartol used Allston's *Belshazzar* as a weapon against the theology of perfectionism, espoused by some of the more radical revivalist preachers and Transcendentalist philosophers (see chapters 7 and 8). Based upon Allston's frustrating experience with *Belshazzar's Feast*, Bartol concluded that "the idea is, not that we should grasp perfection as an immediate result, but make it our aim."[51] The clergyman, in short, sanctioned millennial desire, but not millennial perfection. For, as Allston had proved, "absolute perfection cannot be reached here on earth."

For most of Allston's apologists, the fact that he left the painting unfinished was not really an indication that he lacked the necessary technical skills or even the temperament for large history paintings. The lack of finish was rather a sign of his spiritual greatness, his willingness to grasp at that which was beyond his, or any mortal's, reach.

In a fundamental sense, Allston ultimately may have realized that not finishing the work might actually be preferable to its final resolution. Hadn't Edmund Burke and other art theorists argued that objects of great labor, left unfinished or in a state of ruin, were a source for the sublime? According to Burke:

When any work seems to have required immense force and labour to effect it, the idea is grand. Stonehenge, neither for disposition

16

nor ornament, has anything admirable; but those huge, rude masses of stone, set on end and piled on each other, turn the mind on the immense force necessary for such a work.[52]

Allston's own painting was akin to Stonehenge, a great modern-day ruin, the object of years of labor. In the words of one critic, *Belshazzar's* disconnected parts were "like the gigantic fragments of the Temple of the Colonna Garden."[53] Its ruined state actually reinforced a central theme of the biblical subject, the ephemeral, transient nature of worldly affairs.

In a manner typical of the eighteenth and early nineteenth century mania for contemplating human ruins, Allston's fragment encouraged meditation upon the mutability of life, the contingencies of history, with its misbegotten projects and interrupted plans. As James Jackson Jarves, an admirer of *Belshazzar's Feast*, wrote in 1855, in terms that could be applied to that tragic painting, the ruined and fading *objets d' art* of Europe, the "old churches" and "mouldering tombs," were artifacts which silently spoke like "sacred writings on the wall," testifying to the transience of earthly existence, while pointing beyond to an eternal realm of physical and moral perfection.[54]

With death and his own entrance into that realm of perfect, eternal forms, Allston finally "finished" his painting. For Allston, *Belshazzar's Feast* had been a living, spiritual force, an extension of his own being. His labor upon it had been a work of performance art, a Jackson Pollock or an Allan Kaprow *avant la lettre*. Allston had been an alchemist and *Belshazzar's Feast* had been his philosopher's stone. Through his attempts to perfect it, to transform it into gold, the artist hoped his soul would be sublimed as well. Death brought both the picture and the drama of Allston's performance to a conclusion. The two would be forever joined in a metonymic relationship, whereby the mention of one would inevitably evoke memory of the other. Thus, as Richard Dana, Jr., gazed upon the countenance of the corpse, he remarked that he could detect the artist's intellect "rising, soaring, from one elevation to one higher, and expanding into infinite space. . . . He had escaped that terrible vision, the nightmare, the incubus, the tormentor of his life—his unfinished picture."[55]

Allston was gone, but *Belshazzar's Feast* was a more powerful image for it, strengthened by the body and blood of America's most beloved artist. *Belshazzar's* "terrible vision" was only slightly more optimistic in its message than Thomas Cole's famous series of paintings, *The Course of Empire*, which described the remorseless, inevitable cycles of history.[56] In contrast to fatalistic, cyclical theories of history, *Belshazzar's* tale of divine providence offers a glimmer of salvific hope. Yet, as a moral allegory, it admonished self-confident Americans, brash and impatient for change, to assume a Hebraic attitude of humility under the threat of holy retribution.

In contrast to later American paintings, such as Emanuel Leutze's *Westward the Course of Empire* (fig. 5), where the panoramic space suggests an identity or oneness between the new chosen people and the object of their desire, the promised land of the American West, Allston's unfinished masterpiece suggests ceaseless spiritual struggle or a lack of identity between subject and object.[57] In *Belshazzar,* we look inward—not outward—within the dark recesses of the troubled self as symbolized by the indefinite contours of Belshazzar's murky inner apartment. The satanic idol continues to shine in that unholy place, thanks to a man-made source of light.

While a new generation of artists traveled westward and represented the pioneers of the American frontier in the image of a "new chosen people," already spiritually sanctified, back in New England's more sober climate, *Belshazzar's Feast* continued to challenge and sternly reproach its beholders for their moral failings. Its grand, aristocratic manner refused to compromise with the easy optimism of the new democratic age. Like its creator, *Belshazzar's Feast* kept its distance from America's hurly burly. Isolated amidst the quiet grandeur of the Boston Athenaeum, it silently spoke of the artist's sacred mission, to elevate a people upward toward the moral and physical beauty of God's idea.

Unfortunately, most Americans still did not value intellectual, much less artistic, endeavor. Art remained essentially marginal in American society, restricted to the private, domestic realm and therefore, more suited to the production of smaller landscape and genre paintings. Allston's history painting thus symbolized the plight of the artist, his marginal existence in a materialist culture. The prophet, after all, had always been someone isolated and alienated from contemporary society. Yet, Allston's friends used the fate of his great painting and the fact of his cloistered existence to write jeremiads denouncing the nation's neglect of its greatest artist.

C. Edwards Lester thus attributed Allston's failure to finish *Belshazzar's Feast* to his persistent financial difficulties, blaming not the artist's poor fiscal management but rather the crude, profit-hungry nature of American enterprise:

. . . we cannot suppress a burst of indignation when we think that the sordid soul of some sordid wretch, who weighed dollars against Allston's art, and could see nothing in *Belshazzar's Feast* but three hundred yards of canvas, should have locked up that half-formed vision, when a few more weeks of the master's magical pencil

Figure 5
Emanuel Gottlieb Leutze,
*Westward the Course of Empire
Takes Its Way,* 1861, oil on
canvas, 33¼ × 43⅜ in.
National Museum of
American Art, Smithsonian
Institution, Washington,
D.C.; Bequest of Sara Carr
Upton.

would have given the world a creation that our countrymen three hundred years hence would speak of as the Italians now speak of the Last Judgment of Michelangelo.[58]

Though not referring specifically to *Belshazzar,* George W. Peck also recognized that Allston's calm, cerebral style was not popular with the democratic, mass audience that required "stories where the passion overpowers the judgment, and sometimes runs riot with the intellect." As Peck sadly concluded, "a great, pure soul, that was born a worshipper of truth, is as much alone in the moiled rabble of the common world, as if it had been dropped from some planet nearer the sun."[59] William Wetmore Story joined in this litany, criticizing the lack of sympathy and understanding experienced by artists in America, claiming that "Allston starved spiritually in Cambridgeport," for "there was nothing congenial without & he introverted all his powers & drained his memory dry."[60]

Allston, himself, had prepared the ground for such attacks upon the American climate for art, for he had repeatedly complained, prior to his 1839 retrospective, that indebtedness prevented him from completing *Belshazzar's Feast.* Furthermore, like Story, he attacked "the matter of fact char-

19

acter of the present age" in which "men are too busy with the palpable useful to open their minds to those higher influences which in other times were considered as the natural cravings of an immortal spirit."[61]

As an expression of the moral sublime, Allston's masterpiece sought to stir millennial desire or "the natural cravings" of man's "immortal spirit." It sought to agitate or exercise the viewer's conscience, forcing a choice between the dark deformities of a sinful life or the Hebraic beauty of humble obeisance before divine law. The composition's spatial dualism was the product of an apocalyptic frame of mind, not only the artist's but the nation's as well. In a very real sense, Allston's painting explored the spiritual meaning of American history. Despite its lack of contemporary costume, it was an emphatically American history painting, for it was commonly acknowledged that the jealous God of Old Testament Israel had chosen a new people to draw the curtain upon history's final act. Whether Americans would ever be worthy of this task was the anxious concern of Allston and his zealous supporters.

CHAPTER 2

The Tradition of Belshazzar's Feast

Washington Allston was not merely an artist and poet. More importantly, an admiring American public acknowledged his stature as a man of God, indeed, a latter-day prophet, whose paintings had the power to transfigure the spirit of the beholder. For Allston, painting was not so much a profession as a divine calling. The true artist could not be troubled by the problems of earning a living, turning a profit, or painting for the market. Art was not an end in itself but an instrument for the greater glory of God, the realization of His principles on earth.

When, therefore, Allston decided to concentrate his attention upon the painting of biblical subject matter, more was involved than a question of aesthetics. To understand his liking for themes based upon Old Testament prophecy, one must examine not only the art historical tradition but also the religious and political traditions within which such themes flourished. As my reading of his career will show, the conservative Allston could not and would not dissociate art from questions of religion, morality, and politics.

Belshazzar's feast, or the legendary tale of the fall of the Babylonian empire, captured Washington Allston's imagination for more important reasons than its supernatural drama, exciting as it may be. As an American who interpreted his world as if it were a moral text, Allston was interested in the story's allegorical, apocalyptic significance. During an age of revolutionary and counterrevolutionary violence, the Old Testament theme suggested the cosmic meaning of current events.

Traditionally, God's judgment against Belshazzar has possessed a dual significance for Christians. On the one hand, it served as a historical type of the weighing of souls and the fate of the damned in the Last Judgment. On the other hand, Belshazzar's death heralded the end of the Jews' seventy-year captivity in Babylon. As had been foretold by Second Isaiah and other prophets of the Babylonian exile, the Jews were to be restored to their holy city of Jerusalem. In the

21

Old Testament and the New Testament's Book of Revelation, Babylon's destruction is contrasted to the building of a "new Jerusalem," or "a new heaven and a new earth."[1]

For the author of Daniel, the rebuilding of Jerusalem would begin a new age of divine rule. Daniel's prophecy of the rise and fall of four world empires, superseded by a holy fifth kingdom (Daniel 7), influenced Saint John's vision in Revelation of a blissful thousand-year preparatory reign of Christian harmony here on earth, that is, the millennium.[2] According to Revelation 20:4–6, the millennium would be a period when those martyred saints, who had been loyal and steadfast in the faith, would rise again to rule the earth with Christ, prior to the final judgment. Whether interpreted literally or figuratively, some variant of the millennial idea pervaded nearly every social and religious group in America during Allston's lifetime.

Like Revelation, the Book of Daniel is an apocalyptic text, prophesying the end of time. It was actually written several centuries after the Babylonian exile, during the Maccabean revolt against the Greek ruler Antiochus Epiphanes (175–163 B.C.). Yet, the author of Daniel disguised his address so that he appeared to be writing in the sixth century. His gaze into the future, hundreds of years beyond the Babylonian Captivity, thereby proved to be amazingly accurate, while his chronicle of Babylon's fall is seriously marred by numerous errors.[3] For instance, Cyrus, emperor of Persia, not Darius the Mede, conquered Babylon. Furthermore, Belshazzar was never actually king but was merely a coregent under his father, Nabonidus (not Nebuchadnezzar).

The author of Daniel was not so much interested in history as in offering his contemporaries hope for the future. The punishment of Belshazzar and the fall of Babylon were vivid symbols of God's providence during a new period of persecution for the Jews, this time at the hands of the Greeks. The reconstruction of a spiritual Jerusalem was still, therefore, an unfulfilled dream. Yet, in Daniel's apocalyptic visions and tales of Providence, the prophet foresaw that the Greek empire, the fourth and final world empire, would fall just like the Babylonian had under King Belshazzar.

Even though the fall of the Greek empire resulted in the rise of yet another world empire, the Roman, an event unforeseen by Daniel, Christians throughout history have continuously reinterpreted Daniel's enigmatic prophecy to accord with their own prophetic calendars. Belshazzar's feast thereby continued to serve as an allegorical figure, an apocalyptic type for Daniel's fourth and final world empire; and Daniel's prophecy of a divine fifth kingdom became popular among many Christians as proof of a future millennium.[4]

Allston was aware of the eschatological meanings of Belshazzar's feast. As will be demonstrated, his painting of the subject differed from earlier pictorial interpretations by virtue of its dual focus, featuring not only the usual judgment against Belshazzar, as described in Daniel five, but also the millennial promise of good, in the person of the liberated Jews, who gratefully celebrate their restoration to Jerusalem, as prophesied by Isaiah, Jeremiah, and others.[5]

In his explicit reference to the captive Jews, his clear representation of their liberation, Allston was influenced by poems, sermons, and sacred dramas, which told the story of Belshazzar's doom primarily from the point of view of the exiled Jews. In Allston's painting, the fact of the Jews' captivity becomes a key counterpoint against which the Babylonian king acts out the last hours of his depraved existence.

In contrast, most painters, who undertook the representation of Daniel five, focused solely upon the fate of Belshazzar for the very good reason that he is the central character in the chapter. The Jews' captivity is simply understood as a given in this text, though alluded to by reference to the gold and silver vessels confiscated from the Jewish temple in Jerusalem (Daniel 5:3). Unlike literary reinterpretations of the theme, which often featured a chorus of Jews longing for their restoration to Jerusalem, painters obviously felt more restrained to narrow their conception to a single moment in time, usually the sudden appearance of the handwriting, so that even the Jewish prophet is excluded from most pictures. In harmony with Daniel five, painters would often merely suggest the captivity of the Jews by displaying gold and silver vessels in the foreground of their pictures.

In medieval art, Belshazzar's feast was generally interpreted in apocalyptic terms as an Old Testament type for the Last Judgment, warning heretics and the unfaithful to mend their sinful ways. The subject appeared in a variety of illuminated manuscripts including a commentary on Dante's *Inferno*.[6] Its most continuous source of representation, however, was in Spanish Romanesque painting, particularly illustrated commentaries on the Book of Daniel, which were often appended to Beatus Apocalypse manuscripts.[7]

In Pierpont Morgan ms. 429, a commentary on the Book of Daniel, dating from the thirteenth century, the illumination for chapter five visualizes the story through the juxtaposition of isolated, emblematic imagery (fig. 6). The prophet points to a disembodied hand, as it emerges from behind a flaming candlestick. Meanwhile, at the bottom of the page, Belshazzar, oblivious to the message of doom, idly reclines on a couch before a banqueting table accompanied by members of his court.

Figure 6

Unidentified Spanish artist, *Belshazzar's Feast*, manuscript illumination for a commentary on the Book of Daniel by Saint Jerome, Daniel V: 1–28. Morgan ms. 429, folio 159 recto, 13th century. The Pierpont Morgan Library, New York, N.Y.

Conjoining commentaries on the Book of Daniel and the Revelation of Saint John the Divine, medieval exegetes identified Belshazzar as an Old Testament type for the Antichrist, the demonic agent of Satan, who oppresses and persecutes the faithful prior to the final triumph of Christ (Rev. 20:7–10). According to the influential Spanish theologian Saint Isidore of Seville (c. 570–636), Revelation's apocalyptic battle between the city of Jerusalem, or the true church, and the city of Babylon, or the kingdom of the heretics, merely repeated the image of cosmic struggle in the Book of Daniel. Furthermore, in Spain and elsewhere in Europe, the figure of Belshazzar and his exotic, oriental court, became a logical symbol for the hated caliphs and sultans of the Arab empire.

24

The centuries of crusades against Islam, having as their central spiritual goal the Christian rebuilding of a new Jerusalem, assured the topical relevance of Daniel's tale of retribution and liberation.

By the sixteenth and seventeenth centuries, when the Bible was translated into the vernacular, the imagery of Belshazzar's feast had become thoroughly integrated into ordinary, popular discourse. Isolated names and phrases from the Belshazzar legend, "handwriting on the wall," "weighed in the balance and found wanting," and even "Mene, Mene, Tekel, Upharsin," evoked feelings of wonder and fear in sermons, poetry, and political broadsides. The image of a disembodied human hand, emerging from a cloud of smoke or fire, became generalized in the visual arts to signify an act of divine intervention or justice. One of the more powerful paintings of the subject, Jusepe de Ribera's *Vision of Belshazzar* (c. 1635), features only the hand, protruding mysteriously from a cloud, to write the message of doom upon the wall.[8] Ribera's decision not to depict the narrative context, but rather to make a figure of speech—"the handwriting upon the wall"—frighteningly palpable, endows the theme with a more universal meaning applicable to any number of historical situations as a sign of God's providence.

Most Renaissance and Baroque painters, who undertook to represent Belshazzar's doom, were attracted to the rich pictorial and dramatic potential of the oriental subject. The story's sudden reversal of mood and expression was a challenge to those interested in representing human gesture and physiognomy. Artists who excelled in vivid contrasts of light and dark exploited the possibilities of an intense, supernatural light emanating from the handwriting on the wall. Other artists concentrated upon the pictorial effects of exotic costumes, a banqueting table laden with food and surrounded by gold and silver vessels, and the architectural fantasies suggested by the palace of an oriental despot.

The visual possibilities of the story were often so diverting that many painters seemed uninterested in its moral or religious content. This seems to have been particularly true among Venetian artists. Tintoretto and various of his followers, as well as disciples of Veronese, produced pictures of the subject that are essentially interchangeable with other banqueting scenes by Tintoretto or Veronese, whether it be *Wedding Feast at Cana* or *Feast in the House of Levi.*[9] The versions indebted to these two artists tend to subordinate the dramatic narrative to the rendering of a magnificent architectural space, the rhythmic movement of figures and the elaborate trappings of a sumptuous banquet. The handwriting on the wall, if visible at all, sometimes appears enframed within

an escutcheon, that is, relegated to the ornamental detail of the architecture (fig. 7).

Northern artists seem to have been more attentive to the religious and moral content of the narrative. For instance, in a Southern Netherlandish *Belshazzar's Feast,* the recession of the banqueting table directs the viewer's eye to the disembodied hand and the supernatural writing on the wall (fig. 8).[10] In a far more powerful and direct manner, Rembrandt van Rijn's memorable version of the subject reduced the number of figures in the composition and brought them closer to the picture plane, thereby involving the viewer in the supernatural drama during the moment when the handwriting suddenly appears (fig. 9). Furthermore, Rembrandt placed Belshazzar's startled gaze immediately next to the handwriting, forcing the beholder to contemplate the image of doom as the proper fruit of a dissolute life.

Changes in religious practice and belief may help to account for the apparent increase in attention among artists to the theme of Belshazzar's feast. Belshazzar's eschatological content was supplemented by a new appreciation of its moral value, as the conviction grew in both Catholic and

Protestant Europe that man played an active role in the
accomplishment of his own salvation and that art was an
important instrument to that end. While Protestant reformers
opposed the worship of images, banned them from
churches, and rejected many traditional subjects such as the
lives of the saints and the Virgin Mary, they did not entirely
reject the private or public display of religious art.[11]

Reformers suggested guidelines for the painting of biblical subjects, encouraging those with a strong moral message,
represented in a clear realistic manner. Emphasis upon
human, didactic themes tended to increase the popularity of
the Old Testament, since its stories had more to do with the
practical problems created by sin and human weakness.
Thus, Belshazzar's traditional typological relationship to the
Last Judgment became more instrumental in the sense that it
encouraged moral reform in preparation for the final days.
The growing popularity of Belshazzar's feast and similar
themes was based upon the assumption that Christ's mille-
nial rule was indeed attainable through human effort.

The Hebraic character of Protestant theology also
encouraged the representation of Old Testament themes. For
many Protestant reformers, the centerpiece of Scripture was
God's covenant with Abraham and his seed (Genesis 17).[12]
Protestant covenant theology became a powerful cultural
force in European and American history, because it revived
the archetypal theme of a chosen or "elect" people, thus
encouraging the development of modern nationalism.[13]

Figure 9
Rembrandt van Rijn,
Belshazzar's Feast, 1635, oil
on canvas, 67 × 84 in.
Reproduced by courtesy of
the Trustees, National
Gallery of Art, London.

Promoting an assumption, which continued to dominate American politics during the lifetime of Washington Allston, covenant theology held that every individual was accountable to God not only for his own sins but also for those of the nation at large. There were, in effect, two covenants in Protestant thought, one between the individual and God and the other between God and the polity to which the citizen had sworn allegiance. While a nation of elect believers was destined to prosper, God would administer a collective punishment, if individual citizens fell from virtue into sin. Thus had God caused the Babylonian Captivity to punish the sins of Israel and Judah.

Protestant reformers in Europe and America took it upon themselves to guard their respective national covenants just as the Old Testament prophets had once guided Israel's spiritual and temporal destiny. Based upon Jeremiah's denunciations of the sins of Israel prior to its Babylonian Captivity, Protestant clergymen developed a genre of political sermon known as the "jeremiad."[14] The jeremiad was a harsh critique of moral decline within a polity. It held up the ideal of a community's original covenant with God as a means of condemning unhealthy, corrupting influences in the present. Covenant theology became a revolutionary, destabilizing political force in Europe and America. Many clergymen sought to impose limits upon the powers of kingship, arguing that monarchs were just as subject to the laws of God as the common man.

John Calvin and others cited the example of Belshazzar to demonstrate that kings were mere humans, frail and weak when confronted with God's damning judgment.[15] In his treatise *Eikonoklastes*, John Milton attacked the growing royalist idolization of the Stuart monarch Charles I by comparing him to Belshazzar, whom God caused to shake ''worse than a storm, worse than an earthquake.''[16] Yet, Belshazzar's fate as a pagan monarch was inconsequential compared to the destiny of God's elect held captive in a spiritual Babylon.

During the seventeenth century, the convenantal idea of a new chosen nation developed in conjunction with a growing belief in the millennium. In Europe and America, many Protestants believed that just as God had required the Jewish nation to wage a perpetual war against impiety, so did He now need a new chosen nation to fight the armies of Babylon. The ''new Israel'' would lead the world to Christ's thousand-year reign. Protestant theologians, interpreting Revelation, Daniel, and other biblical texts, were divided over the question of whether Christ would literally return to rule the world or whether, instead, Christian principles would bring spiritual enlightenment to all who had previously lived in darkness.

While Catholic theologians argued that Christ's earthly reign had begun already with His Resurrection and the establishment of the Church, Protestant reformers claimed that the papacy was the Antichrist, Rome was the Babylon of Revelation, and the struggle for millennial rule had begun only with the Reformation.

In seventeenth century England, ideas of the millennium and a ''new Israel'' were woven into the very fabric of the national consciousness. According to Barbara Tuchman, ''the history, traditions, and moral law of the Hebrew nation became . . . the most powerful single influence'' on English culture until the early twentieth century.[17] During the period of Civil War, when they overthrew the monarchy of Charles I, Protestant revolutionaries thought of their country as an ''elect nation'' fighting the papacy or forces of Babylon. In his essay ''Of Reformation in England,'' John Milton referred to the imagery of Belshazzar's feast to characterize papist tendencies in the Church of England, arguing that the English prelates ''revell like Belshazzar,'' and that ''if the splendor of Gold and Silver begin to hord in once againe in the Church of England, wee shall see Antichrist shortly wallow heere, though his chiefe kennell be at Rome."[18]

With the Restoration of the Stuart monarchy in 1660, the Puritan dream of an earthly millennium suffered a severe defeat. Nevertheless, millennial ideas continued to inspire a significant number of English writers, including the Cambridge Platonists, whose philosophy would be of such importance to Washington Allston's intellectual mentor, Samuel Taylor Coleridge.[19] Cambridge philosophers of the late seventeenth century, like Henry More and Ralph Cudworth, were influenced by the prophetic writings of the Puritan preacher Joseph Mede.

During the English Civil War, Mede's prophecies had fueled millennial speculations. Mede helped to popularize the notion, still common, as we shall see, during Allston's day, that a necessary precondition for the advent of the millennium would be the conversion of the Jews to Christianity and their literal restoration to Palestine. The conversion of the Jews, the original chosen nation, but now (ironically and maddeningly) the most stubborn of non-believers, would be one of the most certain signs that the Gospel had prevailed over infidelity. Furthermore, the belief spread that the nation which assisted in bringing the Jews to Christ would be favored by God as the new chosen nation. Who, it was asked, would be the new Cyrus, conqueror of Babylon?

The bloodless Revolution of 1688 rekindled the flames of millennial desire. Indeed, latitudinarian defenders of the Protestant succession found in Queen Anne a most receptive ear for biblical prophecies regarding the conversion of the Jews.[20] While the eighteenth century has been noted more for its Hellenism than its Hebraism, Jewish conversion, with all of its millennial promise, continued to fascinate intellectuals, including such men of reason as John Locke, Sir Isaac Newton, and Joseph Priestley. Though millennialism may have been more prevalent among dissenting Protestant sects, important members of the Anglican clergy could scarcely resist the temptation to prophesy. Bishop Thomas Newton's *Dissertations on the Prophecies* (1758), which focused extensively upon the subject of Jewish conversion, enjoyed a wide readership.

The continuation of millennial thought in the eighteenth century meant that interpreters of Belshazzar's feast did not forget the reverse side of Babylon's fall, that is, the theme of spiritual liberation. However, Belshazzar's millennial content was best understood when the text of Daniel five was supplemented by references to earlier Old Testament prophecies. The Books of Jeremiah and Isaiah, in particular, feature

the longing of the captive Jews and repeatedly prophesy
Babylon's fall within the context of Jewish restoration to
Jerusalem.

Literary interpreters of the subject were understandably
better able to combine the imagery of the various texts than
were painters who felt constrained by the demands of pictorial unity and space. Thus, George Frederick Handel's
English oratorio *Belshazzar* (1745) differs substantially from
painted versions of the feast in that the focus of the work is
not upon the doom of Belshazzar but rather upon the spiritual longing of the captive Jews.

Composed for three musically differentiated choruses,
representing the three different nations in the story, Jews,
Babylonians, and Persians, the oratorio is also, in part, a pan-
egyric to the earthly power of the Persian, read British,
empire.[21] Unusual attention, for instance, is paid to the valor
and virtue of Cyrus, the Persian king.

The unhappy example of the Babylonians, by way of
contrast, served as a useful moral warning for the British that
bloated empires, corrupted by luxury and pride, are doomed
to certain ruin. Yet the suggestion that history is governed by
the cyclical, and perpetual, rise and fall of empires, is modi-
fied by the oratorio's reference to Daniel's fifth, millennial
kingdom and the repeated allusion to prophecies of Jewish
restoration and the rebuilding of the city of Jerusalem.[22] The
Jewish chorus, in other words, seems to point the way
beyond the remorseless cunning of history toward an age of
spiritual bliss.

The libretto, written by Handel's friend, Charles Jennens, is not the work of a religious radical. The tenor of the
work as a whole is moralizing rather than apocalyptic. Nevertheless, Jennens' celebration of the Persian empire as a
nation chosen by God to restore the Israelites to Jerusalem
could not help but keep alive the millennial idea that England
would fulfill biblical prophecy in guiding the Jews back to
Palestine. For those Anglicans who believed that the millennium had begun already in 1688, such an event would be a
fitting culmination to Christ's earthly rule.

Handel's numerous English oratorios based upon Old
Testament themes were extremely popular in America, particularly in New England, where Washington Allston cultivated a taste for such sacred music.[23] English religious poets
of the eighteenth and early nineteenth century drew inspiration from these magisterial vocal works. Oliver Goldsmith
even wrote his own oratorio *The Captivity* (1764), which was
based upon Handel's *Belshazzar*. In Goldsmith's composition,
Cyrus, the Persian king, is once again portrayed as the deliv-

erer of the Jews, being proclaimed the "great restorer" and "benefactor of mankind," who "comes pursuant to Divine decree, / To chain the strong, and set the captive free."[24]

Thanks to Handel's *Belshazzar*, the theme of Belshazzar's feast became more frequently associated with millennial desire or the building of a new Jerusalem. Yet the more common meaning of Belshazzar's feast as a story of divine retribution against pride and luxury, an emblem, that is, for the Last Judgment, continued to predominate. In Goldsmith's and Handel's oratorios, the fall of Babylon, the just result of internal vice and corruption, was a lesson for the British empire, which, in its eighteenth century global expansion, seemed to be suffering the ill effects of excessive luxury and pride.

A number of writers pointed to Old Testament Israel as an exemplar of moderation and virtue. Bishop Robert Lowth, whose *Lectures on the Sacred Poetry of the Hebrews* did much to promote the Bible as a work of literary value, stressed the fact that the Jews had been, for the most part, uncorrupted by the vices of luxury and pride. For Lowth, the Hebrews were "a people superior in dignity" to their contemporaries, "poorer only in luxury, levity and pride of artificial civilization."[25]

By contrast, Babylon symbolized all the vices that a nation had to avoid in order to survive. The eighteenth century Hertel edition of Cesare Ripa's *Iconologia* had codified Belshazzar's feast as a symbol for pride and luxury. Its personification of luxury, a drunken satyr, was juxtaposed against a background representation of the biblical story (fig. 10). Meanwhile, in a number of eighteenth-century English caricatures, a balance, weighing each side of a political issue, implicitly warned that the losers faced the same fate as Belshazzar.[26] Thus, in a print entitled *The Ballance* (1745), Jacobite opponents of the Revolutionary Settlement of 1688 and their Catholic allies in Europe have been weighed and found wanting, as the scales tip in favor of the Holy Bible and a copy of the Magna Carta, both symbols of English liberties (fig. 11).

Eighteenth-century historians continued to excavate the past primarily as a source for lessons in virtue. One of the most popular such history texts in Europe and America was Charles Rollin's multivolume *Ancient History*.[27] One volume of Rollin's history chronicled the fate of the Babylonian empire, attributing its fall to overweening pride, self-confident idleness, and debauchery. The frontispiece, engraved by Hubert François Gravelot, illustrated the story of Belshazzar's feast (fig. 12).

Gravelot's *Daniel Explaining the Hand Writing on the Wall* differs from most earlier pictorial versions of the story in that the artist chose a later moment in the narrative, when Daniel

Figure 10
Gottfried Eichler the
Younger, *Luxuria*, engraved
illustration from *Baroque and
Rococo Pictorial Imagery: The
1758–60 Hertel Edition of
Ripa's "Iconologia"* (New
York: Dover Publications,
1971), pl. 132.

is present to interpret the writing. Belshazzar still recoils in
fear and astonishment, but the object of his fear has been
transferred from the sudden supernatural appearance of the
hand to Daniel's actual interpretation of the writing. In harmony with the didactic purposes of Rollin's text, the teaching
role of the prophet has acquired central importance. One's
eye is drawn to this mysterious figure who ominously stands
in shadow, with his back to the viewer, pointing authorita-
tively, like Moses with the original tablets of stone, to the
words which have been seared into the wall.

Art historians have demonstrated how other Gravelot
engravings for Rollin's *magnum opus* were influential for the
history paintings of Allston's teacher Benjamin West.[28]
West's *Daniel Interpreting to Belshazzar the Handwriting on the
Wall* (1775), the principal contemporary prototype for All-

Figure 11
Unidentified artist, *The Ballance*, engraving, published 18 November 1745 in London, 10¾ × 6½ in. Peel Collection (II, 57:179), The Pierpont Morgan Library, New York.

ston's painting, differs considerably from Gravelot's more baroque composition (fig. 13 and pl. V). But the choice of the later moment in the story, when Daniel interprets the writing, is identical. Both artists relegate the banqueting table to the background, thus avoiding the temptation to render sumptuous still life elements, which would have detracted from the human drama. Both artists are concerned with the variety of human emotion and response to the event. However, in Gravelot's work, the figures are somewhat dwarfed by the grandiose architecture of the palace, as columns and pilasters rise beyond the frame, accentuating the vertical shape of the picture. By severely limiting the background space and placing all the main figures of the drama in the foreground plane, West created a much more classical, frieze-like composition, which emphasized the teaching role of the prophet to an even greater degree than Gravelot.

West's stately composition and his portrayal of Daniel as a noble orator were influenced by the artist's deep admiration for Raphael's heroic representations of the Acts of the Apostles in his Sistine Chapel tapestry cartoons, which were on display at Hampton Court. English artists and critics of the eighteenth century routinely cited Raphael's tapestry cartoons as models of aesthetic and moral perfection, and it was to Hampton Court that West first journeyed after he had arrived in London in 1763.[29] Raphael's portrayal of Saint Paul as a noble public orator stirred patriotic feelings among England's political elite, who were proud of their country's

34

Plate I
Washington Allston,
Belshazzar's Feast, 1817–43, oil
on canvas, 12 ft. ¹/₈ in. ×
16 ft. ¹/₈ in. © 1987 The
Detroit Institute of Arts,
Michigan; Gift of Allston
Trust.

Plate II
Washington Allston, *Jeremiah Dictating His Prophecy of the Destruction of Jerusalem to Baruch the Scribe*, 1820, oil on canvas, 84 × 98½ in. Yale University Art Gallery, New Haven, Connecticut; Gift of S.F.B. Morse, B.A. 1810.

Plate III
Washington Allston, *Miriam the Prophetess,* 1821, oil on canvas, 72 × 48 in. William A. Farnsworth Library and Art Museum, Rockland, Maine.

Plate IV
Washington Allston, *Head of a Jew*, 1817, oil on canvas, 30¼ × 25¼ in. Museum of Fine Arts, Boston; Gift of Henry Copley Greene, 41.291.

Plate V
Benjamin West, *Daniel
Interpreting to Belshazzar the
Handwriting on the Wall*, 1775,
oil on canvas, 50³/₄ × 73¹/₂ in.
The Berkshire Museum,
Pittsfield, Massachusetts.

Plate VI
Washington Allston, *Self-Portrait*, 1805, oil on canvas,
31½ × 26½ in. Museum of
Fine Arts, Boston; Bequest of
Miss Alice Hooper, 84.301.

Plate VII
Washington Allston, *Study for Belshazzar's Feast*, 1817, oil on cardboard, 25½ × 34¼ in. Museum of Fine Arts, Boston; Bequest of Ruth Charlotte Dana, 06.1875.

Plate VIII
Washington Allston, *Study for Belshazzar's Feast* (monochrome), 1817, oil on cardboard, 25 × 34 in. Fogg Art Museum, Harvard University, Cambridge, Massachusetts; The Washington Allston Trust.

Figure 12
Hubert François Gravelot, *Daniel Explaining the Hand Writing on the Wall*, 1749, engraving, published as a frontispiece for Charles Rollin, *The Ancient History of the Egyptians, Carthaginians, Assyrians, Babylonians, Medes and Persians, Macedonians and Grecians*, 6th ed., vol. 2. London: J. and F. Rivington *et al.*, 1774. New York Public Library, New York.

strong parliamentary tradition. As Ronald Paulson has noted, in discussing the influence of the Hampton Court cartoons on William Hogarth's *Paul before Felix* (1748), Saint Paul had become "a type for the principles of the Glorious Revolution of 1688," that is, "the principles of liberty and the superiority of law to the executive power."[30]

As in Raphael's *St. Paul Preaching in Athens* or *The Death of Ananias*, Benjamin West's *Daniel Interpreting to Belshazzar* contrasts the noble character and gestures of God's eloquent spokesman with the expressions of fear, anger, and consternation of his opponents. In no previous representation of Belshazzar's feast are the Chaldean astrologers or soothsayers so clearly part of the drama, standing, as they do, immediately next to the handwriting on the wall. West's drama has a "parliamentary" flavor to it as opposing parties vie for the ear of the king. The painting's focus is upon Daniel's oral exegesis rather than the writing itself. As West's friend the Reverend Robert A. Bromley argued, while praising Raphael's portrayal of Saint Paul, the mere gestures and attitude of an orator have a superior persuasive power over even "the best writing in the world."[31]

43

Figure 13
Benjamin West, *Daniel Interpreting to Belshazzar the Handwriting on the Wall*, 1775, oil on canvas, 50¾ × 73½ in. The Berkshire Museum, Pittsfield, Massachusetts.

To a nation wary of religious painting and fearful still of religious enthusiasm, West's decision to feature the noble Daniel as a mediator for God's awful judgment served to mute the supernatural nature of the event. To appreciate West's restraint, one need only contrast the difference between West's painting and Rembrandt's version of the subject, which West easily could have seen, since it was in an English collection.[32]

West's painting shares the golden warm hues of Rembrandt's picture. West even seems to have borrowed the twisting, recoiling pose of the woman to the right of Rembrandt's Belshazzar for that of his muscular bare-legged soothsayer, who also leans backward, toward the viewer, away from the glowing handwriting. West's soothsayer, however, like his other figures, is placed safely at a distance from the surface of the picture plane, while Rembrandt's woman, and the wine spilling from her goblet, threaten to break through into the viewer's space. Though he may have been influenced by Rembrandt's dark billows of smoke and the brilliant light of the handwriting, West eliminated the mysterious hand and subordinated the pyrotechnics, choosing a later moment in the story, Daniel's act of interpretation, and an appropriate Raphaelesque composition that would

44

appeal to the viewer's reason or conscience rather than his "baser" emotions of fear.

West's didacticism is similar in spirit to the religious dramas of the popular English moralist Hannah More, whose works were widely read in America and undoubtedly known by Allston.[33] More's sacred drama *Belshazzar,* published during the decade following West's painting, placed an unusual emphasis upon the opportunity for Belshazzar to repent and be saved. Playing loosely with her biblical source, More has Belshazzar ask: "If Heav'n's decrees immutably are fix'd, / Can prayers avert our fate?"[34] Daniel replies in the affirmative, assuring the king that prayers "dispose Omnipotence to mercy" and would, therefore, avert "th' impending bolt." In the hands of More and West, the theme of Belshazzar's feast was adapted to the age of reason and enlightenment. If Belshazzar himself is ultimately doomed, the audience which witnesses the drama is taught that it can act differently. Daniel seems to offer a moral choice and a means for avoiding the monarch's fate.

When West's painting was exhibited at the Royal Academy in 1776, it is likely that he intended to make a veiled reference to the American rebellion against the British empire. The painting may be regarded as a kind of personal political statement, since it was not painted on commission for any known patron, nor was it sold during West's lifetime, remaining in his studio until his death in 1820, when it was exhibited again at the British Institution.[35] Yet, like his *Hagar and Ishmael,* originally exhibited in the same momentous year as the *Belshazzar,* West continued to retouch and work on the painting, a habit which may not have been lost on West's impressionable student, Washington Allston.

Art historians have recognized the relevance of West's *Hagar and Ishmael* to the signing of the Declaration of Independence, since its biblical source refers to the founding of a new nation from the seed, albeit adulterous, of Abraham.[36] But West also chose the story of Belshazzar's feast for the topicality of its metaphorical reference, the contemporary popularity of its imagery. American radicals and the Whig opposition in Parliament were charging that "Asiatic luxury" was leading to "Asiatic principles of government," and that George III was under the unholy influence of sycophantic courtiers and flatterers.[37]

Popular prints employed Daniel's prophecy of doom to characterize this state of affairs. Providential hands, emerging from clouds, weighed the king and his cabinet in enormous, emblematic balances and found them wanting (fig. 14).[38] Meanwhile, from 1769 through 1772, a series of letters,

signed with the pseudonym of "Junius," appeared in the
English press, publicly addressing George III as if he were
the Babylonian monarch deceived by the sweet words of
Chaldean courtiers. Benjamin Waterhouse, an American
acquaintance of West's, who lived in London during the time
that the artist painted and exhibited his *Daniel Interpreting to
Belshazzar*, wrote that the Junius letters seemed written by
a "second Daniel" for the benefit of "another Belshazzar."[39]

It is tempting to speculate that Waterhouse discussed the
Junius letters with West when they met in the spring of 1775,
the year West painted his picture. Waterhouse was a connois-
seur of art and may even have had Rembrandt's painting *Belshazzar's Feast* in mind when he compared the Junius letters
to a "Rembrandtian" painting, in which "the figure starts
horribly from the canvas."[40] Waterhouse elsewhere referred
to the letters in pictorial terms as "that startling exhibition of
flaming Letters, reflected on the interiors walls of [Belshaz-
zar's] palace, by an Unknown Being."[41] If Rembrandt's
painting helped to inspire Waterhouse's imagery, West's version of the subject, representing Daniel's act of interpretation, was more nearly suited to Waterhouse's analogy. Like
Junius, West's Daniel wages a kind of debate against a group
of courtiers, who had heretofore influenced the mind of the
king.

While West's precise political opinions are not fully
known, he clearly sympathized with the American cause and
admired the statesmanship of William Pitt, whom
Waterhouse and many others identified as the author of the
Junius letters.[42] West's *Belshazzar* may be interpreted as an
expression of the pessimism among opposition Whigs that

the British empire had passed its zenith of power and was now in a state of decay. The statesmanlike wisdom and calm of a Daniel seemed the last fading hope for altering the course of events.

In his role as history painter to George III, West himself seemed to be a kind of Daniel, opposing those courtiers who hurled personal insults at his American origins and loyalties. He cultivated his identity as a humble American Quaker before sophisticated European and English audiences. West's primitivism seemed to give him moral license to pass judgment upon a decaying European civilization. Yet, he did so in a manner calculated to give no offense to his devoutly religious patron George III. West's *Belshazzar* is certainly open to alternative interpretations. As an allegory, it enforced no specific political viewpoint but rather expressed the moral and religious tenor of political discourse. Thus, other history paintings, which have been interpreted as antimonarchical, could also have been interpreted as reaffirmations of the limited, constitutional monarchy that Britain, in fact, enjoyed.[43]

West's high moral stature as a kind of Danielic adviser to the king of England guaranteed his influence over the next generation of American artists who traveled abroad. Furthermore, West's royal commission to decorate Windsor Chapel with a series of paintings on the history of revealed religion surely must have impressed upon Allston and other aspiring American painters the idea that biblical pictures were not incompatible with Protestant theology and were, in fact, among the most sublime of all history paintings. The fact that the artistic scheme for the Windsor Chapel decoration was based, in large measure, upon Daniel's apocalyptic prophecies also may not have been lost on Allston, who met West soon after George III had put an end to the ambitious project, but not before West had exhibited numerous paintings for the Chapel at the Royal Academy.[44] Thus, in the summer of 1801, soon after he had arrived in London, Allston wrote a friend describing the apocalyptic wonder of West's sketch for *Death on the Pale Horse:*

No fancy could have better conceived and no pencil more happily embodied the visions of sublimity than he [West] has in his inimitable picture from Revelation . . . a more sublime and awful picture I never beheld.[45]

In the same letter, Allston praised another painting with apocalyptic content, Henry Fuseli's *Sin Separating Death and Satan* from John Milton's *Paradise Lost.* He even composed a poem in honor of Fuseli's conception, shuddering in horror at the thought of Satan's rebel forces. Yet, as we shall see in the following chapter, Allston's interest in such subjects clearly antedated his first trip abroad. Like Benjamin West, Allston seemed ordained from birth to assume the mantle of artist-prophet.[46] His patrician nationalism, sown upon his family's South Carolina rice plantation, blossomed in the harsher New England climate, where he became acculturated to the Hebraic myth of a chosen people. With his Harvard diploma in hand, the aspiring artist then voyaged to Europe with the intention of succeeding the elderly West as a Daniel exiled to Babylon.

CHAPTER 3   *The Mantle of Prophecy*

Washington Allston's birth in 1779 virtually coincided with the agonizing birth of the American republic. His christening in honor of the new nation's commander-in-chief bestowed a special significance to this coincidence. It surely instilled in the youth a sense of mission, that his future was intimately associated with the sacred destiny of his native land. Patriotic American orators, after all, repeatedly enunciated the name of Washington as if it were part of a holy incantation.[1]

The famous hagiographer of George Washington, Parson Weems, certainly believed that the name would forever be synonymous with the highest moral virtues and the greatness of the new nation. It was, therefore, a supreme compliment when, in 1809, Weems saluted the thirty-year-old Allston for already proving "himself to be highly worthy" of such an "illustrious" name.[2] Coming at such an early point in the artist's career, Weems's commendation could only have motivated Allston to further exert himself for the benefit of his fellow countrymen.

Weems's reference to the artist was really an addendum to his commemoration of Allston's father, Captain William Allston, who had served in the American Revolution under the command of General Francis Marion, the "Swamp Fox." William Allston had died a martyr's death, having been taken ill after the Battle of Cowpens. Rumor was that he had been poisoned by a servant, who, presumably, was in the pay of the British or Loyalist opposition.

According to family legend, the dying William asked that his infant son Washington be brought to his bedside, whereupon he prophetically announced that "He who lives to see this child grow up will see a great man."[3] William's wife Rachel apparently was the source of this story, which so resembles deathbed rituals of the Old Testament patriarchs. According to Jared B. Flagg, Washington Allston's nephew and biographer, Rachel "cherished the prediction of the dying father as a sacred legacy" and she reared the young Washington "as in the light of that prophecy."[4]

49

Washington Allston's special identity, the linkage of his future with that of the new republic's was a fact which the child apparently was not allowed to forget. To visitors, he was Washington, "the little general," and every and any indication of genius "would recall the words" of his father's prophecy.[5] Furthermore, Allston's tie to the "father" of the new nation developed a more personal dimension, when, in April 1791, President Washington visited Brookgreen, the Allstons' South Carolina rice plantation.[6] Unfortunately, his young namesake was then away at school in Newport. Nevertheless, Allston was able to repay the honor eight years later when he was chosen to give the students' eulogy at Harvard's official memorial service for the deceased president. According to his former classmate, Leonard Jarvis, Allston delivered a heartfelt address. There was such "a peculiar sweetness and depth and plaintiveness in the tones of his voice" that the mourners could not restrain "murmurs of approbation."[7]

Regrettably, we have no record of what specifically Allston said upon that solemn occasion, but, based upon even a casual reading of other eulogies for Washington, one can well imagine that he would have compared him to biblical heroes, particularly Moses, the savior of the Jewish nation. George Washington was commonly referred to as a second Moses, because he had led a nation out of bondage and had presented his people a new code of law, as if by divine command. Even such vocal deists as Benjamin Franklin and Thomas Jefferson had first proposed that Moses and the exodus from Egypt be featured in the seal of the United States.[8]

In preparation for his poetic eulogy to President Washington, Allston may have consulted Timothy Dwight's famous epic poem *The Conquest of Canaan*, which suggested that Israel's taking of the Promised Land was a type for America's holier, Christian mission in God's providential plan. Dwight's poem had certainly inspired Allston's older colleague, John Trumbull, whose drawing of 1786, *Joshua Attended by Death at the Battle of Ai*, bears comparison to his battle pictures of the American Revolution.[9] As expressed in Trumbull's drawing and Dwight's epic, the Israelite commander Joshua had been another popular Hebraic type for George Washington.

Old Testament stories of the ancient Israelites became prophetic allegories for the events of the American Revolution. While Allston was too young to have known his father, who died in 1781, the young boy would have heard personal tales of the war from his stepfather, Dr. Henry Collins Flagg, who had been chief of the medical staff for the army of General Nathaniel Greene in Rhode Island.[10] Flagg would have been able to tell his stepson details of soldiers' bravery in battle, their defiant spirit inspired by a sense that they were fulfilling Old Testament prophecy. The young boy surely heard songs of the Revolution, particularly from the songbooks of William Billings, their popular lyrics interweaving a running history of the war with paraphrases from biblical history.[11]

As one who would become a great admirer of George Frederick Handel, the young Allston also may have attended patriotic ceremonies in which that composer's oratorios, based upon Old Testament history, were used to commemorate American independence.[12] The city of Charleston's Saint Coecilia Society, one of the few musical organizations in the nation with roots in the colonial era, often performed the works of Handel. Though Handel's *Belshazzar* oratorio was scarcely his most popular, it does not seem too fanciful to imagine that Allston became aware of the work at a fairly early age. Booksellers and printers frequently advertised the sale of sheet music for Handel's oratorios, including the *Belshazzar*.[13]

Allston's christening, the martyrdom and prophecy of his father, the pride of his mother, and the professional and military prestige of his stepfather, all conspired to reinforce Allston's sense of belonging to America's "natural" aristocracy. Being descendent from a wealthy plantation family, Allston easily came to identify with the conservative Federalist elite, whose political hero was, after all, George Washington. In opposition to the democratic ideas of Jeffersonian Republicans, the Federalist elite assumed that wealth and property were necessary prerequisites for holding public office. The economic or social elite, in fact, had a moral obligation to govern the nation and prevent "mob rule."

That Allston maintained antidemocratic views long after it had become unfashionable and the Federalists had ceased to exist as a party is a fact which demonstrates how deeply rooted were his beliefs in the patterns of social hierarchy dominating Southern plantation life.[14] As befit their social station, his parents had been married in the established Anglican church of South Carolina.[15] Allston's mother, however, being descended from Huguenot refugees, probably practiced a certain liberality and tolerance in matters of religion, a virtue which became a necessity when the Revolution disestablished the Anglican church forcing its reorganization.[16] Her son would inherit this genteel spirit of toleration in matters of religion, though maintaining membership in the Episcopal church, which retained its status as the church of the social elite.

Though he left the place of his birth at an early age to attend school, Allston had fond memories of Brookgreen plantation, located on the Waccamaw River near Charleston. Art historians have properly emphasized the importance of the plantation for the development of the artist's imagination, particularly his predilection for the sublime and tales of supernatural terror like Belshazzar's feast. Allston later recalled his delight in the superstitions, ghost, and witch stories that had been told him by the plantation slaves.[17] As a little boy, he was allowed to mingle and socialize with the black slaves, absorbing the mystery of their exciting, magical tales.

Yet the master-slave relationship obviously also had importance in that it habituated the artist to the idea of a natural social order or hierarchy. It increased the artist's sense of otherness and superiority to the less fortunate. While it is true that one of his early paintings was of a Santo Domingo black boy with a liberty cap (now lost), he apparently also represented the figure with a boot in one hand and a shoe brush in the other, performing a typically menial task.[18] Furthermore, Allston's later efforts to grant freedom to the slaves he inherited from his parents and stepfather would not necessarily contradict but probably enhanced his sense of paternalism.[19] Acts of charitable benevolence were, after all, the special responsibility of a ruling elite, particularly in reform-minded New England.

Allston thus asserted in his *Lectures on Art* that cultivation and education were necessary for enjoyment of the "mental pleasures." He insisted that "no one . . . would refer to the savages of Australia for a true specimen of what was proper or natural to the human mind; we should rather seek it, if such were the alternative, in a civilized child of five years old."[20] While the slaves in America were surely a few steps above the "savage state" of the Australian aborigines, one cannot help but think that Allston was here remembering his childhood relationship with the plantation blacks. As Allston's nephew Jared B. Flagg stated with a bemused, patronizing tone:

The boy Washington was sensible and sturdy enough to be able to listen without injury to stories of ghosts and goblins in which the African delights. The Southern negro is never so happy as when relating to infantile gentry legends and myths to startle and alarm.[21]

Allston was expecially proud of his intellectual accomplishments and the superior development of his taste. He accepted his social rank as a matter of course; his education, his growing knowledge of art and literature, also clearly distinguished him from the great mass of American society. By selling the nearly nine hundred acres of plantation property bequeathed him by his father in order to finance his study abroad, Allston typified his generation of young Federalists who advocated education as a means to counter the growth of democracy.[22] With property losing exclusive political rights, perhaps the cultivation of talent and virtue could stem the tide.

While, in theory, Allston seemed to recognize that any individual could sublime himself upward, beyond the savage animal state, toward the manners and taste of a gentleman, he could never really discard his belief in a natural chain of being. He conceived the body politic in traditional, organic terms. Some people were the hands and feet of society, mechanically reproducing the material conditions of life, while others, the natural leaders of society, engaged in intellectual labor, reproducing the spiritual necessities of life. Thus in his most famous self-portrait, painted in Rome in 1805, the artist represented himself as a gentleman-scholar (fig. 15 and pl. VI). The touch of dandyism in hair style and dress is mitigated by the picture's poetic somberness, while the intellectual and moral seriousness expressed in the face is iconographically accented by the gold Phi Beta Kappa key that hangs from the chain of his watch.[23]

Though Allston's formal education began at a boarding school in Charleston, Allston's stepfather soon sent him northward to be educated in Newport, Rhode Island. According to Allston's memoirist, Jared B. Flagg, the family was uneasy about the boy's budding interest in art and hoped that a sterner schooling in Newport would help overcome his inclination to become a painter.[24]

Of course, family opposition to a career in art is a standard cliché found in countless biographies and novels and, in Allston's case, one must take his biographer's contention with a grain of salt. We know, in fact, that Henry Collins Flagg had brought with him from Newport a number of paintings, consisting mostly of family portraits.[25] Furthermore Flagg's father, Ebenezar, had been a business partner of Henry Collins, one of the most wealthy merchants in Newport, who also happened to possess a large collection of paintings.[26] Not only had Collins helped to support such painters as John Smibert and Robert Feke, but he also helped to finance the construction of important public buildings in Newport, including Peter Harrison's Redwood Library and Brick Market. If, therefore, Allston's stepfather had wished to discourage the boy's interest in art, the rich cultural environment of Newport scarcely would seem to have been the solution.

Whatever the case may have been, it was not unusual for Southern boys to be educated in the North, and George Gibbs Channing, a friend of Allston's, recalled that the Newport preparatory school, supervised by Robert Rogers of

Brown University, practiced a severe discipline.[27] Thus, although Allston retained the genteel manners and social conservatism of his Southern plantation background, he was formally educated within the spartan environment established by New England Puritanism. The sudden change in moral atmosphere may have contributed to a certain tension and sense of guilt in Allston's mind. Having been used to the more leisured pace of plantation life, he found himself apologizing to Mr. Rogers for his habitual laziness and tendency toward procrastination, a condition that later, of course, contributed to the tragic incompletion of *Belshazzar's Feast*.[28]

At Newport, Allston began to meet many of the future leaders of New England society, including William Ellery Channing who would become the chief advocate of unitarian theology in Boston. Also, despite what may have been hoped, he continued his interest in painting, coming into contact with the portrait painter Samuel King and befriending the miniaturist Edward Greene Malbone. He also would certainly have seen some of the early portraits of Gilbert Stuart and works by John Smibert, the English painter who had journeyed to Newport with Bishop Berkeley in 1740.

Allston would have been interested in hearing of Berkeley's mission to found a college in Bermuda with the purpose of spreading religion and culture in the New World. Furthermore, Berkeley's belief that Europe was in a state of permanent decay and that America was the land of the future, where civilization and the arts would flourish once again, surely must have had an impact on Allston's own sense of mission, his desire, as he later wrote his mother, to be "the first painter" in America.[29]

One further aspect of Newport culture and history must be mentioned for its influence upon Allston's career, particularly his interest in painting themes from Jewish history. Prior to the Revolution, Newport had had a small but extremely influential population of Jews who worshipped in Touro synagogue, one of the city's most famous buildings. The Revolution had, however, wreaked havoc upon this community, whose commercial enterprises were disrupted by the British occupation of Newport and patriotic reprisals against Loyalist merchants. George Gibbs Channing recalled that services at Touro synagogue "gradually subsided, and finally died out," as Jewish families were forced to leave the city.[30]

It must have seemed to many who witnessed their departure a reenactment of the Diaspora after the Babylonian Captivity. Allston was very likely sensitive to this sad event for, at the very least, it directly affected the livelihoods of his portraitist friends who had depended upon commissions from these families.[31] Yet, on a more spiritual level, Newport's loss of this community ended a relatively close relationship with the Christian majority, a relationship that had been cultivated by the Congregationalist clergyman Ezra Stiles, who prided himself in his knowledge of Hebrew and had even attended services at the synagogue.[32]

Allston was, perhaps, aware of Samuel King's portrait of Ezra Stiles, painted many years before, in which King represented the clergyman as a Latin and Hebrew scholar. More certainly, Allston was moved by a letter from George Washington to the diminishing Hebrew congregation in Newport. Dated 17 August 1790, Washington's correspondence assured the Jewish community that Americans "have a right to applaud themselves for having given to mankind examples of an enlarged and liberal policy . . . which gives to bigotry no sanction, to persecution no assistance."[33] The Newport letter was widely hailed as a landmark in the history of religious freedom. American Jews joined their Christian brethren in linking Washington with "Moses, Joshua, Othniel, Gideon, Samuel, David, Maccabeus and other holy men of old, who were raised up by God, for the deliverance of our nation, His people, from their oppression."[34]

As the Touro congregation, nevertheless, continued to decline in numbers, the synagogue and neighboring cemetery acquired the status of romantic ruins, evoking melancholy musings upon the unhappy history of this persecuted people. Allston's friend Henry Wadsworth Longfellow eventually wrote a poem dedicated to "The Jewish Cemetery at Newport." While contemplating the "sepulchral stones, so old and brown," he wondered, "What burst of Christian hate, / What persecution, merciless and blind, / Drove o'er the sea—that desert desolate—/ These Ishmaels and Hagars of mankind?"[35] It is not too difficult to imagine that Allston's sympathetic feelings for the Jews, his compulsion to relate their history, were also stirred amidst these abandoned ruins, which symbolized their homeless wandering.

In 1796, Allston began study at the center of New England culture, Harvard College. During his first year in Cambridge, he lived in the home of a friend of his father's, Dr. Benjamin Waterhouse. If, as Jared Flagg claims, Allston's stepfather had hoped to discourage the young student's inclination toward painting, he certainly made a mistake in asking Dr. Waterhouse to provide Washington's room and board. For this was the same Dr. Waterhouse who had been in London, enjoying the company of Benjamin West, viewing that artist's entries in the Royal Academy exhibition of 1776 (see chapter 2).

Allston must have eagerly listened to what the doctor could tell him about the history paintings and the artistic fame of West. Perhaps, also, he heard stories about the great statesmen of England, like William Pitt, and the political tremors caused by the mysterious letters of Junius, which, according to Waterhouse, had shaken the public and the king as the handwriting on the wall had shaken Belshazzar.

As an aspiring young painter, Allston had much to gain from Waterhouse, who had been an intimate friend of Gilbert Stuart's as well as an acquaintance of West's.[36] Waterhouse, himself, had practiced anatomical drawing in the company of Stuart. He surely impressed upon Allston the high calling of art, the artist's responsibility to promote virtue through both his social conduct and his painting. In a letter dated 21 October 1796, soon after his arrival in Cambridge, Allston wrote his stepfather that Dr. Waterhouse "has shown a friendship for me that I wish may never be forgotten."[37]

Yet, as in his relationship with Robert Rogers, Allston's southern genteel background must have continued to make it difficult to adapt to the more disciplined regimen of New England life. Within the same sentence praising Dr. Waterhouse, Allston complained about "the great distance" from the house to the campus, which "makes my exercises rather disagreeable." In this matter, he certainly would have gotten little sympathy from the robust Dr. Waterhouse, who prided himself in delivering orations upon the virtues of exercise and the evils of intemperance and luxury.[38] Steeped in the tradition of New England Puritanism, he admired the rugged strength of the American forefathers and equated them with such Old Testament patriarchs as Moses or Joshua.

Nowhere was the Old Testament cited more often as a guide to American history than in the area of Boston. Allston would have attended services at the First Congregational Church of Cambridge, where the Reverend Abiel Holmes, a close friend and neighbor of Waterhouse's, preached to Harvard's undergraduates.[39] Holmes's sermons were liberally laced with typological associations between ancient Israel and America. Allston may also have remembered Sundays when Holmes used the negative example of Babylon to admonish his listeners against pride and luxury. One can only imagine the old clergyman's delight when a mature Allston returned to Boston in 1818 with his huge canvas of *Belshazzar's Feast*, a painting that he would surely have interpreted in apocalyptic terms, as foreshadowing the fall of Babylon in the Book of Revelation.[40]

Holmes was scarcely alone in his typological interpretation of Old Testament history. For the Reverend David Tappan, Hollis Professor of Divinity during Allston's tenure at Harvard, the Hebrew theocracy was a model for the new republic. Tappan claimed that even during its captivity in Babylon, Israel had been a "light" in a "dark world."[41] Daniel and the other prophets were, in fact, the primary role models which Harvard students were expected to emulate. The college's former president, Increase Mather (1685–1701), considered the ancient Hebrew schools of the prophets as spiritual prototypes.[42] In the eighteenth century, Harvard presidents were called prophets. Thus, Abiel Holmes, in his sermons, addressed the students of the university as "Sons of the Prophets."[43] The prophets and sons of the prophets were to transform the American wilderness into a millennial paradise of enlightened piety. They would teach their intellectual inferiors to curb base, selfish instincts and, instead, to practice self-sacrifice and benevolence for the public good. Lest their pride should ruin the nation, Americans needed to be reminded that ultimate sovereign power rested not with the people but with God and His law, as interpreted by the schools of the prophets, especially Harvard, Princeton, or Yale.

During Allston's years at Harvard, the mission bestowed upon its students had become urgent. The nation was beset by social and political unrest fueled, in part, by the libertarian ideas of the French Revolution. The Francophile deist Thomas Paine scathingly attacked the Bible, particularly the Old Testament. His *Age of Reason*, which began appearing two years prior to Allston's arrival in Cambridge, staggered the Harvard faculty with its viciously sarcastic prose.

Rejecting the Bible altogether as a reliable revelation of God's will, Paine argued that nature's perfect design was the only clear proof of God's existence. Religion was not mysterious. Man's reason could easily comprehend its truths. Paine attacked the writings of the Old Testament prophets as purposely obscure and deceptive. Old Testament prophecy was a figment of poetic imagination without real truth value. The American revolutionary attempted to undermine the Hebraic tradition in America with his relentless criticism of the immorality and bloodthirsty brutality of the ancient Jews. He scorned the notion that the Jews had been a "chosen nation" worthy of America's emulation.[44]

Clergymen and American Federalists watched in alarm as thousands of copies of *The Age of Reason*, published in Paris, were sold cheaply in America. Eight American editions of *The Age of Reason* were published in 1794, and nine the following two years. Fifteen thousand copies of the second part of the treatise were shipped to the United States in the spring of 1796. Much to the horror of the Harvard administration, students purchased and read Paine's treatise. A "French mania" had stirred the campus during the early 1790s, creating an atmosphere of irreligious experimentation in morals, and a rebellion against established authority.[45]

William Ellery Channing, whom Allston had befriended while at school in Newport, recalled that Harvard:

> . . . was never in a worse state than when I entered it [1794]. Society was passing through a most critical stage. The French Revolution had diseased the imagination and unsettled the understanding of men everywhere. The old foundations of social order, loyalty, tradition, habit, reverence for antiquity, were everywhere shaken, if not subverted. The authority of the past was gone. The old forms were outgrown, and new ones had not yet taken their place. The tone of books and conversations was presumptuous and daring. The tendency of all classes was to skepticism.[46]

Even at more conservative Yale College, the Reverend Lyman Beecher remembered that in 1795 the school was in "a most ungodly state."[47] Fellow students greeted each other by using the names of such infamous French infidels as Voltaire, Rousseau, and d'Alembert. The president of Yale and author of *The Conquest of Canaan*, Timothy Dwight, later concluded that the ideas of Voltaire and the French Revolution had lured college youth more than any other group in America:

Youths particularly, who had been liberally educated, and who with strong passions, and feeble principles, were votaries of sensuality and ambition, delighted with the prospect of unrestrained gratification, and panting to be enrolled with men of fashion and splendour, became enamored of these new doctrines.[48]

However, by the time Allston entered Harvard, a conservative reaction had begun. During his freshman year, Allston expressed the drift of the campus toward the right in a series of three Hogarthian caricatures entitled *The Buck's Progress*. The caricatures satirized a small but highly visible group of Harvard students who enjoyed the reputation of being the "town bucks" or dandies. Citing Allston's stylish manner of dress and his love for the social clubs, most scholars have interpreted the series as a humorous self-portrait of the artist and his circle of friends. Yet the most recent scholar to suggest Allston's identification with the bucks admits that the series was an "acidic satire" upon liberal thought and that "the story reveals the speciousness of the personal refinements that the bucks were advocating by their dress and behavior."[49]

The highly moral message of the parody shows that Allston had little sympathy with the irreligion, vanity, and violence of buckism. In the first sketch entitled *The Introduction of a Country Lad to a Click of Town Bucks*, an unsophisticated newcomer, obviously ill at ease, is introduced to the group by a reassuring friend (fig. 16). The other bucks stand or are seated around a table. While one tips a drinking glass in greeting, the others, in various states of inebriation, critically scrutinize the new arrival's awkwardness.

In the second sketch we see the bumpkin being fitted with a brand new set of clothes and a new hair style (fig. 17).[50] The chaotic scene with an overturned chair, bottle of wine, and broken wine glass reveals the anarchic ethos that existed beneath the surface veneer of liberal, Enlightenment rationalism. Upon the fireplace mantle, Allston significantly placed a set of books with the title of Thomas Paine's *Age of Reason*.

The concluding sketch depicts the social impact of the bucks' Francophile ideology and lifestyle. In the sketch, subtitled *A Midnight Fray*, the bucks are shown in the middle of a

Figure 16
Washington Allston, *The Buck's Progress: Introduction of a Country Lad to a Click of Town Bucks,* 1796, pen and watercolor on paper, 9½ × 11⅝ in. Location unknown. Photograph courtesy of the National Park Service, Longfellow National Historic Site, Cambridge, Massachusetts.

street brawl, disrupting the peaceful citizens of the town (fig. 18). In the distance, Allston placed a church steeple, highlighted by a full moon, which stands in silent judgment upon the immorality below.

Allston did not share the bucks' confidence in Paine's extreme rationalism. As Leonard Jarvis, a former schoolmate, recollected, Allston had never been "a scoffer or an encourager of scoffing in others."[51] The young artist's absence or tardiness for chapel probably reflected more upon the dullness of the services than the student's lack of devotion. Jarvis and others agreed that Harvard's religious exercises, as led by President Joseph Willard, tended to be repetitious and wanting in emotion. As we shall see, Allston preferred the imaginative religious poetry of an Edward Young or a William Cowper. Yet, he was also interested in rational proofs for religion. In the spring of 1800, he checked out from the Harvard library a copy of "Jennings evidences," probably a reference to Soame Jenyns' *A View of the Internal Evidence of the Christian Religion.*[52]

The libertine ethos of the Harvard bucks was alien to Allston's experience. The social clubs to which he belonged were anything but seditious. For instance, when he joined the Hasty Pudding Club in 1798, the organization had become thoroughly committed to the conservative principles of the Federalist Party. In celebrating President Washington's birthday that year, the members even lifted a toast to the "constituted authorities" of Harvard and expressed the hope that "the government of our own choice never be assailed by Jacobinism."[53]

Belonging to the generation born after the Declaration of

Figure 17
Washington Allston, *The Buck's Progress: A Beau in His Dressing Room*, 1796, pen and watercolor on paper, 9¹/₂ × 11⁵/₈ in. Location unknown. Photograph courtesy of the National Park Service, Longfellow National Historic Site, Cambridge, Massachusetts.

Figure 18
Washington Allston, *The Buck's Progress: A Midnight Fray*, 1796, pen and watercolor on paper, 9¹/₂ × 11⁵/₈ in. Location unknown. Photograph courtesy of the National Park Service, Longfellow National Historic Site, Cambridge, Massachusetts.

Independence, Allston did not experience the optimism and noble heroism of the previous revolutionary generation. He, instead, shared his youth with an American republic struggling for domestic stability and international respect. The patriotic unity generated by opposition to a common foe dissipated in the aftermath of the Revolution. During the 1790s, the new nation viewed with growing alarm the creation of political parties.

Party or factional opposition to the government was considered illegitimate and treasonous by most Americans of the period. Federalists associated the popular violence of Shay's Rebellion (1790) and the Whiskey Rebellion (1789) with the

Republican party's opposition to the government. The formation of secretive democratic societies added a conspiratorial flavor to the threat perceived by Federalists, who increasingly feared that Jacobin violence would result in the dictatorship of the mob.

Paranoia had reached a frenzied pitch when Federalist clergymen rang the alarm over the so-called conspiracy of the Bavarian Illuminati.[54] Founded in Bavaria in 1776, the Illuminati had been only one of many Enlightenment societies devoted to the propagation of liberal principles. It had been suppressed after ten years of existence, but not in the minds of certain paranoid conservatives, who managed to trace the origins of the French Revolution to the Illuminati, and who argued that the organization continued to exist in the 1790s as an international conspiracy against the established order of church, family, and state.

By the spring of 1798, the accusations, which had begun in Europe, had reached the United States. Fearing the growth of democratic societies, the Reverend Jedidiah Morse and Harvard's Hollis Professor of Divinity, David Tappan, led the counterattack, warning of an international conspiracy against the natural social order and the Christian religion.

Interestingly, Allston made a contribution to all the excitement by anonymously placing advertisements in Harvard Chapel for the meeting of a secret society. According to Leonard Jarvis, "All these papers were ornamented with altars, daggers, swords, chalices, death-heads and crossbones, and other paraphernalia of German romance . . ."[55] While Jarvis claimed that Allston intended his caricatures as ridicule for the conspiracy charges made by Morse, Tappan, and others, the artist's real intent was probably quite the opposite, that is, to ridicule the secret democratic societies that threatened the stability of the American government.[56]

Allston was not immune from the paranoid mentality which motivated the fearful reports of the Bavarian Illuminati conspiracy. His avid consumption of Gothic romances during this period of revolutionary violence typifies the taste of conservative reactionaries, who became obsessed with man's diabolical capacity to violate willfully the laws of nature. Conservative fears found expression in Gothic tales of terror, where the authors almost invariably described the machinations and intrigues of secret societies as a means for attacking the moral relativism espoused by the Enlightenment.[57]

If Allston had disbelieved the specific charges of the Illuminati conspiracy, he knew that dangerous, secret democratic societies existed nevertheless. Only a few days after Reverend Morse's sermon warning of the conspiracy, the *Columbian Centinel* published an open letter to President John

Adams signed by nearly every member of the Harvard student body. Written by Allston's close friend William Ellery Channing, the letter condemned France for conspiring to export her principles of revolution to America:

Though removed from active life, we have watched with anxiety the interests of our country. We have seen a nation in Europe grasping at universal conquest, trampling on the laws of God and nations, systematizing rapine and plunder, destroying foreign governments by the strength of their arms or the pestilence of her embraces, and scattering principles which subvert social order, raise the storms of domestic faction and perpetuate the horrors of revolution.[58]

Allston would certainly have signed the letter in the *Centinel*. Through his position as class poet and secretary for the Hasty Pudding Club, he displayed commitment to Federalist principles. Certainly, his poetic eulogy to the Federalists' leading hero, George Washington, had been warmly received. Furthermore, during the presidential campaign of 1800, Allston, in a satirical letter to his friend John Knapp, vented his wrath upon Thomas Jefferson whose election aroused a near universal cry of dismay from Federalist Jeremiahs. For Federalists, Jefferson's deistic faith and Jacobin support for democratic values meant that atheistic mob rule would now destroy the republic and its sacred covenant with God. Americans had accepted the devil within their midst.

Allston's satirical letter and certain pictures that he painted during this period echoed these conservative sentiments. In his letter, Allston described Jefferson as both an "assassin who lets himself for hire" and "the unruly madman of society."[59] Several paintings, now all lost, *Satan at the Gates of Hell* (probably a pastiche of Henry Fuseli's interpretation of the scene from Milton's *Paradise Lost*), *Judas Iscariot*, and *St. Peter When He Heard the Cock Crow*, speak of the imminence of satanic evil, the willful betrayal of Christ through greed, moral weakness, and cowardice, all sins alluded to in his letter to Knapp. Finally, a small painting which still exists, *Man in Chains*, is a study in human madness, and, if not a metaphorical reference to Jefferson, "the unruly madman of society," is certainly an expression of the dark cloud of pessimism which hung over conservative political circles.[60] If America were to abandon God, then the spiritual gifts which elevated man above the beasts would be lost. The faculties of reason and conscience would be overcome by an unrestrained animal passion.

During his years at Harvard, Allston showed great interest in man's nonrational behavior. The increase in lawlessness and banditry which followed the American and French Revolutions revealed the fragility of human civilization, its

63

vulnerability to the forces of nature. In his senior year at Harvard, he wrote a short story, "Procrastination is the Thief of Time," a line made famous by Edward Young's poem, "Night Thoughts" (1742–45).[61] In his tale of a young artist named Bernardo, Allston reiterated the central theme of Young's famous poem, the transience of man-made empires and dreams.

Bernardo's grand designs for artistic fame are dashed against the rocks of earthly desire. Lured by the transient pleasures of carnal love, he abandons the sacred calling of art. The "crown of glory" that ought to have been "o'er his head" is lost to another and then "Death came, and shov'd him in the grave."[62]

The sudden, unexpected arrival of death was a theme that haunted Allston throughout his life and it surely contributed to his obsession with the painting of *Belshazzar's Feast*. In "Night Thoughts," Edward Young had employed the metaphor of Belshazzar's feast to warn that time was too fleeting for one to procrastinate or to waste upon earthly power and riches. Death could strike with "Belshazzar-like" suddenness, preventing the accomplishment of important spiritual goals (Night II). Ironically, Allston's own death would prevent him from finishing the picture that was to have established his fame. This unfortunate fact gives his story "Procrastination is the Thief of Time" an eerie, prophetic aura.

At Harvard, Allston realized that his calling as an artist necessitated his departure for Europe. Bernardo had gone to Rome to become a painter, where art seemed to flourish as the natural outgrowth of a mature civilization. America was yet a young nation which required instruction in taste. As Allston wrote only months before leaving New York harbor:

The same taste (or rather no taste) the same architecture, and the same sentiments are to be found in all parts of the United States. If one meets with a curiosity, it is either a bear, a dancing dog, or a learned pig.[63]

Nowhere were there "better citizens" than in the United States, but Allston knew that these citizens required a great deal of education before they could take their place at the forefront of civilization. He traveled to England in the spring of 1801 because he believed its art represented the highest development in taste.

In other respects, however, he was appalled by what he saw in London. Napoleon Bonaparte's continental blockade had made unemployment and inflation rampant. Food rioting was endemic in the countryside and, in London, the young American expressed shock at the disparity between rich and poor: "Scarcely a luxury but you may command here; and scarcely a scene of wretchedness but you may witness at the corner of every street."[64] Perhaps even more disturbing for Allston was the extreme pridefulness of the wealthy and the sycophancy of the middle classes:

I had no idea before of pride unaccompanied by some kind of merit. But here no one has pride without fortune. Indeed, the most respectable among the middle ranks appear to have no consequence except in boasting of the acquaintance of some one in rank; and among the greater part, so shameful is their venality, they will condescend to flatter the most infamous for a penny.[65]

Allston's response to London's social ills had been conditioned by his familiarity with the Whig literary tradition exemplified by such poets as James Thomson and William Cowper. Whig criticism of English virtue seemed to reflect all too accurately the reality he witnessed for himself. In a poem which he wrote after his first visit to England, Allston lamented its corrupted moral state:

Alas, poor Cowper! could thy chastened eye
(Awhile forgetful of thy joys on high)
Revisit earth, what indignation strange
Would sting thee to behold the courtly change!

How wouldst thou start to find thy native soil,
Like birthday belle, by gross mechanic toil
Tricked out to charm with meretricious air,·
As though all France and Manchester were there![66]

During his second residency in London, when relations between America and Great Britain degenerated into the War of 1812, Allston became even more aware of the moral discrepancy between England's Christian conscience, expressed by her best poets, and the actual behavior of its people. According to Samuel Morse, it was Allston's opinion that the English think of Americans as:

. . . an inferior race of men, and such is their want of delicacy or even of common politeness, that whenever an American chances to be in their company, the abuse of America is the common topic of their conversation.[67]

Despite his criticism of English pride, Allston was, nevertheless, witness to a moral and religious revolution in England, a revolution which was already influencing the Second Great Awakening in America. Led by the Reverend William Wilberforce and the polemicist Hannah More, the evangelical movement within the Anglican church was largely inspired by fear of the French Revolution. In attempting to block the spread of infidelity and social revolution, Anglican evangelicals minimized their doctrinal differences with other Christian denominations. They formed an "evangelical united front" through the formation of a host of interdenominational moral, missionary, and Bible societies.[68] The societies founded in England, such as the Society for the Suppression of Vice and the Religious Tract Society, were soon copied in America. Anglican evangelicals believed that moral reformation was best achieved through attention to the manners of the ruling elite, the moral exemplars of society. Reform them, and the middle and lower classes would naturally follow. The validity of this strategy must have been readily apparent to Allston who had noted how the English middle classes slavishly aped the aristocracy.

Given that its audience was the ruling elite, the evangelical revival had a definite impact upon art. Toward the end of the eighteenth century, signs pointed toward a renewed interest in religious painting. Benjamin West's Windsor Chapel project and his series of apocalyptic pictures for William Beckford's Fonthill Abbey attracted wide attention. Thomas Macklin, meanwhile, employed a large number of artists to produce paintings which would be engraved for his illustrated Bible.

By 1801, when he arrived in England, Allston would have discovered that other American artists, like John Trumbull and Mather Brown, had been following West's lead in the painting of religious subjects. It is not surprising, therefore, that Allston's biggest project during his first year under West's tutelage was a religious painting, *And Christ Looked at Peter* (now lost), repeating the theme of betrayal he had attempted earlier in America.[69]

This picture anticipates the major biblical works that the artist would paint during his second trip to England, but Allston would largely abandon New Testament subjects in favor of the Old Testament. He would become increasingly interested in themes related to the travails of the ancient Jews, culminating, of course, in his quarter century obsession with *Belshazzar's Feast*.

This preference for Old Testament history, prepared for by his New England education and the biblical flavor of so much of American political discourse, was further abetted by certain "apocalyptic" events taking place on the European continent and in the Middle East, or Holy Land, itself. With the arrival of the revolutionary armies of Napoleon Bonaparte near the city of Jerusalem in the spring of 1799, millennialists began to prophesy that defeat of the Ottoman Turks would result in the restoration of the Jews and the building of a new holy city. Termination of the Diaspora would herald

Christ's thousand year reign. Whether Christ would rule in a literal, personal sense or merely figuratively, through the universal establishment of Christian principles, was left open to debate.

Certainly, Napoleon Bonaparte, the supreme propagandist, did everything he could to present himself as God's instrument, the new Cyrus, liberator of the Jews. On 20 April 1799, he issued a proclamation to the exiled Israelites of the world, "the Rightful Heirs of Palestine," calling upon them to return to their homeland under his protection.[70] A month later, the *Moniteur,* the official newspaper of the French government, reported the issuance of the proclamation, but, in the meantime, Bonaparte's Near Eastern campaign had floundered and the proclamation was quickly withdrawn.

Nevertheless, in England, news of Napoleon's designs upon Jerusalem revived the old Puritan prophecies, largely dormant since the mid-seventeenth century, that the restoration and conversion of the Jews was imminent. Edward King wrote in *Remarks on the Signs of the Times* (1798) that the French, in returning the Jews to Jerusalem, were about to fulfill the prophecy of Isaiah.[71] The English Baptist minister, James Bicheno, in his *Restoration of the Jews: The Crisis of All Nations* (1800), argued that the French revolutionary army was an instrument of God which would destroy the forces of Antichrist, including the Ottoman Turks and the papacy in Rome.[72] Bicheno and other self-styled prophets still hoped, however, that England would ultimately play the central role in leading the Jews back to Palestine.

Bishop Samuel Horsley and George Stanley Faber contended, contrary to Bicheno, that Napoleon was actually the Antichrist and, though God may have designated him to lead the first contingent of Jews back to Palestine, England would have the far more important task of actually converting the Jews to Christ. In fact, the final conflagration leading to the second coming of Christ would be a great battle between armies of unconverted Jews, allied with the French, and converted Jews, allied with Britain. Thomas Witherby, another prophet who supported this view, in opposition to Bicheno, wrote that "no atheistical democracy, no revolutionary government, but a pious sovereign, great in power and greater in piety and virtue, beloved by his subjects as their father, was to become the new Cyrus for the Jewish nation."[73] George III, an avid admirer of Handel's Old Testament oratorios, certainly seemed the more reasonable choice for Cyrus.

Though Napoleon's military campaign in the Near East failed, he did not relent in his effort to become the second Cyrus, who would usher in the new earthly millennium of equality, freedom, and justice. In 1807, he convoked a Great

Sanhedrin, the Supreme Court of the ancient Jewish state, which had not met in eighteen hundred years. Allston's friend and former classmate at Harvard, Joseph Stevens Buckminster, was in Paris at the time of the Sanhedrin, when the *Moniteur* published an extract from a seventeenth-century book of prophecy by Isaac La Peyrere, entitled *Rappel des Juifs*, which predicted that the Jews would be returned to the holy land by a king of France. Buckminster, who was no friend of the French Revolution, initially referred to the "fanciful" nature of Peyrere's prophecy and yet he was clearly impressed when he saw an actual copy of the treatise, terming it a "rare and extraordinary work."[74]

Most Englishmen viewed Bonaparte's posturing as an absurd farce. For Protestant England, liberation and restoration of the Jews were questions subsidiary to the primary problem of Christian conversion. In response to Napoleon's Jewish policies, the Anglican evangelical elite founded the London Society for the Promotion of Christianity among the Jews. The purpose of the new society was not to grant the Jews full civil liberties nor, primarily, to restore them to Israel. Jews would effect their own "emancipation" when they accepted Christ as their Messiah.

Thanks to a temporary period of peace between England and France, Allston was given an opportunity to judge at first hand whether Napoleon was a Cyrus or a Belshazzar. During the period of his residence in Paris from the end of 1803 until 21 September 1804 the artist saw Bonaparte's reputation as a ruthless tyrant firmly established.[75] In March 1804, Napoleon unjustly executed the duc d'Enghien for conspiring to restore the Bourbon monarchy. Two months later, he had himself declared emperor of France. Finally, he resumed military operations and threatened to launch an invasion of England.

While Allston marveled at the artistic treasures that Bonaparte had collected for the Louvre, it was impossible for him to ignore the manner in which they were acquired as the spoils of war. When he arrived in Rome during the first few days of 1805, the artist could witness for himself the emperor's appalling disrespect for the art which had been looted in 1796. Allston believed that the French were a corrupted people who lacked a sense of the sacred and ineffable. As he later told Richard Dana, Sr., "I never met with a French artist who had a sense of the sublime."[76] Without a sense of man's higher nature or art's divine purpose, it was little wonder that the French felt no guilt in confiscating great works of art from their original temples, churches and monasteries.

The act of looting sacred objects from ancient temples and churches may have contributed to Allston's identification of Napoleon as a Belshazzar, since one of the Babylonian monarch's principal sins had been the profanation of the holy vessels from the Jewish temple. Allston's friend, Charles Sumner, wrote that the artist had gladly left Paris from a revulsion over Napoleon's sacrilege:

At Paris were then collected the masterpieces of painting and sculpture, the spoils of unholy war, robbed from their native galleries and churches to swell the pomp of the Imperial capital.[77]

Sumner interpreted Allston's journey to Rome in symbolic, moral terms as an escape from the unholy struggle for empire to the timeless, spiritual realm of art.

In Rome, Allston found a colony of German artists who shared his conception of the artist as a kind of minister or prophet. Instead of a Jacques-Louis David, who flattered the pride of an ambitious despot, the American artist discovered saintly characters like Gottfried Schick, who declared his wish to live like a monk, avoiding completely the temptations of earthly fame and glory, or Joseph Anton Koch, whose sublime landscapes evoked the "elemental character" of Hebrew poetry.[78]

Allston arrived in Rome during a period of enormous excitement over the future of European painting. The fashion for classical Greek and Roman subjects was waning. Under the influence of Herder, Novalis, Wilhelm Heinrich Wackenroder, and others, German artists had begun to turn toward the Bible for subject matter and inspiration. When Gottlieb Schick exhibited his *Sacrifice of Noah* in the Pantheon in 1805, critics hailed it as marking the rebirth of Christian art. Madame de Staël chose Schick's *Sacrifice of Noah* as the most important example of modern German art, proclaiming that, "the new school maintains the same system in the fine arts as in literature, and affirms that Christianity is the source of all modern genius."[79]

The Nazarenes, Friedrich Overbeck and Franz Pforr, were greatly influenced by the success of Schick's *Noah*. Pforr wrote to a friend in 1809:

. . . why choose subjects so remote that they scarcely hold any interest for us? Why not treat more relevant subjects? The ancient history of the Israelites offers more material than any other. . . .[80]

More important than Schick's influence during Allston's residence in Rome was the friendship of the English poet Samuel Taylor Coleridge, whom the artist described as his most important intellectual mentor.[81] Coleridge was familiar with the works of German idealism, including the biblical criticism of Herder, Johann Gottfried Eichorn, and Gotthold Lessing. In his 1795 *Lectures on Revealed Religion*, he continued

69

the seventeenth-century Puritan and eighteenth-century English Whig tradition, endorsed by Herder and the Germans, of using the Old Testament Hebrews as a model for national unity.

Coleridge's poetry and philosophy of the imagination were also deeply indebted to the Bible. He argued that classical Greek poetry was a product of "fancy, or the aggregating faculty of the mind, not imagination or the modifying and coadunating faculty."[82] In contrast, the ancient Hebrew poets had used their imaginations to transform the objects of nature, giving each thing a life of its own and yet infusing every object with their own subjective perception. Coleridge also associated sublimity with Hebrew poetry. In his *Table Talk*, he asked:

Could you ever discover anything sublime in our sense of the term in the classical Greek literature? Sublimity is Hebrew by birth.[83]

Coleridge did not share Edmund Burke's theory of the sublime, believing that his explanations were too mechanical. He, instead, agreed with the early eighteenth-century theorist John Dennis who found sublimity not in wildness, disorder, and irregularity but rather in "Divine Ideas, or Ideas which shew the Attributes of God, or relate to his Worship."[84] For Dennis, the Bible rather than nature was the greatest source of sublimity. Its mysterious stories of God's wrath and miracles excited extraordinary or "enthusiastic passions" that exalt men with great souls to a state of being beyond "the ordinary course of life."[85] Thus Coleridge thought that sublime, deep feelings were aroused by the contemplation of obscure spiritual and moral ideas. Sublime feeling occurred "when the self turns inward" to examine the ground of its being and its relationship to the infinite world of spirit.[86]

The growing Romantic enthusiasm among the English and German visitors in Rome for Hebrew poetry helped inspire Allston's first attempt at Old Testament subjects, two small oil sketches, *David Playing before Saul* and *Moses and the Serpent* (figs. 19, 20). The recent experience of Napoleon's tyranny probably motivated the thematic choice for both these images of royal guilt and pride. From Coleridge, the artist would have heard a steady stream of criticism against the French emperor. Coleridge had angered Bonaparte with a series of derogatory articles he had written for the *Morning Post*.[87] In May of 1806, the poet had to flee Rome for fear of Napoleon's approaching army.

The two small sketches anticipate Allston's painting of *Belshazzar's Feast* in that he chose similar dramatic moments in all three stories. In the two sketches and in *Belshazzar*, he

represented a corrupted king just at the point when his conscience is thrown into torment by a prophet of God. Saul,
who has been rejected by God, starts angrily from the throne
as the recently anointed David plays the harp before him. In
Moses and the Serpent, the Pharaoh darkly glares at the miracle
of Moses' staff being transformed into a serpent, while those
around him quake in fear.

In March of 1808, Allston, like Coleridge, was forced to
leave Rome since American neutrality in the European war
was in growing doubt. Had communications between Italy
and England not been broken off, he may have tried to return
to England to complete his studies.[88] As it was, Napoleon's
aggression compelled him to discontinue his education
before he had the opportunity to establish his reputation as a
history painter.

Upon returning to Boston, Allston found that the Napoleonic threat had stirred New England's moral and religious
fervor. Faced with the common foe of French infidelity, New
England's fractious clergy were temporarily able to unite,
exciting public opinion against the foreign menace. Many

71

Figure 20
Washington Allston, *Moses and the Serpent*, c. 1805–8, oil on canvas, 15 × 18 in. Collection of the Carolina Art Association, Gibbes Art Gallery, Charleston, South Carolina.

preachers began to speculate that the religious awakening in America and abroad signaled the approach of the Christian millennium. Excitement over the prospect of Jewish conversion to Christ inspired the hopes of revivalists and nonrevivalists alike. According to the Reverend Timothy Dwight of Yale, the awakening of the Jews, that ''wonder of wonders, will awaken in all nations a full conviction of the reality, and excellence, of Christianity.''[89] Meanwhile, Hannah Adams, a religious liberal from Boston, urged Americans to subscribe to the London Society for Promoting Christianity among the Jews.[90]

Though Allston painted no explicitly religious works during his relatively brief return to Boston, he now felt himself part of a new community of artists, poets, and scholars conscious of the need to organize in behalf of Christian civilization. While Allston had been away in Europe, a number of his friends had helped to found the Boston Anthology Society. The Anthology Society's purpose was to preserve traditional cultural and social values from the leveling effects of the French Revolution and Jeffersonian democracy. Since

Christianity was the principal bulwark of the traditional moral order, artists and poets were told that they shared with preachers or ministers a responsibility to promote religious truth. When Allston finally returned to England in 1811, he immediately began his career as a painter of biblical subjects. His *Dead Man Restored* (1811–14) seemed to be animated by the new public spirit of religious reawakening. More importantly, his work upon *Belshazzar's Feast* was undertaken after he, too, had been born again in Christ.

CHAPTER 4

The New England Clerisy and Allston's Rebirth in Christ

During the Enlightenment, Christianity defended itself upon the grounds of scientific reason. Skeptics had forced theologians to produce empirical and historical evidence for the existence of God and the accuracy of biblical prophecy. However, by the end of the eighteenth century, the failure of the French Revolution had cast doubt upon the Enlightenment conception of human reason. Philosophers in Germany and Britain admitted the cognitive limitations of man's understanding and the Christian faithful turned increasingly inward to discover God. Man's intuition and feeling replaced scientific reason as the locus of religious truth. Scottish Common Sense philosophers, like Dugald Stewart and Thomas Reid, argued that man possessed an internal "moral sense" through which he could intuit "first principles," including "the reality of the soul, the existence of God, and the verity of standards of morality and truth."[1]

In Germany, the tendency toward an anti-empirical religion of the heart was more extreme. J. G. Herder, J. G. Hamann, and Friedrich Jacobi were the leading exponents of *Gefühlsphilosophie* or faith-philosophy.[2] Jacobi argued that faith alone, originating from man's innate moral nature, had immediate access to the truths of religion. Encouraged, perhaps, by the tutelage of Samuel Taylor Coleridge, Washington Allston was familiar with the work of Jacobi and the German philosopher's identification of man's faith with a kind of "higher reason."

Scottish Common Sense philosophy was influencing a number of New England intellectuals by the late eighteenth century. At Harvard, the Reverend David Tappan introduced Scottish texts into the curriculum. At Princeton and Yale as well, there was a growing preoccupation with the moral concerns presented by Scottish philosophers. The study of man's internal nature replaced the more traditional interest in defining church doctrine. Courses in moral science were among the most important taught in American colleges, since they were designed to instill virtue within the nation's future statesmen and men of letters.[3]

The moral concerns of Scottish philosophy began to influence the content of sermons in New England. Over the opposition of orthodox clergymen like the Reverend Jedidiah Morse, more liberal preachers tended to deemphasize theology in favor of affecting the emotions of their congregations through the use of narrative and illustration.[4] Ministers increasingly rejected sermons that were abstract, speculative, or metaphysical. They instead, composed homilies having practical spiritual value in preparing the heart for God. Liberal clergymen assumed that man was not innately depraved but was capable of aiding in his own salvation through careful obedience to divine law. Moral instruction therefore seemed more imperative than an intellectual knowledge of church doctrine.

In the Boston area, Congregational ministers who tended toward unitarianism purposely refrained from publicly stating their controversial belief that Christ was not part of the Godhead. The Reverend Elias Boudinot, visiting Boston from Princeton in 1809, noted with some surprise that the sermons he heard preached were "universally practical" with no hint of disbelief in the divinity of Christ.[5]

Liberal Congregational ministers, like the Reverends Joseph Stevens Buckminster and William Ellery Channing, preferred to ignore the controverted, metaphysical question of Christ's nature and his relation to the Father. Jesus Christ was instead presented as a moral exemplar. According to Buckminster, the intelligent Christian "does not disturb his mind with endeavouring to explain . . . the precise boundaries between his [Christ's] nature and that of the Father," but rather "looks to him as the great leader, whose steps he is to follow, whose character he is to resemble. . . ."[6]

Washington Allston was a close friend of both Buckminster and Channing. He shared their inclination toward a more ecumenical, less doctrinaire form of religion, one that emphasized benevolent feeling and morality rather than rational proof and argumentation. Allston rejected the idea that any one denomination in Christendom was significantly superior to another. As in his art, so also in his religion, he observed an eclectic policy. Believing that no one denomination or sect had a monopoly upon truth, he once proclaimed "I am neither an Episcopalian nor a Congregationalist, I endeavor to be a Christian."[7]

Allston cherished the ideal of religious freedom that had been proclaimed by the American Revolution. Though his family had belonged to the established Anglican church, they also had ties with dissenters in Charleston.[8] Allston was sensitive to the evil of religious persecution. Though troubled by the unitarian beliefs of Buckminster and Channing, he nevertheless accepted their right to freedom of conscience and adopted many of their own views regarding religion and moral philosophy.

As Harvard classmates, Allston, Buckminster, and Channing had been dissatisfied with the relatively arid atmosphere characteristic of the college's moderate brand of Calvinist theology. According to Allston's friend Leonard Jarvis:

Whatever the religious exercises of the University may be at the present day, they were at that time not calculated to encourage religious emotions. Our worthy president had a worthy face, wore a white wig, and had a strong nasal intonation, and always repeated the same prayer, which had nothing to recommend it on the first hearing. What, then could be expected of its effect, *milies repetita?* Under these circumstances it is not to be wondered at that the summoning of the chapel-bell should have been rather irksome, and I do not believe that among the three hundred undergraduates of Harvard, in my day, twenty could be found who would gainsay me, and certainly Allston would not have been one of the score.[9]

Channing concurred with Jarvis that "the government and teachers of the college, most of them of mature years, and belonging to the old school [understood] little of the wants of the times."[10] Harvard theologians had opposed the emotional revivalism of the Great Awakening begun in the 1740s. Fearing the disruptive nature of mass revivals, they had argued that genuine conversion to Christ was a gradual progression of the mind rather than the result of an immediate supernatural insight into God.[11]

Channing, Buckminster, and other young Boston ministers did not dispute the gradual nature of conversion or the role of man's intelligence in judging religious truth, but they sensed the existence of a poetic truth that was "higher than the mere language of reason."[12] They realized that rational arguments proving the existence of God provided little spiritual sustenance for the increasing number of souls who grew anxious as opposing rational arguments by deists and skeptics undermined traditional Christian beliefs and values.

Channing, Buckminster, and Allston had been joined by other classmates at Harvard, including Edmund T. Dana and Arthur Maynard Walter, in their rebellion against the deistic arguments of Thomas Paine and their college's own brand of religious rationalism.[13] After their departure from school, Channing, Buckminster, Dana, and Walter helped publish the *Monthly Anthology,* Boston's first important literary journal. As a group, they contributed a dissenting romantic flavor to the *Anthology* whose pages were chiefly devoted to the defense of classical rules and standards. Channing, for instance, wrote in 1803:

The higher kinds of poetry have often a veil thrown over all their beauties. The man of fancy and ardent genius labours with conceptions, which words but faintly convey. He forms unusual combinations of language to express the ideal beauty and excellence, which he discerns in the regions of the imagination. Aloof from vulgar apprehensions, he is forced to clothe himself in darkness and mystery. . . .[14]

Even while he was in Europe Allston managed to add his voice to his friends' advocacy of individual beauty and genius. Walter published several letters from Allston in the *Anthology*. In one of them, the artist dared to favor the expressive power of Michelangelo over the work of Raphael, whose *Transfiguration* he characterized as being somewhat mechanical.[15] When he returned to Boston in 1808, he submitted several poems and essays for publication.[16]

Those who contributed to the *Monthly Anthology* organized themelves into the Anthology Society. The journal and the Society were dedicated not only to the cultivation of letters in America but also to the propagation of morality and religion. The Boston clergy were heavily represented in the Society. Besides Channing and Buckminster, the Reverend John S. J. Gardiner, rector of Trinity Church, the Reverend William Emerson of the First Church, and the Reverend John Thornton Kirkland of New South Church were important members of the Society. Gardiner was the Society's president and Emerson was vice-president.[17]

Although liberal in theology, the Anthology Society was uniformly conservative in politics. As Federalists, its members opposed the democratic and egalitarian policies of the Jeffersonian Republicans who had come to power in 1800. Having been barred from political influence within the national government, the Federalist intelligentsia after 1800 sought to modify American political and social life through their control of education and culture.[18] As Reverend Channing assured *Anthology* readers in 1804:

The most enviable power is that which is exercised over the minds of men. He, who enforces the conviction, bends the will and commands the affections, has resistless power; he is a despot; he raises his throne in the heart; . . .[19]

Led especially by the youthful Reverend Buckminster, Allston's literary and religious friends in Boston consciously began to organize the New England intelligentsia into a kind of "national church" or Coleridgean "clerisy."[20] As clergymen increasingly tended to be conscious of literary eloquence

78

and narrative style in their sermons, they recognized the usefulness of the arts and humanities in propagating national religion and morality. Poets, scholars, and artists would join the clergy to form "a spiritualized literary authority responsible for the intellectual and spiritual well-being of the nation."[21]

Buckminster's address before Harvard's Phi Beta Kappa Society in 1809 was a manifesto for the Anthology Society's notion of a clerisy:

Scholars! I dare not say that the cause of religion depends upon the fidelity of the learned; but I do say that gratitude and every motive of virtue demand of you a reverence for the gospel. . . . Without this for the guide and terminus of your studies, you may "but go down to hell, with a great deal of wisdom." My friends, infidelity has had one triumph in our days; and we have seen learning as well as virtue, trampled under the hoofs of its infuriated steeds, let loose by the hand of impiety. Fanaticism, too, has had more than one day of desolation; and its consequences have been such, as ought always to put learning on its guard. Remember then the place where we have been educated. . . . Think of the ancestors who have transmitted to us our Christian liberties! Nay, hear the voice of posterity, pleading with you for her peace, and beseeching you not to send down your names, stained with profligacy and irreligion.[22]

Whereas the arts and letters had been mobilized in the eighteenth century to encourage the atheism and skepticism which had caused the French Revolution, Buckminster urged American intellectuals to organize themselves for the propagation of Christian values.

Buckminster's emotional Phi Beta Kappa address had an enormous impact upon Boston's community of poets and scholars. Allston probably attended this emotionally charged oration. In fact, Buckminster's address held deep personal meaning for him since the young minister used the occasion to commemorate their friend Arthur Maynard Walter, who had died suddenly in 1807. Buckminster eulogized Walter as a pure spirit whose scholarly endeavors and religious devotion had proven that there was no contradiction between learning and Christianity.

In his many articles written for the *Monthly Anthology,* Walter, like Buckminster, had formulated an image of the man of letters as a kind of Christian knight in combat against infidelity and irreligion. The Christian scholar or poet did not hide in his library but actively engaged the forces of evil upon the public battlefield in an effort to establish what Walter repeatedly referred to as "the empire of morals."[23]

While on a two-year tour of Europe beginning in the fall of 1802, Walter enjoyed the company of Allston and E. T.

Dana. He already began to write the series of political essays that he would publish in the *Monthly Anthology*. He first submitted them to his friends Allston and Dana, receiving their encouragement and approval.[24] Then, when he finally returned to America, Walter published three letters he had received from Allston during the artist's trip to Paris and Rome. In introducing the letters he compared the paintings of an artist to the sermons of a clergyman. Painting, like poetry, was not a frivolous luxury but a useful instrument for moderating the nation's unregulated desire for material wealth and social advancement:

He who equalizes the passions by exhibiting the harmonies of Nature, though he pipes in the fields or pencils on the canvas, may without levity be considered as sermonizing with the preacher on the loveliness of Divinity. It is not the contemplation of Nature or her resemblances that weakens the sinews of a nation. . . . Luxury is born of the body and rebel to the soul; and we may say with Fuseli, that towards the aggrandizement of character and the cultivation of Genius, gold, gold, had done nothing.[25]

The content of Allston's three letters reinforced the introductory points made by Walter. In the first two letters, the artist described his impression of the great masterpieces in the Louvre. While he criticized Raphael's *Transfiguration* for failing to convey a sense of divine wonder among the witnesses to Christ's "preternatural power," he praised Paolo Veronese's *Marriage at Cana* for the "sublimity" of its color:

There is something so pure, so divine, in the atmosphere that breathes it throughout, so grand and impressive is the aspect of the whole, that you forget you are looking at an entertainment, and fancy yourself in the presence of some aerial court, surrounded by genii, and respiring the ambrosial gales of enchantment. So powerful is the effect of colour even without sentiment![26]

The Venetian colorists of the sixteenth century convincingly demonstrated to Allston that great artists magically transformed the essential material of the craft into something ethereal, nonmaterial and nonsensuous. One saw through the transparent, carefully harmonized glazes of the Venetians into a world beyond normal sense experience. Such an art form which transcended ordinary material existence could scarcely be subject to the common criticism that it was a luxury or mere useless bauble.

For this reason, Allston adapted the glazing techniques of the Venetians, carefully controlling the color of his pictures with layered veils of paint and subtle gradations of tone.[27] He concealed the brushstroke to achieve a transparent glow of light that seemed to penetrate beneath the surface of objects. He thereby believed that he had subordinated the material means of his craft to a higher, spiritual end, one which reflected the purity of his own moral being.

By associating painting with the life of the spirit, Allston hoped to strengthen the ranks of the American clerisy. His former Harvard classmates and the members of the Anthology Society wished to support him in this hope. As Walter suggested, his pictures would be interpreted as sermons in paint. He, too, would become a Christian knight, fighting the spread of irreligion in America. Allston wrote in his poem "The Two Painters," that the task of the artist is "to raise man's grovelling heart, / Refining with ethereal ray / Every gross and selfish thought away."[28]

However, when Allston had returned to Boston in 1808, he must have felt frustrated that he had not yet begun to fulfill his calling. From 1808 until 1811, he had to confine most of his painting to portraiture as there was still no substantial encouragement for history painting in America. The young artist was nevertheless able to establish his ranking in the clerisy through poetry. In "Eccentricity," probably delivered as his Phi Beta Kappa poem in the year following Buckminster's stirring address, Allston echoed the Anthology Society's demand for a fusion of learning with Christian feeling and belief. The poem is addressed to poets and scholars, who, instead of following truth and their own genius, follow the paths of common sense and quick reputation. The bankrupt poet, who thirsts for fame, ignores God and the simplicity of nature. He rather seeks out the artificial environment of the city, where "courts and taverns echo around his name."[29] To win the applause of the crowd, he must falsify nature, dress and redress her in perpetually odd and eccentric ways, "till, fairly knocked by admiration down, / The petted monster cracks his wondrous crown."

Philosophers and sages, meanwhile, use intellectual gifts granted them by God to prove that God does not exist. Instead, they deify their own reason and craft as if there were nothing higher, no distinction between creation and a creator. The unbelief of scholars poisons the whole of society down to the lowest classes:

> 'Twere labor lost in this material age,
> When schoolboys trample on the Inspired Page,
> When cobblers prove by syllogistic pun
> The sole they mend and that of man are one.[30]

Men of letters must lead man to truths that have an existence independent of his own limited will and reason. Knowledge of God and Nature should be approached with the humility of an Old Testament prophet:

81

> *Presumptuous man! wouldst thou aspiring reach*
> *True wisdom's height, let conscious weakness teach*
> *Thy feeble soul her poor, dependent state,*
> *Nor madly war with Nature to be great.*[31]

Praise and fame "by genuine merit wrung" will ultimately fall upon the scholar or poet who loves truth better than the "mob's applauding stare." The artist must turn inward away from the world. Within himself, he will discover the life of the spirit which "feels the heavenly fire."[32]

For Allston, man's extroverted, common sense understanding was ill-suited to the task of perceiving the harmony of God's universe. The senses experience objective reality as separate, distinct phenomena, without apparent unity. The synthetic imagination, however, penetrates into truths beyond the cognitive powers of analytical reason. It harmonizes that which the senses had apprehended separately, blending them with the memory images of the distinct past and the dimly perceived visions of man's future in heaven.

The Anthology Society encouraged Allston's defense of painting as a spiritual activity, the equal of poetry. At the 17 April 1810 meeting of the Society, the artist submitted two brief, anecdotal articles on Luca Giordano and Annibale Carracci.[33] The articles were read for the members and immediately approved for publication. In both, Allston emphasized the long years of learning necessary to achieve mastery in painting. He criticized the facile execution of Luca Giordano as puerile and contrasted it with Carracci's arduous, but virtuous, labour. Luca's work was justly forgotten because it contained so little thought and evidence of spiritual reflection:

> . . . if mere manual dexterity, without the aid of mind, be sufficient to the constitution of genius, no one had ever juster pretensions to the reputation of that faculty; for no artist in so short a life has ever painted so great a number of pictures at the expense of so little thought.[34]

Members of the Anthology Society gave Allston and other artists cause to hope for institutional patronage in the city of Boston. When the Society established the Boston Athenaeum in 1807, providing a reading room and library for its subscribers, it also promised that a repository for the fine arts would be organized as soon as funding became available. This repository would be designed especially to assist "our native artists."[35]

A letter written by Anna Cabot Lowell, sister of John Lowell, an important contributor to the *Monthly Anthology,* indicates Allston's high standing within the New England clerisy. Miss Lowell lamented that genius received little encouragement in America but she optimistically reported that Boston now had a young man who promised to surpass America's greatest painters, including West, Copley, Stuart, and Trumbull. Speaking highly of Allston's character, she informed her friend:

He has visited England, France and Italy to improve himself. He returned to fulfill an engagement of the heart, but as we have few or no purchasers for such pictures as his he will soon go to England, where I hope the sunshine of patronage may await his labours. Few young men deserve it more. His manners are polished; his mind improved and elevated, his morals pure. . . . Does not this production of great painters prove that genius may spring up in our soil? although circumstances may prevent the growth of some sorts of it.[36]

Allston's fulfillment of "an engagement of the heart" was his marriage to William Ellery Channing's sister, Ann. The marriage had been delayed some ten years, apparently because the artist feared it would interfere with his professional ambition. The frightening power of carnal love to dominate the mind and soul caused Allston to conclude in a letter to Charles Fraser that "love and painting are two opposite elements; you cannot live in both at the same time."[37]

Nevertheless, after the lengthy engagement to Ann Channing, during which time he had dedicated himself to his first love, painting, Allston must have finally felt emotionally secure enough to risk marriage. Ann was surely under no illusion as to her husband's priorities. In 1811, she bade farewell to her family and endured a difficult trip to London so that her painter-husband could fulfill the promise engendered by his first European tour. Ann's quiet, introspective temperament was perfectly suited to the demands of Allston's career.

Charles R. Leslie concurred with Coleridge's opinion that Mrs. Allston "is an Israelite indeed in whom is no guile."[38] In referring to Ann as an "Israelite," Coleridge probably meant that she had an intuitive Old Testament faith in the God of Abraham, Isaac, and Jacob. She believed in the personal being of Jehovah, rather than God as an abstraction or a product of scientific testing and logic.[39] Ann's love and respect for her brother, Reverend Channing, was profound. Leslie recalls that she invariably referred to him proudly as "little Saint William."[40] It may easily be supposed that she expected no less a standard of saintliness from her husband.

Besides being a source of spiritual inspiration, Ann was an invaluable helpmate. In 1813, Allston suffered a severe and extended stomach illness. Having been advised to try a change of air, he and Mrs. Allston, accompanied by Samuel

Morse and Charles Leslie, traveled to Clifton near Bristol. While Allston was placed under the professional care of a Dr. King, Leslie recalled the indispensable comfort that Ann bestowed upon her husband during the period: "Never did I witness greater devotion in a wife to a husband than Mrs. Allston's throughout his long and severe trial."

Unfortunately, the emotional and physical strain of nursing her husband back to well-being may have contributed to the ruin of her own frail health. After returning to London, Ann became ill and died 2 February 1815. Ann's sudden death caused a spiritual crisis in Allston's life. Having become dependent upon his wife's love and care, the artist realized his worst fears regarding the irreconcilable relationship of love and painting. Possibly Allston felt a measure of guilt for Ann's patient self-sacrifice during his own illness. More certainly one may assume that he was overwhelmed by the thought that a being so pure in heart and soul could now lie decaying in an earthly grave. In a poem, "The Mad Lover," Allston had anticipated the anguish he now deeply suffered. The poem described the grief of a young man mourning the death of his mistress. Death's injustice threatened to drive him toward evil and insanity.[41]

Allston's depression after Ann's death echoed the worst fears expressed in "The Mad Lover." The biographer William Dunlap emphasized the shock of the death by contrasting it with the high hopes that had attended the couple's return to London from Bristol. According to Dunlap, Mrs. Allston's death "produced a temporary derangement or prostration of the artist's intellect."[42] Based upon the account of an essay that he attributed to Washington Irving, the critic-novelist John Neal believed Allston suffered from a sense of betrayal, that his sacred mission as an artist and man of letters had been irreparably harmed by Ann's untimely death:

. . . [Allston's] own wife had abandoned him in a land of strangers, and gone alone into the sky—leaving him *alone,* upon the earth, unsustained, weary, and heart-sick, to waste his continual inspiration upon the darkness and emptiness of the world about him. . . .[43]

As one of the principal eyewitnesses to Allston's condition after Ann's death, Charles R. Leslie reported in his autobiography that the artist experienced "extreme depression of spirits," and that "he was haunted, during sleepless nights, by horrid thoughts; and he told me that diabolical imprecations forced themselves into his mind."[44]

Allston's depression lasted nearly a year. His productivity as an artist suffered to the degree that he began and finished only one picture in 1815, *Donna Mencia in the Robbers Cavern.* As he told his nephew, George Flagg, many years later, he had painted it while deep in sorrow and "constantly in tears."[45]

Almost nine months after Ann's death, Coleridge still felt the necessity of comforting his friend and encouraging his faith in God:

I have, perhaps, felt too great an awe for the sacredness of grief. But those of our Household know, with how deep and recurrent a sympathy I have followed you: and I know what a consolation it has been to *me* that *you* have in every sense the consolations and the undoubting Hopes, of a Christian. . . .[46]

Without knowing the precise content of the "horrid thoughts" and "diabolical imprecations" entering his mind, one may infer that Allston had suffered doubts regarding the justice and wisdom of God's providence. That he could seriously entertain such doubts must only have compounded the problem, increasing his sense of guilt and calling into question his mission as an artist-prophet of God.

Allston's crisis of faith following Ann's death was further complicated by events in Boston which jeopardized the moral and literary calling of the New England clerisy. After the artist's departure for London, debate had intensified between theological conservatives and liberals who tended toward unitarian belief. The Anthology Society dissolved in 1811, partly because the Episcopalian divine, John S. J. Gardiner, could no longer tolerate the religious liberalism of his fellow anthologists.[47] One suspects that Allston may have sympathized with Gardiner's principled resignation as president of the Society. Possibly because of its unitarian bias, Allston himself, though nominated, had not become an official member of the Society.[48]

Allston had befriended the family of the Reverend Jedidiah Morse, the harshest critic of unitarianism in the Boston area. Anthology Society authors often criticized Morse's theological conservatism in the pages of the *Monthly Anthology* and had even called into question his moral character.[49] Reverend Morse earned the enmity of the Anthology Society members largely because of his position on the Board of Overseers at Harvard College. As an orthodox Calvinist, he had vigorously opposed the appointment of Henry Ware, Jr., a unitarian, to become Hollis Professor of Divinity. For Morse and other more orthodox Calvinists, like the Reverend Abiel Holmes, Ware's successful appointment threatened New England with a potentially catastrophic religious crisis. In fulfillment of their worst expectations, the Harvard presidency and other professorships were soon filled by theological liberals. Despite Morse's angry counterattacks against the unitarians, which included many of Allston's friends within the

Anthology Society, the artist won the trust of the conservative clergyman. When Allston returned to London in 1811, Reverend Morse had agreed to place his son Samuel under Allston's professional tutelage and protective care.

Reverend Morse must have known that he was not entrusting his beloved son to a unitarian heretic. Despite his deep friendship with Ann's brother, William Ellery Channing, Allston was committed to the more orthodox theology of Morse's friend, the Reverend Abiel Holmes. He must have been disturbed by Reverend Channing's and other Anthology Society members' disbelief in Christ as the third person in a triune God.

While the unitarian controversy festered in the years following the Harvard elections for President and Hollis Professor of Divinity in 1805–6, the debate became even more bitter, open, and personal during the period of Allston's mourning for Ann. Reverend Morse, with holy vengeance, had once again launched an attack upon his liberal foes less than a year before Ann's death. In June 1814, his son Samuel, who had been enjoying thoroughly the companionship of Mr. and Mrs. Allston in England, received a book authored by his father. His mother wrote that Reverend Morse had been under severe attack from Boston liberals since the treatise's publication. Apparently realizing that Samuel's mentor already shared their belief in the Trinity, the proselytizing Mrs. Morse cautioned her son not to mention the book or the bitter dispute to Mr. Allston, considering the close personal ties that existed between the Allstons and Reverend Channing. Samuel's mother reminded him that the brother so dear to the heart of Ann Channing Allston "feels with the rest [of the unitarians] as it respects your father."[50]

Acutely aware of the delicate, personal nature of the theological debate, Samuel's father also took care to warn his son in regard to Allston's feelings:

This book perhaps you had better keep pretty much to yourself. There has been a most violent answer to it—ascribed to Mr. John Lowell—the effect of which will be destroyed by its own violence. I would send it if I had a copy—It may be sent to Mr. Alston [sic]—If it be sent to him, you may lend him the *Appeal*—I commit it to your discretion.[51]

As the debate heated up, Jedidiah Morse and his orthodox allies became more insistent in their demands that Channing and Boston's other liberal Congregational clergy confess to being unitarians, a label they had avoided for fear of causing a schism within the Congregational church. Channing and Buckminster had been reticent in public when it came to discussing the nature of Christ's being and his relationship to the Father.

Jedidiah Morse was determined, however, to expose them for what they were. In 1815, the orthodox clergy forced the issue in a series of polemical articles. They insisted that the liberals accept unitarianism as the proper name for their creed since they denied the divinity of Christ. The orthodox clergy announced that they could no longer join them in Christian communion or fellowship. Schism was preferable to the abandonment of fundamental church doctrines.

The doctrine of atonement was a central issue in the debate. Channing denied his critics' arguments that liberals had abandoned the doctrine simply because they believed that Christ was an intermediate divine being, more akin to an archangel than God.[52] But Samuel Worcester, in a published reply to Channing, argued that the atonement was impossible if one held to unitarian belief:

As it respects the doctrine of atonement . . . it matters not whether Jesus Christ be regarded as mere man or as a creature of super-angelick divinity. If he is a mere creature, whatever rank you choose to assign to him, his death could not have been of the nature, of the meritorious efficacy of a propitiatory sacrifice for the sins of the world . . . those who hold him to be a mere creature, *do actually* deny the doctrines of atonement and justification, as held by orthodox Christians.[53]

Channing, in his reply to Worcester, intentionally kept his conception of the atonement vague and ambiguous. He firmly denied, however, that it was God who had died on the cross: "In not *one* solitary text," he said, "is the efficacy of Christ's death in obtaining forgiveness of sins ascribed to his being the Supreme God."[54] Channing believed that Christ's death had atoned for the sins of man, but "On the question . . . how the death of Christ has this blessed influence . . . the scriptures have given us little light. . . ."[55] In his later writings, Channing argued that it was Jesus's moral example of self-sacrifice rather than the bloody death itself that achieved atonement. He thus wrote:

I am astonished and appalled by the gross manner in which "Christ's blood" is often spoken of, as if his outward wounds and bodily sufferings could contribute to our salvation; as if aught else than his spirit, his truth, could redeem us.[56]

Channing's orthodox critics denounced him for his rationalism. They charged that he wished to deprive Christianity of its mystery and tradition. What, they asked, is left when all the mysterious and sacred doctrines of the church are discarded either because they are too vague or too controverted?

What remains, said Reverend Worcester, is "mere natural religion" or "in this enlightened age, rational Christianity."[57]

During his period of mourning and mental anguish over the death of Ann, Allston could not possibly feel the confidence of Reverend Channing's more optimistic view of human nature or the clergyman's belief that man could reasonably hope to emulate the life of Christ. The enthusiasm and ambition of Allston's youth had suffered a severe shock. In the wake of his own debilitating illness of 1813–14, from which he never completely recovered, and his wife's untimely death, Allston now felt the helplessness of man, his inability to control events. He became far more conscious of the forces beyond man's woefully limited capabilities and the need to rely upon a source of power infinitely greater than man himself.

According to Charles R. Leslie, it was the advice and comfort of Coleridge that brought Allston back to stable psychological health. Coleridge advised Allston to ignore the "diabolical imprecations" described by Leslie that had forced themselves upon the artist's mind. Allston should say to himself that the evil thoughts "are no part of me, and there can be no guilt in them."[58] According to Leslie, after telling Allston of Coleridge's advice "I did not hear him again complain of the same kind of disturbance."

As a result of his opium addiction, Coleridge was sympathetic to persons suffering, like Allston, from periods of severe mental derangement. He entertained the seemingly contradictory opinion that while men were responsible for the acts which they commit, evil's existence was independent of time and space and ultimately beyond the capacity of any one man to control. Scholars have argued that Coleridge was torn between an optimistic "Greek" and a pessimistic "Hebrew" view of human nature. During periods of optimism and creative activity, Coleridge stressed man's divinity and his responsibility for his actions, but during periods of illness or depression, the poet saw with the eyes of the Hebrew prophets man's weakness and the depravity of his being.[59] As early as 1798, the poet wrote to his brother George that he believed "most steadfastly in original sin" and that "our organization is depraved, and our volitions imperfect; and we sometimes see the good without wishing to attain it, and oftener wish it without the energy that wills and performs."[60]

According to Arthur D. Lovejoy, Coleridge believed in the Calvinistic notion that all individuals suffer from "the inherently sinful nature of the immutable noumenal self" and that this nature is "the result of no act of conscious choice on the part of any one of them, but simply an inexplicable eternal property of theirs—inexplicable unless, . . . it was conceived to be attributable to the (in itself 'mysterious') will of God.''[61] For Coleridge, sin was not merely attributable to the conscious actions of man but emanated from his very being. The poet suffered greatly during periods of self-doubt and creative paralysis and, therefore, did not wish to believe that he was personally or solely responsible for the nature of his being. Refusing to curse the injustice of God, Coleridge instead blamed the sinful nature of mankind, his generic rather than his individual self, for the burden of his infirmities.

Toward the end of his life, Allston recalled his recovery from depression for Elizabeth Palmer Peabody. Although he does not state the precise year, it must be presumed that he was referring to 1815 and the aftermath of his wife's death. The time of year was November, more than nine months after Ann had died and one month after Coleridge's letter urging Allston to find his consolation in Christian hope and love. The artist spoke of his return to mental health in terms of a religious conversion:

Ah, yes! That is the solution, . . . to recognize the divinity in Christ; and this was revealed to me—I say *revealed to me,* for I cannot call it any thing else. It was not spun out of my brain, *I know.*It was a dim, misty night in November that I was walking in London; the fog enveloped the lamps, so that each looked like a huge bundle of cotton-wool; the air was comfortless; my own spirit was even drearier than the outward scene; a heavy weight was on my heart and in my brain. Then this question of memory and dread of imprisonment in my own self forever, with the sense that it would be a relief to get out of such a dungeon, even into the cold, raw, wretched November, were hardly living, but obscurely burrowing in my brain. Suddenly there came to me a train of thought in verse, as if it were whispered by a spirit objective to mine, who made me the automaton of its utterance. I actually uttered it in words, which I subsequently wrote down.[62]

Allston recited again for Miss Peabody this spontaneous, divinely inspired poem, entitled ''The Atonement,'' in which he expresses his consciousness of sin's eternal presence followed by his feelings of relief and joy at Christ's removal of the burden of sin. In overcoming his grief for Ann, Allston had felt compelled to reject her brother's unitarianism. He makes a point of distinguishing between Christ and the creatures created by God, because Christ is God:

> Ay, such, O Man, thy wretched lot had been
> Had He forbade not,—He who knew no sin;
> Who to his own, the creatures he had made,
> Veiling his empyrean glory, came,
> E'en in their form. . . . [63]

Unlike Channing, Allston refused to shrink from the bloody image of the crucified Christ. Instead, he flees to the protection of the cross where "the sweat of blood, the nameless agony, . . . wrought the final doom of Sin and Death." He does not claim to understand the mystery of Christ's atonement. His feelings tell him of his need and dependency upon Christ:

O blessed truth! in my soul's need I feel
In thee alone my ever-during weal.

Mental anguish and a physical state weakened by lengthy illness combined to create an acute sense of human fraility in the artist. Channing, too, felt the sinfulness of man but he was better able than Allston to overcome any latent pessimism in human nature. Like Channing, Allston believed that man possessed free will, yet he more deeply felt the need for divine assistance, having far less confidence in the power of human reason and man's ability to resist sin. To relieve himself of feelings of personal guilt that Ann's death had been a kind of punishment for sins of commission or omission, Allston, perhaps, more than ever needed to believe in the general guilt of mankind:

Hopeless, alas, of sinful man the lot,
(And who can say of sin, he knows it not?)[64]

Sin and death were burdens too great for Allston to bear alone. He sought comfort by pleading human weakness. Accepting the continuing reality of Adam's sin, he transformed his personal remorse into something suprapersonal and abstract and, therefore, bearable. Joining with the orthodox theologians, Allston believed that only an infinite atonement could redeem man from the burden of sin. Since infinite atonement is beyond the finite power of man, God had come down to earth in the form of Jesus Christ.

Like Coleridge, Allston found relief for his own feelings of guilt and moral weakness in evangelical religion. His "Atonement" was a poem of humility recited in propitiation for his own pride and the pride of all mankind. He felt secure in the knowledge that redemption was bestowed from a source entirely outside his own, unreliable, mutable being. Christ's atonement guaranteed to Allston that he and Ann would one day be reunited in an infinitely more blissful realm. In triumph he concludes his poem with the cry, "Where now, O Death, thy sting, O grave thy victory?"[65] This affirmation brings him back from that madness which had threatened the mourning bard in his earlier poem, "The Mad Lover."

While Allston did not share Channing's confidence that man had the moral ability to save himself, he was far more dissatisfied with the antinomian implications inherent in the orthodox Calvinist doctrine of predestination. Man willingly had to cooperate with God in his own salvation. In one of his sketchbooks, he wrote that the regeneration of the soul is impossible, "against the desperate will that rejects it."[66] During the 1830s, when he was writing his *Lectures on Art*, the artist also wrote a related but fragmentary essay on religion and morality. In it, he struck a compromise between the Calvinists' notion of original sin or innate depravity and Reverend Channing's optimistic view of human nature.

Allston argued that man's "inbred Ideas of Right and Wrong (in other words, conscience)" were not destroyed by Adam's fall, "for had this constitutive ground of his moral nature been removed, he would have ceased to be a *man*, and have been left a mere animal."[67] In retaining his conscience man is able to cooperate with God in effecting his own spiritual rebirth:

. . . no man, though partaking of the *imperfect*, as the descendent of the sinning Adam, is left *wholly* without light. God took not away from Adam, when he fell, this *ground* on which he and his posterity *might*, through *productive* power (influence) of his Holy Spirit, be regenerated.

Allston concluded that man possessed "the fearful power of choice between good and evil," yet because it is a "fearful" power, it is not desirable in and of itself. Man rightly wishes to be freed from his ability to choose, thereby merging his will with the infinitely superior will of God. According to Allston, the "immutable freedom of holiness," whereby an unerring God chooses for us, is far more desirable than the uncertain "fearful responsibility" of freedom of choice. Thus, while Allston admits man's ability to act for himself, he displays a distinct uneasiness with his natural freedom and severe doubt that man will choose correctly more often than not.

Allston's loss of self-control in 1815 caused him to believe, if he had not already believed it before, that, despite his free will, man could not be held entirely responsible for his thoughts and actions. For Allston, as for Coleridge, evil had an absolute existence independent of the individual human will. The artist possessed an essentially apocalyptic, supernatural view of reality. As a visual analogue for his cosmology, he drew a diagram illustrating the Manichaean opposition between the forces of God and the forces of Sin (fig. 21). The archetypal ideas of Beauty, Truth, and Holiness

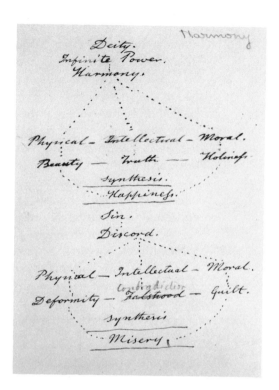

Figure 21
Washington Allston,
Diagram of the Ideas of the
Deity and Sin, from an
unpublished manuscript
entitled ''Fragments on
Religion'' in the Dana
Papers, Massachusetts
Historical Society, Boston.

are diametrically opposed to the equally real ideas of Deformity, Contradiction, and Guilt. Man's dual nature, physical and spiritual, was a microcosm of the cosmic war between good and evil in the universe.

Both good and evil have an archetypal existence and, in their purity, cannot be perfectly realized on earth. In his *Lectures of Art,* Allston argued that only ''a devil, or some irredeemable incarnation of evil'' could have a selfless, disinterested hatred of the good.[68] Man was incapable of loving evil for its own sake. Thus, the French Revolution and its evil ideas were not simply spun from the minds of evil men but from Satan himself. No longer in the form of a serpent, ''The King of Hell'' had simply decided to take ''a Nation's congregated form,'' the French, in order to tempt the rest of mankind.[69] Tempted by forces that are not entirely under his control, man must seek supernatural help to do what is right and good. Unassisted by God's gift of heavenly grace, individual humans cannot resist evil.

Allston believed that man's moral being was most efficaciously safeguarded through participation in the traditional institutions and sacraments of the Christian church. Though man-made and splintered by numerous denominations, the Christian church and its essential sacraments were divinely sanctioned and had withstood the test of time. While Reverend Channing tended to minimize the role of the church and the clergy in favor of the independent moral development of the individual believer, Allston's intuitive distrust of man's nature convinced him that the external regulation and guidance of the church was an absolute necessity.

Just as Coleridge had finally rejected the egoistic philosophy of pantheism for the more reassuring truths of the Anglican church, so too did Allston hastily retreat from the abyss separating the individual from the universe, seeking instead, the more secure mediating ground of the Episcopal church. As Doreen Hunter has argued, when doubts overtook Allston and other first generation American romantics, including Allston's close friend Richard Henry Dana, Sr., "they questioned their ability to know the truth but never the existence of that truth or its divine author."[70]

The artist's Christian humility and belief in human weakness, including his own, prevented him from advocating a religion of art or the imagination as a number of the more radical European romantics did. He would not fall into the same hubristic trap as that of the deists and Enlightenment skeptics who had created a religion of reason and man. For Allston, the unitarians' demotion of Christ from a person in the Godhead to the level of mere archangel, divine messenger, or worse, mere human was a comfortless compromise with Enlightenment rationalism.

After Ann's death, nothing earthly or remotely human could earn the artist's confidence and trust. He had learned through bitter experience that only Christian love could quell the human heart. In his Gothic romance entitled *Monaldi*, written in 1822, Allston wrote that earthly love is temporal and ultimately results in bitter disappointment. Inspired in part by his emotional reaction to Ann's death, the story is a theodicy justifying the existence of pain and evil in the world.

Monaldi, a successful artist, dearly loved the virtuous Rosalia, whose Roman family was a near relation to the pope's. It could be said that Monaldi loved Rosalia too well. She completely filled his heart leaving no room for Christian love and feeling. Though Monaldi had never been irreligious, his faith had been rational and intellectual in nature. His understanding assented to the truths of Christianity, but his heart was too satisfied with the earthly present, the love of Rosalia. Lacking a knowledge of the heart, Monaldi easily fell prey to the evil designs of those who wished to destroy his marriage to Rosalia. Rather than trusting the innocent purity of her moral being, he gave credence to the circumstantial evidence created by his enemies that his wife was faithless. Convinced that he had lost the love of Rosalia, Monaldi was paralyzed as a moral being, left with nothing:

To Monaldi's heart she was all; and his all was now gone, leaving it empty. An empty human heart!—an abyss the earth's depths cannot match.[71]

In a fit of jealous rage, he attempts to murder her. However, he soon realizes his mistake and is filled with remorse and guilt. Monaldi describes how his remorse was finally transformed into repentance before God. One day, standing at the edge of a cliff, he looked down to see the skeleton of a mule and the skull of its unlucky rider. This *memento mori* led him to conclude that even "the surest foot . . . may stumble at last."[72] For the first time since his attempted murder of Rosalia, Monaldi was able to fall to his knees in prayer. However, when he discovers that it had been one of his best friends who had betrayed him into believing Rosalia's faithlessness, he is again driven to the brink of insanity. He now perceives the objective existence of evil and the powerlessness of man to combat it without the aid of God.

Inwardly driven by some supernatural force, Monaldi is able to paint one final picture before he dies. Working in utter secrecy, he allowed no one into his studio, becoming angry when a servant momentarily intruded. After months, he finished. So horrible was the image that he had been called to paint that he loudly wept after he laid down the brush. The painting depicted a man, actually Monaldi's own self-portrait, prostrated in agony before an enthroned Satan. It symbolized the struggle of man's conscience against the passions of his own will that inclined him toward evil. Monaldi told his father-in-law that the picture was a warning against the evil invariably lurking beneath the surface of earthly beauty. Unless physical beauty is accompanied by a moral, spiritual beauty, it is false. Pointing to the deceptively attractive figure of Satan, Monaldi tells Rosalia's father " 'though only a picture—*I* have known the original. What is there, I have *seen*.' "[73]

Upon completion of the picture, Monaldi is able to die in peace, confident of life in a happier world beyond that of earth. Evil and suffering have been transformed into something good. The artist's painful remorse had opened his heart to God's grace. Monaldi thus refers to the "virtue" of his sorrow, and asserts that the "Supreme Love" of God "turneth the very misery from our misdeeds into a cleansing fountain."[74] The prior of a monastery who listens to these dying words of Monaldi agrees:

Thou sayest well, my son . . . for the sufferings of this world are healthful medicine to the soul; even the holy apostles tasted it. Let those who grieve then remember the words of Him who suffered for us—"blessed are they that mourn, for they shall be comforted."

The concluding paragraphs to *Monaldi* bear a remarkable similarity to the sentiments and words that Coleridge had expressed in his 25 October 1815 letter to Allston, consoling him after Ann's death:

Blessed indeed is that Gift from above, the characteristic operation of which is to transmute the profoundest sources of our Sorrow into the most inexhaustible sources of our Comfort. The very Virtues, that enforce the Tear of earthly regret, fill that Tear with a Light not earthly. There is a capaciousness in every *living* Heart, which retains an aching Vacuum, what, and how so ever numerous, it's [*sic*] present Freight of worldly Blessings may be—and as God only can *fill* it, so must it needs be a sweet and gracious incarnation of the Heavenly that what we deeply loved, but with fear & trembling, we must now love with a love of Faith that excludeth fear! love it in God & God in it![75]

For a period of approximately nine months after Ann's death, Allston had been unable "to transmute" his sorrow into a source of comfort. As he recollected years later, a heaviness had weighed upon his heart. He had felt entrapped within his own material being like a prisoner in a dungeon. Finally, "a spirit objective" to his own had entered his heart. Like an Old Testament prophet, inspired by a supernatural power of speech, he spontaneously recited "The Atonement." Allston's love for Christ's selfless act of sacrifice overcame the "learned ignorance" and "reasoning pride" that had led him to the brink of madness.

In 1816, Allston returned to his painting with renewed vigor. His revitalized Christian love expressed itself in the most productive period of his artistic career. He finished *The Angel Liberating St. Peter*, begun in 1814, and sold the *Dead Man Restored* (fig. 22). As allegories for spiritual liberation or revival, these two pictures almost seem to have anticipated Allston's conversionary experience.[76] In addition to *Belshazzar's Feast*, Allston also began to paint other Old Testament subjects during his final years abroad. Both *Jacob's Dream* (fig. 23) and *Elijah in the Desert* (fig. 24) express the problem of man's dual nature and the incommensurability between heaven and earth.

In *Jacob's Dream*, the radiant supernatural light and the glory of angels beckon the viewer to rise above the earth's dark void. However, Jacob is unable to move his limbs. His heavy body contrasts with the graceful angels, who appear less corporeal the further their position is along the heavenly steps. Unable physically to act, Jacob can only dream of transcendence.

In *Elijah in the Desert*, Allston represented the prophet as he seeks refuge from the wrath of King Ahab. Like all genu-

Figure 22
Washington Allston, *The Dead Man Restored to Life by Touching the Bones of the Prophet Elisha*, 1811–14, oil on canvas, 156 × 120 in. Pennsylvania Academy of the Fine Arts, Philadelphia.

ine prophets, Elijah lived in the world without being of the world. The rugged, barren landscape is a metaphor for man's difficult pilgrimage through life, while the great expanse of sky and the aspiring mountain in the distance offer hope for a life beyond earthly existence. God, meanwhile, provides for the needs of the faithful. Miraculously, ravens fly down to feed pieces of bread to Elijah. The antithesis of prideful man, the prophet accepts the heavenly gift upon his knees.

After Ann's death, friends commented upon Allston's eagerness to discuss religion and theology. William Collins, who traveled with Allston to Paris in 1817, wrote that the two of them discussed religious principles as much as they discussed art.[77] After Allston's death, Collins told Richard H. Dana, Sr.:

You speak of a period of uncertainty in our dear friend's religious opinions. If such was ever the state of mind, it must have been before I knew him. . . . I can safely bear testimony to the consistency

and orthodoxy of his theory; and the beauty of his practice, during our whole acquaintance.[78]

While in Paris with Collins, Allston met Gulian C. Verplanck of New York, who also became impressed with Allston's knowledge of religion. When Verplanck, as Professor of Revealed Religion at the Episcopalian General Theological Seminary in New York, published his lectures in 1824 he dedicated the book to Allston as "a Slight Mark of Respect, for his Talents, Works, and Character."[79]

Verplanck's arguments for revealed religion, based upon a mixture of Scottish Common Sense philosophy and romantic idealism, were similar to Allston's. Like Allston, he did not believe that the intellect was the most basic faculty for perceiving spiritual truth. Intuition or knowledge of the heart was of more fundamental importance. Quoting some verse from Wordsworth, Verplanck taught that man must pay reverence to the voice of his inner conscience, " 'God's most intimate presence in the soul, and his most perfect image in the world.' "[80] Powerful forces are at work in an attempt to silence the voice of conscience, including "our selfish or animal propensities," man's pride, will, and evil passions.[81] Yet Verplanck recognized the irrefutability of intuitive knowledge. Knowledge of the heart was a superior knowledge not only because it was so accessible to everyone but also because all the intellectual, so-called rational arguments that

Figure 24
Washington Allston, *Elijah in the Desert,* 1817–18, oil on canvas, 48³/₄ × 72¹/₂ in. Museum of Fine Arts, Boston; Gift of Mrs. Samuel Hooper and Miss Alice Hooper.

skeptics brought against it were useless. Their arrows, ''can never reach'' such knowledge, said Verplanck.[82]

Thanks to his conversionary experience, Allston knew that an act of humility and self-abasement was a necessary prerequisite before man's intuitive feeling could operate effectively. The pride engendered by reason was an impediment to knowledge of the heart. Acknowledgment of the empty, aching void within the self, described in Coleridge's letter of consolation to Allston and then by Allston himself in *Monaldi,* prepares the way for God to fill the heart with spiritual light and divine love.

Belshazzar's Feast was to be Allston's plea for a humble, self-abasing attitude before God. Pride had blinded the heart or conscience of the king until it was too late. Glorification of the self had led him down the path of materialism and luxury. Like the human skull which initiated the spiritual rebirth of Monaldi, the story of Belshazzar's fate was a *memento mori,* reminding the individual that life is too short and death too unpredictable to waste upon objects of earthly desire.

Allston had vividly seen evil's objective existence in 1815. His love for Ann had not been adequately immersed in that spirtual love that could transcend earthly woe. Paralleling the strategy he employed in *The Atonement,* in *Belshazzar's Feast* Allston sublimated his private, subjective experience of evil and divine retribution onto the relatively impersonal and emotionally distant plane of a public history painting. His own sinful pride and suffering was, after all, merely a microcosmic manifestation of all mankind's history of declension and punishment since the Fall.

Furthermore, the artist may have been struck by the remarkable coincidence that his own release from feelings of guilt occurred during the same year that the world itself had finally been freed from captivity in a spiritual Babylon. From Allston's apocalyptic viewpoint, not since the Flood had transformed the earth into "one universal ocean" had the world seen such devastation as the French Revolution.[83] Napoleon's defeat offered the hopeful prospect of a new millennial age.

Allston thus began *Belshazzar's Feast* as both a celebration and a warning. Differing from earlier versions of the subject, his painting was far more than an image of divine retribution. Like Handel's oratorio, it seemed to prophesy a brighter, Christian future. This delicate hope was contingent, however, upon the moral reformation of man and his rejection of the prideful principles of the French Revolution.

CHAPTER 5

Allston Interpreting to Napoleon Bonaparte the Handwriting on the Wall

Washington Allston began to compose *Belshazzar's Feast* during what appeared to be a momentous turning point in world history, the dawn of a new morning, following the nightmare of French revolutionary violence and Napoleon's military rule. On a personal level, too, the artist felt as if he had recently discovered a new source of spiritual energy, following his mental depression of 1815. In a letter to his friend Washington Irving, dated 9 May 1817, he excitedly described a finished sketch for his projected masterpiece:

I think the composition the best I ever made. It contains a multitude of figures, and (if I may be allowed to say it) they are without confusion. Don't you think it a fine subject? I know not any that so happily unites the magnificent and the awful: a mighty sovereign, surrounded by his whole court, intoxicated with his own state—in the midst of his revellings, palsied in a moment under the spell of a preternatural hand suddenly tracing his doom on the wall before him; his powerless limbs, like a wounded spider's, shrunk up to his whole body, while his heart, *compressed to a point*, is only kept from vanishing by the terrific suspense that animates it during the interpretation of his mysterious sentence: his less guilty, but scarcely less agitated queen, the panic-struck courtiers and concubines, the splendid and deserted banquet table, the half-arrogant, half-astounded magicians, the holy vessels of the Temple, (shining, as it were, in triumph through the gloom), and the calm, solemn contrast of the Prophet, standing like an animated pillar in the midst, breathing forth the oracular destruction of the empire! The picture will be twelve feet high by seventeen feet long.[1]

Allston's enthusiasm for the subject was widely shared by contemporaries. William Blake and other English artists had earlier interpreted the theme (fig. 25), while the German philosopher, Johann Gottfried Herder, wrote that Babylon was simply "another name for pride, magnificence, arrogance, oppression of the people and of nations."[2] In the private gallery of Benjamin West, Allston saw that artist's *Belshazzar* (pl. V), which had warned the ministry of George III against repression of the American colonies (see chapter 2).

101

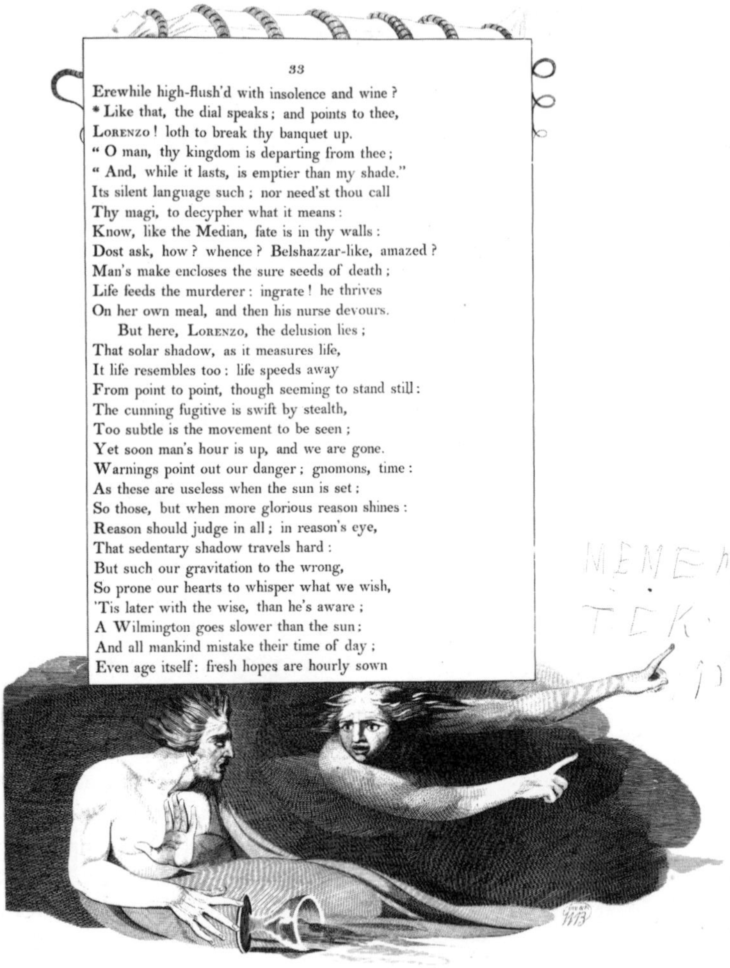

Figure 25
William Blake, illustration of Belshazzar and the handwriting upon the wall from Night II, page 33, Edward Young, *Night Thoughts*, London, 1797 (RB 431729). The Huntington Library, San Marino, California.

However, by the time of Allston's arrival in Europe, Belshazzar and his court had gained a new, imperial referent in the person of Napoleon Bonaparte. Though Bonaparte's supporters hailed him as the savior of French revolutionary ideals, his opponents characterized him as a satanic force, the Antichrist of Revelation, challenging the sovereignty of God. Critics claimed that Napoleon had craftily disguised his true nature. He was not really a Cyrus, or liberator, as argued by some, but a Belshazzar, a prideful and arrogant oppressor.

Indeed, this was the message of James Gillray's caricature, *The Hand-Writing upon the Wall*, published 24 August 1803 (fig. 26). The famous cartoonist's portrayal of Napoleon as a startled Belshazzar, feasting in a captive London, reportedly angered the French court, and Gillray's metaphor was later copied by caricaturists throughout Europe, when the emperor was defeated and forced to abdicate.[3] Daniel, chapter five, was frequently cited to describe how the hand of God struck down tyrants for their overweening ambition.

MENE MENE,
TEKEL,
UPHARSIN

On 6 April 1814, after the surrender of Paris, the London *Times* thus proclaimed that "Babylon the great is fallen!" Immediately afterward, patriotic revelries occurred throughout England. At night, the streets of London's fashionable business and living districts were brightened by illuminations or painted transparencies. The *Times* reported on 13 April that a transparency, which "attracted particular attention," featured an Old Testament prophetic denunciation of tyrants.

Besides on the front page of the *Times* and in various political caricatures, the fall of Babylon and the Belshazzar theme were popular in poetry of the period. In 1814, Lord Byron published his "Ode to Napoleon," borrowing a phrase from Daniel's interpretation of the handwriting on the wall, "weighed in the balance," to proclaim that "hero dust / Is vile as vulgar clay" (stanza XII).[4] In 1817, the Reverend Thomas S. Hughes won a prize from Cambridge University for his epic poem "Belshazzar's Feast." Allston was familiar with this poem, because he recommended it to his friend and fellow-artist John Martin.[5] Hughes's exultation in the utter annihilation of the Babylonian monarch perfectly suited Martin's fiery temperament. Though the English artist's panoramic vision of *Belshazzar's Feast* was exhibited several years after Allston's departure for America, the two had

103

had ample opportunity to exchange their ideas about the subject, and Allston, later, defended Martin's picture from hostile American critics (see chapter 1).

Allston's friendship with Samuel Taylor Coleridge was also critically important for the conception of *Belshazzar's Feast*. Traveling to Bristol in June 1814, Allston visited the poet and actively participated in that city's celebration of Napoleon's defeat. According to one eyewitness, artists competed to present the most striking transparencies:

In the evening [of 27 June 1814] the city was illuminated. A lofty triumphal arch, erected in Corn Street in front of the Commercial Rooms, was, when its pictorial embellishments were lighted up, an especial attraction; but the inhabitants of the chief streets appear to have vied with each other in the production of fanciful allegories, the description of which fills many columns of the newspapers.[6]

Coleridge, himself, contributed a design to the competition, yet he admitted that Allston's transparency was artistically superior to all the others: "a truly Michael Angelesque Figure, and of course beyond all comparison the finest in the City."[7] Allston described the appearance of his work to Samuel Morse:

I painted a large transparency for Mr. Visger, which attracted great notice. Twas a gigantic figure of Boney in an attitude of terror, shrinking from an imp, who is sitting on his shoulder and setting fire, with a torch, to his brimstone crown. Tis entitled the coronation at Hell-Bay. Some verses underneath explain the reason of his being represented as a giant. The figure, which is sitting, would be, if standing, 8 or 9 feet high.[8]

Allston did not quote the accompanying verses. However, his image of an enthroned Bonaparte shrinking in terror from an agent of doom is virtually identical in conception to the king's fear in *Belshazzar's Feast*.

Coleridge would have encouraged Allston to think in terms of the Old Testament prophets. During the winter of 1816–17, when Allston was beginning to mull over ideas for his great picture, Coleridge published his *Lay Sermons Addressed to the Higher Classes of Society.* In these jeremiads, the English poet argued that the Old Testament prophets were the most reliable guides for solving current political problems, for not only were the authors divinely inspired, but also, God was an active participant in the history of Israel, directly intervening in the course of events. Thus, Coleridge angrily compared proponents of French revolutionary ideals with Babylon's Chaldean soothsayers. Citing the forty-seventh chapter of Isaiah, he argued that the Old Testament prophet had "revealed the true philosophy of the French

Revolution more than 2,000 years before it became a sad irrevocable truth of history.''[9]

Coleridge made it clear to his upper class audience that Isaiah's denunciation of Babylon applied not only to French materialism and skepticism but also to English utilitarianism and empiricism. In *The Friend*, published in 1818, he admonished the English public that simply because Napoleon had been defeated, there was no reason for complacency. Other apocalyptic events, another fall of empire could be expected.[10] Coleridge was well aware that labor unrest and government repression were fueling radical, Jacobin ideas at home. At public meetings during the autumn of 1816, while the poet-philosopher was writing his lay sermons, many Englishmen ominously referred to the approaching day of reckoning.

Coleridge's solutions to social and economic unrest were moral and religious rather than explicitly political. He renounced imperial pride as well as radical demagoguery, believing that the English were victims of a commercial spirit, which resulted in an excessive attachment to temporal, material objects. A change in ideas toward eternal and universal principles would favorably alter the course of history.

Allston's *Belshazzar* was undertaken in a spirit similar to that of the *Lay Sermons*. Since the poet-philosopher had championed Allston's first Old Testament painting, *Dead Man Restored* (1814), it seems highly probable that they would have discussed the fall of Babylon as a particularly timely theme.[11] Allston's desire to incorporate ideas from the prophecies of Isaiah and Jeremiah, as will be discussed shortly, may have been due to Coleridge's influence as a biblical scholar and an admirer of Hebraic poetry.

By 8 May 1817, when Allston initially described his conception of the painting to Irving, he said that he had already made a "highly finished" sketch (fig. 27; pl. VII). In addition to drawing numerous figure studies, he had also made a monochrome study of the entire composition (fig. 28; pl. VIII). Given his sense of excitement in the letter to Irving, Allston had probably just completed the sketches that spring. Significantly, he did not refer to his composition as a Belshazzar's feast but rather as "The prophet Daniel interpreting the *handwriting on the wall* before Belshazzar."

His conception was thus very close to that of his teacher, Benjamin West, in which a later moment in the story is represented, when the banqueting table has been "deserted" and Daniel assumes his central role as orator and prophet. Though Allston mentions in his letter "a preternatural hand suddenly tracing [Belshazzar's] doom on the wall before him," there is no such hand in the small sketches nor would

Figure 27
Washington Allston, *Study for Belshazzar's Feast (color)*, 1817, oil on cardboard, 26 × 35 in. Museum of Fine Arts, Boston; Bequest of Ruth Charlotte Dana.

there be one in the large canvas. Allston did not even choose to delineate the glyphic writing, in contrast to West's picture, where the wall is seared by mysterious letters. In Allston's composition, whether in the sketches or the large canvas, the upper right corner is simply a nebulous glow of light. Nor is there a dramatic, billowing circle of smoke to enframe the "handwriting," as there is in West's version.

Even more than West, Allston de-emphasized supernatural pyrotechnics. Sublime terror was strictly subordinated to the painting's purpose as a moral allegory. As Allston boasted to Irving, the figures are arranged "without confusion." Thus, "the half-arrogant, half-astounded magicians" on the right side of the composition are in clear moral contrast to the "calm" and "solemn" prophet, standing directly in the middle. While Daniel assumes an open, forthright position, the heavily garbed soothsayers stand suspiciously and secretively in a closed circle. One of them holds a divining rod, a mechanical device for discovering truth. Another holds a scroll, now rolled up, its conventional words or signs having proven ineffectual for decoding the message. The Old Testament prophet relies, instead, upon the spiritual light of God's word.

106

Figure 28
Washington Allston, *Study for Belshazzar's Feast (monochrome)*, 1817, oil on cardboard, 25 × 34 in. Fogg Art Museum, Harvard University, Cambridge, Massachusetts; The Washington Allston Trust.

As discussed in chapter one, Allston's interest in the moral sublime motivated his concern for the rendering of physiognomy. By delineating vivid contrasts of human expression, the artist made visible the great moral gap between fear created by a guilty conscience and the calm grandeur of one obedient to God's command. Allston thus drew careful studies for Belshazzar's tense, clutching hands (fig. 29). In the large canvas, he increased the degree to which Belshazzar's eyes appear to bulge from their sockets. He accentuated the strained sinews of the neck, as the figure recoils backward in fear.

Between the earlier, monochromatic sketch and the full color study, Allston already made important compositional changes, with the intention of focusing and intensifying the emotional and moral content of the narrative. In the color sketch, he eliminated the two small, dramatically insignificant boys kneeling in front of Belshazzar's throne, replacing them with several of the sacred vessels, which the Babylonians had confiscated from the Jewish temple. Their presence next to Belshazzar's throne emphasizes the king's sacrilege in using them for an intemperate feast. As Allston wrote, these holy vessels have been made to shine ''in triumph through the gloom.''

107

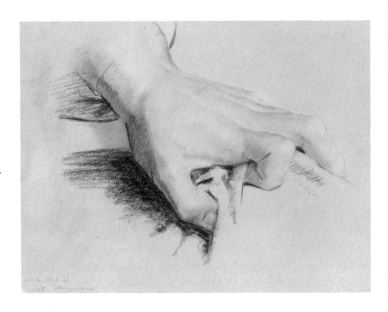

The menorah, whose flames have just been ominously extinguished, is also more prominently displayed above Belshazzar's throne. The throne itself has been enlarged and brought closer to the picture plane, revealing more clearly a large, satanic serpent coiled about its near post. The bizarre elephant at the base of the throne has also been enlarged, while the partial head of a second elephant-caryatid is revealed directly beneath the serpent's tail. Combined with the donkey-headed idols in the background of both sketches, these animals suggest the sensual bestiality of Belshazzar's sins. They recall Daniel's reminder to Belshazzar that his "father," Nebuchadnezzar, had been struck down for his pride to live and eat like a beast with the "wild asses" (Dan. 5:21).

The painting's animal imagery suggests that Allston was strongly influenced by emblematic literature and the satirical political cartoons of his day. As in his own anti-Napoleonic transparency, where an imp rests on "Boney's" shoulder, his Belshazzar is beset by a demonic beast. The snake, menacingly coiling itself around a column of the throne, almost appears to whisper into the king's ear. This juxtaposition of throne and serpent was a traditional device in political caricature to suggest the presence of "evil counsel . . . near the seat of power."[12]

Meanwhile, at the throne's base, supporting the weight of the monarch, are sturdy elephants. According to William Heckscher, the motif of an elephant-caryatid can be traced to ancient Hindu art and mythology, where "the elephant is thought of as carrying the weight of the world; when he falters, the earth quakes. . . . "[13] This original Hindu meaning ultimately was transferred, with modifications, to Western cultures. Thus in medieval bestiaries, the fall of an elephant became an emblem for the fall of man.[14] Many bestiaries thereby claimed that the elephant's natural enemy was the serpent.

Given the proximate juxtaposition of snake and elephants in his picture, Allston surely intended this type of interpretation. He would certainly have known that elephants, from the time of Alexander the Great, were symbols of imperial conquest. He, therefore, placed the spoils of war, the gold and silver vessels, immediately next to Belshazzar's elephantine throne. That one of these vessels has fallen to its side clearly foreshadows the overturning of Belshazzar's rule and the fall of the Babylonian empire.

Furthermore, in European emblem books from the sixteenth and seventeenth centuries, the elephant-caryatid was associated with the struggle of the ancient Jews, led by Judas Maccabees, against their Alexandrian, Greek oppressors.[15] In the *Emblemas Morales* of Sebastian de Covarrubias, illustrating the moral idea of "glory through death," Eleazar, the brother of Judas Maccabees, fearlessly slays one of Antiochus V's tower-carrying elephants (fig. 30). Described in 1 Maccabees 6:40–46, this event symbolized one of the Jews' rare moments of victory over tyranny.

Allston may have intended his elephant-caryatids to suggest the historical continuation of Jewish persecution, linking the Babylonian Captivity with the Maccabean Revolution four centuries later. He was, perhaps, acknowledging the opinion of biblical critics, who argued that the Book of Daniel was actually written during the second century B.C., as an allegory for the Greeks' repression against the Jewish religion (see chapter 2). Certainly, as we shall see, Allston was keenly interested in the history of the Jews and was concerned to address the issue of their destiny in his great picture.

During autumn 1817, Allston interrupted his work on *Belshazzar's Feast* for a six-week visit to Paris. At the Louvre, he copied one of the most famous feasting pictures in the history of art, Veronese's *Marriage at Cana*. At variance with the shallow depth in West's *Belshazzar*, the backgrounds of Allston's two oil sketches had already shown a resemblance to Veronese's sense of architectural space. Henry Moses' noticeable alteration of West's composition in his engraved "copy" of 1815 (fig. 31) perhaps, had influenced Allston, initially, to open up the background to a colonnade and balcony. Now in copying Veronese's picture, Allston apparently wished to sharpen his knowledge of perspective.[16]

Presumably, Allston might have finished *Belshazzar's*

EMBLEMA 24.
Apeteciendo muerte gloriofa,
Eleazar, valiente Machabeo,
Sefue, contra la beftia portentofa
De vn elephante abominable y feo,
Por la barriga larga, y efpaciofa,
La efpada claua, y cumple fu deffeo,
Dexando eterna, y fingular memoria,
Sepultado, en el triûpho de fu gloria.
                                        Mu

Feast prior to his departure for America had he not worked on other pictures during the same period, including two more Old Testament paintings, *Jacob's Dream* and *Elijah in the Desert,* and *Uriel in the Sun,* based upon Milton's *Paradise Lost.* He wrote to Irving that he had spent ten weeks painting *Uriel* and *Elijah,* assuring him that the time "deducted" from *Belshazzar* had not been wasted.[17] In the meantime, he had returned to the large canvas "with redoubled vigor." Of course, work was once again interrupted when he finally left for America in summer 1818.

It is difficult to determine how much work Allston had completed on the large canvas before his departure. According to one letter, he had "more than half-finished" it,[18] while in another he said that there remained "still about six or eight months' work to do to it."[19] When he finally resumed his labor on the canvas in September 1820, he decided to alter the painting's perspective. Allston wrote to Charles R. Leslie in London:

On seeing it at a greater distance in my present room, I found I had got my point of distance too near, and the point of sight too high. It was a sore task to change the perspective in so large a picture; but I had the courage to do it, and by lowering the latter and increasing the former I find the effect increased a hundredfold.[20]

Figure 31
Henry Moses, *Daniel Interpreting the Writing on the Wall*, 1815, engraving after the painting by Benjamin West. Trustees of the British Museum, London.

Although Leslie could not see the results of the perspective changes, he expressed his approval, noting that the epic nature of Raphael's tapestry cartoons for the Sistine Chapel suffered because their point of sight was too high:

I am sure the alterations you have made in your *Belshazzar* must have improved it. A low point of sight is certainly essential to a large picture which must necessarily be hung above the eye of the spectator. The reverse is very injurious to the effect of Raphael's cartoons.[21]

In comparing the oil sketches with the unfinished canvas, it can be observed that Allston did, in fact, lower the point of sight. The horizon line, formed by the edge of the banqueting table, is lower in the large canvas.

He also began to increase the relative size and breadth of the foreground figures. In the large canvas, the figures behind the banqueting table are far more reduced in scale relative to those in the foreground. In the finished color sketch, the difference is less pronounced, as the middle ground figures form part of an almost continuous circular belt, joining with the figures in the foreground. Not only did Allston increase the proportional difference, but he also eliminated a number of connecting heads and figures between foreground

111

and middle ground, thus creating a sense of spatial disjuncture as well as increasing the illusion of distance.

Also striking are the changes in scale and strength for the figures of Belshazzar and the queen. They are no longer the precious doll-like characters of the small sketches. They both have acquired a more masculine, muscular appearance. Prior to his death, Allston had painted over the figure of Belshazzar, intending to enlarge him and the stature of the other figures still further. He had only just begun to repaint the heads of the soothsayers before he died. In lowering the horizon line, diminishing the relative size of the middle ground figures, and increasing the bulk of the foreground figures, he increased the monumentality and spatial depth of the composition. The apparent distance between the foreground and the middle ground of the banqueting table was also accentuated by the more emphatic or convergent orthogonal lines of the palace floor.

However, this apparent increase of distance, from foreground to middle ground, is somewhat mitigated by a concomitant enlargement of the balcony and supporting columns. While the figures behind the banqueting table are thereby dwarfed even further, the foreground characters do not loom as large in front of the balcony as they might have. In enlarging the scale of the balcony, Allston also wished to increase the perception of distance in the background. Beneath and beyond the heavy front of the balcony, tiny human figures run along or ascend two grand flights of steps. At the top flight of the stairs, Allston placed a pagan idol, foreshortened to be seen from below. The idol dwarfs the surrounding humans. Powerfully enframed by the receding columns, the idol arrests the viewer's attention, drawing him into the picture space. The mystery and terror is heightened by the fact that the entablatures of the distance colonnade recede still further into a dark, indefinite space beyond the idol.

The two oil sketches lack the large painting's sense of space and monumentality. Both of their backgrounds ended in a solid wall rather than open space. Instead of the foreshortened idol seated high atop two flights of steps, Allston had depicted two smaller, grotesque idols with donkey ears in niches placed at a lower point just above the level of the banqueting table. While a brilliant chandelier illuminates the background of the large canvas, pillars obscure the light source in the backgrounds of the oil sketches.

Allston explained the meaning of some of these changes to Leslie:

I have, besides [the perspective changes], made several changes in the composition, which are for the better, such as introducing two enormous flights of steps, beyond the table, leading up to an inner apartment. These steps are supposed to extend wholly across the hall, and the first landing-place is crowded with figures, which being just discoverable in the dark have a powerful effect on the imagination. I suppose them to be principally Jews, exulting in the overthrow of the idols and their own restoration, as prophesied by Jeremiah, Isaiah, and others, which I think their action sufficiently explains. The gallery, too, is also crowded, the figures there fore-shortened as they would appear seen from below.[22]

As Allston's letter makes clear, his expansion of pictorial space also entailed an expansion of historical time and icono-graphic reference. In addition to the story of Belshazzar's fate, the artist wished to incorporate the idea of Jewish resto-ration, culled from the Books of Jeremiah, Isaiah "and oth-ers." Perhaps Coleridge, who was especially admiring of Isaiah's sublime poetry, suggested that Allston consider the prophet's song of triumph over Babylon's fall (Isaiah 14:4–27) and his prophecy that Cyrus would restore the Jews to the city of Jerusalem (Isaiah 44:26–28; 45:1–13).

Certainly, Allston's American critics noted the relevance of Isaiah's prophecy for his *Belshazzar.* According to Alexan-der Hill Everett, the fourteenth chapter of Isaiah had, indeed, been an influence on Allston, because its verses evoked the joyous celebrating that erupted following the defeat of Napo-leon Bonaparte.[23] Thomas S. Hughes's epic poem, "Belshaz-zar's Feast," so admired by Allston, had drawn much of its imagery from Isaiah fourteen. Isaiah's angry scorn for the Babylonian's pride perfectly suited this moment of Christian triumph in Europe.

The compositional additions, which Allston described to Leslie, strengthened the theme of Hebraic thanksgiving in *Belshazzar's Feast.* Already in the preparatory sketches of 1817, the artist had placed a small group of Jews, near the foreground, between Daniel and the soothsayers. The most prominent member of this group is the pointing servant boy who excitedly turns back to those behind him. Seated or crouching beside the servant, obscured in dark shadow, is a devout Israelite, who, after many years of captivity, wearily gazes upward in gratitude toward Daniel's message of libera-tion. Behind him stand a pair of women, apparently Jewish, who look calmly and confidently heavenward as if in a prayer of thanks for God's continued providence.

During the 1820s, Allston strengthened the visual pres-ence of this group, thus accentuating the painting's relationship to Isaiah's poetry of praise and thanksgiving. From the oil sketches, he eliminated the startled, richly dressed man standing behind the servant boy, replacing him with a pious-appearing woman. Partially hidden by the soothsayers, there are now two seated men, who attentively listen to Daniel's prophecy. Most importantly, however, Allston added two reverent, kneeling women. One bows in a prayer of thanks, while the other stretches out her hand to touch the hem of Daniel's robe. The praying woman's back and long neck are highlighted by a brilliant passage of "divine" light. This light creates another focal point in the painting, as the humble Jews now provide a strong moral contrast to the recoiling figure of Belshazzar.

Allston's explicit and emphatic reference to the Jews' restoration to Jerusalem clearly reveals his interest in the contemporary Anglo-American campaign for Jewish conversion (see chapter 3). As his friend Charles Lamb acerbically noted, in 1821, evangelicals' efforts to win over Jews for Christ had become such a popular, fashionable phenomenon, that it was difficult to distinguish between "Jews christianizing" and "Christians judaizing."[24] Lamb, therefore, doubted the sincerity of those who had recently converted to Christianity.

Allston, however, seems to have been more enthusiastic than skeptical. Following his own conversionary experience, the painter was, perhaps, more open to portents of a Christian millennium. His portraits of four Polish Jews were painted in London during the same period that he began *Belshazzar's Feast* (pl. IV). Though he may have intended them as studies for the large canvas, they also stand on their own merits, exuding a Rembrandtesque sympathy for the Hebraic temperament. In their gazes heavenward, or spiritually inward, the Polish Jews bear comparison to Daniel or the turbaned Israelites, who sit or crouch behind the soothsayers, in apparent anticipation of Daniel's fifth kingdom of divine rule.

With the inclusion of a chorus of grateful Jews, Allston's Daniel assumes an additional role to that of being God's interpreter. He also becomes the leader of a troubled and persecuted nation. Like Moses, he stands before another pharaoh, persecutor of the Jewish people. Babylon was merely another Egypt.

Yet, unlike the *Moses* of a Michelangelo, Allston's hero is not a particularly dynamic physical presence. One has little sense of the figure's anatomy beneath the bulky drapery. As David Huntington has rightly argued, Allston was not really interested in "the body as an organism."[25] He was more interested in gesturing hands or "demonstrative aspects of separate parts of the body," insofar as they revealed the life of the inner spirit. The dark valued, low saturated color of the prophet's clothing further indicates his otherworldly, spiritual character. Gold and silver, those colors which chiefly define the spendor of the Babylonian court, giving Allston's picture much of its wonderful glow, only threatened to divert the prophet earthward, away from the correct interpretation of God's purpose.

A drawing study for the figure of Daniel suggests that Allston was directly influenced by ancient Roman sculpture in selecting the proper pose and gesture.[26] From Allston's *Lectures on Art*, we know that Daniel's appearance also may have been inspired by the figure of the apostle Peter in Raphael's *Death of Ananias*. The themes of the two pictures are similar. Like Belshazzar, Ananias has sinned against God and must pay with his life (Acts 5:3–5). Furthermore, as Allston noted, Peter is merely a medium for announcing God's judgment:

> . . . the singly-raised finger of the Apostle marks him the judge; yet not of himself,—for neither his attitude, air, nor expression has any thing in unison with the impetuous Peter,—he is now the simple, passive, yet awful instrument of the Almighty. . . . [27]

Here and elsewhere, Allston insists that God's spokesmen, including artists and poets, are essentially no more than passive transmitters of God's ideas. In his letter to Irving, he thus referred to his Daniel as "an animated pillar." That Allston was viewing Raphael's work through the lenses of the Royal Academy does not suffice in explaining the stolid, wooden-appearing Daniel when compared to the energetic and powerful figure of Peter. For even if one compares Daniel with the orator-prophet figures of the English biblical illustrator, Richard Westall, Allston's hero decidedly seems the more passive instrument.[28] Westall's prophet, in a thematically related subject, *Jeremiah Foretelling the Fall of Jerusalem* (fig. 32), angrily directs his glaring eyes downward at the condemned king, while Allston's Daniel impassively stares beyond Belshazzar without focus upon any person or external object. Daniel's eyes have an abstract, distant look, as if his mind has been transported upward toward another realm. As Allston noted in a sonnet, written years earlier, the person who reads "magic words, receives / The gift of intercourse with worlds unknown."[29]

The only sign of outward emotion in the figure of Daniel is his clenched fist. Originally, however, the right hand had hung loosely and open at his side, as can be seen in the small oil sketches. Apparently, it had only been at the urging of Gilbert Stuart that Allston changed the hand to a fist in order to express some evidence of intense feeling. Yet it seems clear

Figure 32
Richard Westall, *Jeremiah Foretelling the Fall of Jerusalem*, engraving for *Illustrations of the Bible* (London: Edward Churton, 1835) II, Jer. XXI: 3–8. Princeton University Library, New Jersey.

that Allston was not entirely happy with Stuart's suggested change, for the only part of Daniel left substantially unfinished is the right hand.[30] Indeed, it was this clenched fist that William Wetmore Story severely criticized, claiming that it ruined Daniel's "calm heroism" (see chapter 1).

Allston's willingness to have Stuart, a portrait painter, criticize his most ambitious history painting is only puzzling until one considers that Stuart was a living, expert witness to the character of George Washington, Allston's boyhood hero and life-long exemplar.

Indeed, Stuart's *Lansdowne Portrait of George Washington* may usefully be compared to Allston's representation of Daniel (fig. 33). Washington's pose, the placement of the feet, the open authoritative gesture, including the spread of the hand and the curling of the fingers are similar to Allston's Daniel. Yet, even more intriguing is the abstract, impassive nature of Washington's gaze, and the fact that he, too, seems to be an "animated pillar." Allston's placement of a sturdy column behind Daniel's left shoulder, emphasizing his strength of character, may have been influenced by the same device in Stuart's portrait.

Whatever the specific artistic models Allston may have employed for his Daniel, George Washington was certainly the living, contemporary, spiritual inspiration. Honoring the memory of Washington was one of the leitmotifs of Allston's career. Shortly after Allston had begun *Belshazzar's Feast*, Boston's Washington Monument Association commissioned him to select an artist for a memorial sculpture. Later, when Horatio Greenough was designing his controversial, partially nude, sculpture of Washington, Allston also offered his professional advice. He wrote Leonard Jarvis, who was on the congressional committee in charge of the project, that in all of

Figure 33
Gilbert Stuart, *George Washington (Lansdowne)*, 1796, oil on canvas laid on wood, 96¼ × 60¼ in. Pennsylvania Academy of the Fine Arts, Philadelphia; Bequest of William Bingham.

history there was no ''grander subject for a portrait statue'' than that of Washington.[31] No one had a more ''noble countenance and majestic stature.''

Significantly, in light of his own work on the figure of Daniel, Allston also cautioned Jarvis that Greenough should not represent Washington as ''an active agent,'' for ''if any man can be said to repose in the fulness of his glory, it is he.'' Arguing that ''no conscious action should break'' the repose, he further advised that Greenough should lower Washington's ''uplifted hand and arm . . . so as to rest on some part of his person, or on the chair.'' One senses from these remarks that Allston had, indeed, been going against his better judgment when he followed Stuart's suggestion to clench Daniel's fist.

Allston had intended that the moral contrast between Daniel and Belshazzar metaphorically express the wide difference in character between a Napoleon Bonaparte and a George Washington, the two most important historical figures of his lifetime.

For Allston and many other American conservatives, these two men represented opposite poles in the spectrum between good and evil. The self-effacing passivity of George Washington, his desire to retire to a private agrarian life at Mount Vernon, was a perfect foil for Napoleon Bonaparte's aggressive military quest for world power. According to Allston's friend and brother-in-law, the Reverend William Ellery Channing, Washington was not a hero in the same sense as the egoistic Bonaparte:

Washington was not a hero in the common sense of that word. We never spoke of him as the French did of Bonaparte, never talked of his eagle-eyed, irresistable genius, as if this were to work out our safety. We never lost our self-respect. We felt that, under God, we were to be free through our own courage, energy, and wisdom, under the animating and guiding influences of this great and good mind. Washington served us chiefly by his sublime moral qualities, and not by transcendent talent, which, we apprehend, he did not possess. . . . His was the glory of being the brightest manifestation of the spirit which reigned in this country. . . . [32]

Washington was, therefore, merely the foremost representative of the new republic. He was more valued for his moral presence than for any particular heroic action. Allston's Daniel embodies the antiheroic qualities ascribed to Washington. He stands nobly and majestically at the center of the composition, yet his gesture toward the handwriting on the wall underlines the fact that true power and authority lie elsewhere. God is the active force in history. Daniel can only point to God's word. He, alone, cannot effectuate the necessary moral changes that each individual must make for him or herself.

On this contingency, Allston frequently expressed a deep-seated pessimism. Thus, the note of triumph, which Daniel and the grateful Jews contribute to the meaning of the picture, is counterbalanced by the single, monumental idol that Allston has placed adjacent to Daniel's head. Its position has the effect of detracting attention away from the prophet, whose central foreground role would ordinarily make him the figure of greatest interest. Daniel's inexpressive face and darkly colored, low saturated drapery diminish his visual importance relative to the shining idol. The receding orthog-

118

onals of Allston's perspective box find their vanishing point in the murky abyss behind the idol, whose gaze upward appears to mimic the image of Belshazzar. Frightened and excited human figures run along the flights of steps. A few hesitantly approach the idol, while others continue to worship it. In the two oil sketches, these tiny idolators are more clearly visible.

The pagan idol's triumphant presence in the background seems to contradict the evidence of God's victory in the foreground. The resulting bifurcation of the picture space was emblematic of the artist's cosmology and world view. Allston's thought was shaped by the dualistic language of the Apocalypse. The two light sources in his picture, the divine light, emanating from the handwriting on the wall and the man-made, idolatrous light, hovering like a nimbus over the pagan statue, symbolize the apocalyptic struggle between the forces of good and evil.

Though Allston lived in millennial hope, he ultimately believed that no earthly resolution to this conflict was possible. Not until the end of history would man be freed from the burden of choosing between good and evil.

To an age obsessed with the idea of liberty, Allston argued that man's inherently sinful nature prevented true freedom. True freedom was freedom from material desire, not from law and the natural social hierarchy. On the contrary, the passive acceptance of God's law and His eternally ordered universe was the essence of Allston's idea of freedom.

The Allstonian hero is not someone who initiates decisive action, because, more often than not, man will act incorrectly. Allston's hero is, instead, a passive receptor, like Daniel, who functions as a kind of lightning rod for God's supernatural rays. The divine light of the handwriting on the wall is the real liberating force, not Daniel. On earth, however, supernatural light offers only a promise of the perfection that lies beyond. It does not overwhelm the artificial light illuminating the pagan idol. Thus, the classical, Raphaelesque clarity of the foreground is countered by the darkly romantic, infinite abyss of Belshazzar's "inner apartment," emblematic of the obscure contours of the troubled human conscience. Allston intended that the viewer reverentially contemplate this infinite moral distance. He demanded that a choice be made between a life of the spirit and a life dedicated to earthly gain. Though the abyss is impossibly great, Allston yet offered the example of the ancient Hebrews as a glimmer of millennial hope that man would ultimately kneel before Providence.

With Channing and Coleridge, Allston believed that

materialism had to be supplanted as the dominant metaphysical system. Man's consciousness had to be directed to spiritual rather than material objects. While he felt that the moral gap between God and man would never be fully bridged on earth, he was sure that only those who strove toward oneness with the deity would be saved. Life was therefore a pilgrimage experienced in a state of perpetual longing for transcendence.

Allston referred to his own life and art in terms of ceaseless spiritual growth. He sought to check his pride, to live simply, apart from the flattering company of society. Like an Old Testament prophet, he wished to avoid the temptations of material rewards. He felt ultimately responsible not to the public nor even to his patrons, but to God. The artist-prophet was society's divine medium, responsible for interpreting to the public the meaning of God's Word and creation.

As a man of letters concerned with the progress of Christian civilization, Allston shared with other intellectuals in Europe and America the belief that the course of history was moving westward. He never really considered his artistic education in England, Paris, and Rome as anything other than a preparation for the time he would return to his native land. He surely believed that the moral and religious message of *Belshazzar's Feast* would have its greatest impact in America, the nation that seemed most favored by God to ignite the spiritual regeneration of mankind.

CHAPTER 6

The Danielic Return from Exile

Allston began *Belshazzar's Feast* as a speculative venture with no certain idea as to its final destination, but tentatively with an American audience in mind. He wrote to Washington Irving:

Should I succeed in it even to my wishes I know not what may be its fate. But I leave its future to Providence. Perhaps I may send it to America.[1]

Irving concurred with the artist's inclination:

As to sending it to America, I would only observe that, unless I got very advantageous offers for my paintings, I would rather do so—as it is infinitely preferable to stand foremost as one of the founders of a school of painting in an immense and growing country like America—in fact, to be an object of national pride and affection, than to fall into the ranks in the crowded galleries of Europe, or perhaps be regarded with an eye of national prejudice, as the production of an American pencil is likely to be in England.[2]

In returning to America in 1818, Allston seems to have acknowledged the truth of Irving's judgment. He had not really become "part and parcel of English artistic society."[3] Charles R. Leslie recollected that "with the exception of Mr. West and Sir Thomas Lawrence," Allston had *not* been "much acquainted with the principal artists" in England.[4] In fact, like West's experience during the American Revolution, Allston, during the War of 1812, sometimes must have felt like a Daniel, an exile in a foreign land.

Both Samuel Taylor Coleridge and Samuel Morse attributed the artist's difficulty in acquiring British patrons to the war between the two nations.[5] Morse wrote to his parents that Allston's one-man exhibition at Bristol had failed because "all public feeling is absorbed in one object, the conquest of the United States; no time to encourage an artist, especially an American artist."[6] For whatever the reasons, it was not until 1818, several years after the war had ended, that Allston began to receive attention from English patrons.

But even that success may have been overrated by the artist who wished to appear more successful in England than he actually was.[7]

Furthermore, while Allston deeply admired English literature and the English school of painting, he never lost his initial distaste for its society which had seemed "composed of princes and beggars," and a venal middle class.[8] When Samuel Morse returned to America in 1815, Allston wrote to the Reverend Jedidiah Morse that London, as evil as it is, had not corrupted his son:

It is a subject of no slight gratification to me that I can with sincerity congratulate you on what religious parents must above all others appreciate. The return of a son from one of the most dangerous cities in the world, with unsullied morals.[9]

Rather than the steady company of English artists, Allston and Morse had preferred the friendship of a small circle of Americans living in London, including Charles R. Leslie, Charles Bird King, and the actor, John Howard Payne.[10] Even Coleridge, the artist's closest English friend, wrote that Anglo-American rivalry had harmed their relationship. In spring 1814 he claimed that "Allston has altogether forgot me: but I have not forgot him!—but I am an Englishman, and he is an American!"[11]

The antipathy that Morse and Allston developed toward English government and society during the War of 1812 did not entirely subside with its conclusion. In the fall of 1816, Allston wrote to Myndert Van Schaick, a patron from New York:

I wish Mrs. Van Schaick and yourself every happiness in our highly favoured country. They would make us believe here in the Ministerial Papers that the United States are more distressed than Great Britain! But I know better things. Heaven grant that our countrymen may not abuse their blessings.[12]

Allston was, therefore, understandably elated when a new American institution for the promotion of art, the Pennsylvania Academy, gave him his first major professional success. After the British Institution had unaccountably failed to purchase *The Dead Man Restored*, a disappointed Allston believed that the picture would never be sold. However, upon receiving news of the Pennsylvania Academy's decision to buy the work, he wrote Samuel Morse:

When you recollect that I considered the *Dead Man* . . . almost literally as a *caput mortuum*, you may easily believe that I was most agreeably surprised to hear of the sale. But pleased as I was on account of the very seasonably pecuniary supply it would soon afford me, I must say that I was still more gratified at the encouragement it seemed to hold out for my return to America.[13]

Morse was nearly as excited as Allston at the news, adding a "Bravo for our country" to his congratulations.[14] Two years earlier, he had speculated to his parents that Philadelphia could become the art capital of the nation thanks to the foundation of the Academy.[15] The purchase of *Dead Man Restored* reinforced his conviction.

Allston may have hoped that the Pennsylvania Academy would purchase *Belshazzar's Feast.* When it bought *Dead Man Restored,* James McMurtrie of the Academy encouraged the artist to paint additional religious pictures. Allston had contemplated painting a finished version of his sketch *Christ Healing the Sick,* which he had made in 1813 under the influence of West's successful version of the subject for the Pennsylvania Hospital. However, he became dissatisfied with his conception of the theme and, in June 1816, he wrote to McMurtrie that perhaps the Academy would be interested in another subject from Scripture "of five or six figures, size of life, which would make a picture about the size of *St. Peter in Prison,* and this I could do for the sum you mentioned, say five hundred guineas."[16]

Desiring "some splendid subject, uniting brilliance of color with strong character and expression," Allston ultimately decided upon a much larger, more ambitious project for his next major religious painting. He thus began *Belshazzar's Feast* without the assurance that the Pennsylvania Academy or any other American institution would be able to afford the picture. In the meantime, he attempted to keep his name alive among the citizens of Philadelphia by asking his patron Myndert van Schaick to send *Rebecca at the Well,* a small pastoral painting, to the Pennsylvania Academy for exhibition.[17]

Philadelphia's establishment of the Pennsylvania Academy had provoked Allston's chosen city of Boston to take measures that it not lose its prize artists. In 1807, at the founding of the Boston Athenaeum, Anthology Society members had promised that a repository for fine arts would be established as soon as sufficient money became available.[18] This proposal languished for a number of years when William Tudor, former member of the Anthology Society and founding editor of the *North American Review,* raised the issue again in a letter to Harrison Gray Otis. Noting that he had already discussed the idea of organizing an institution of fine arts with some of Boston's leading citizens, Tudor expressed his belief that an exhibition of casts and copies from the Louvre would raise a sufficient sum of money "to bring Allston, Morse and one or two other young men here, and would give us the start of New York and Philadelphia, and . . . we should have a more complete collection, than any permanent, public collection that I know of in London." Tudor believed that the transformation of Boston into America's art capital would enhance the city's social and economic future. More specifically, Boston would better be able to attract "the right sort of people" who were emigrating from England and the continent:

I wish most heartily the prosperity of the town, and the enlargement of polished society in it. I have heard a good deal of talk this summer . . . among southern people and foreigners that Boston does and must decline, that New York, Baltimore and Philadelphia must run away with our population and capital. This I do not believe but I believe that exertion is at this time very necessary to secure our standing and future increase. They are straining every nerve in Philadelphia and Baltimore in rivalship, so in New York. The object here contemplated, may with a bold effort at first, go at once beyond them, and will produce permanent advantages. If we can make ourselves the capital of the arts and sciences, and we have already so many powerful institutions that we may do it, our town will increase in that sort of society which is principally to be desired. I think the present state of Europe will drive many to this country. Other events may happen which will keep up the emigration from England of persons who are not mere laborers and mechanics. An object of this kind trifling as it may be in reality will tend more than ten times the sum employed in any other way to give us our share of this increase of population.[19]

While New York and Philadelphia had surpassed Boston as centers of commerce and finance, New England's largest city more than survived the War of 1812. Its merchants, who had suffered from trade embargoes and the warfare at sea, profitably reinvested their money in domestic industries, especially textiles.

Tudor believed that the acquisition of culture would be more than window dressing. It was integral in the very process of building and maintaining the socioeconomic substructure. The foundation of an institution for fine arts may appear trifling on the surface, but it would attract the wealthy and educated elite that Boston needed to achieve a position of preeminence. Patronage of literature and the arts would stabilize and regulate the accumulation and expenditure of wealth in the city.[20] It would contribute to the social cohesion of the elite by creating a refined set of behavioral and intellectual norms. Far from assuming a natural antipathy between the arts and commercial enterprise, Tudor and businessmen like Thomas H. Perkins wished to revive the ideal of Renaissance Florence in which a new class of merchant-prince would lead humanity to ever higher levels of civilization.

The Boston elite professed reluctance to accept economic enterprise as an end in itself. As God-fearing Christians, they believed an unbridled materialism would invite divine retribution in the form of social anarchy. By promoting virtue and the benevolent affections through the founding of philanthropic and religious societies and the patronage of arts and learning, the elite hoped to legitimize and safeguard its role as a ruling class. The employment of private wealth for the public good would engender gratitude and acquiescence to the natural, meritorious leadership of the merchant industrial princes. The elite's selfless generosity and virtue would be a model for soothing the envy and avarice of the subordinate classes. Boston merchants recognized the dangers of the new order of industrial capitalism with its concentration of laborers and mechanics in overcrowded cities. Through a policy of social paternalism and cultural hegemony, they sought to harness capitalism's centrifugal forces, the vices of selfish greed and overweening pride, to prevent the atomization of the traditional social hierarchy.

It was thus with some anxiousness that Tudor wrote about the prospects of luring Allston back to Boston in the January 1816 issue of the *North American Review:*

If there was any prospect of the publick being awakened to a disposition to encourage the arts, he [Allston] would no doubt return to reside among us; we know his strong love of country . . . he would find many friends to cherish and admire him. His accomplished education, the profound knowledge he has acquired in studying for years in all the great schools of art in Europe, would make his experience and science, though a young artist himself, of the greatest importance to a new institution here.[21]

Allston must have felt flattered and encouraged by Tudor's project. He kept in touch with the Boston business community during his residency in London through the New England banker Samuel Williams whose portrait he painted in 1817.[22] When Tudor or T. H. Perkins traveled to England, Allston sometimes dined with them at Williams's home in London. Perkins, one of Boston's wealthiest merchants, made frequent trips to Europe, purchasing "old master" paintings, importing European furniture, and copying European garden designs. Perkins was also an early patron of Allston, having purchased the artist's Hogarthian *Poor Author and Rich Bookseller* of 1811. While Tudor's proposal for an institute of fine arts was not immediately realized, the earnestness and sincerity of the Boston merchant community must have convinced Allston that the creation of such an organization was only a matter of time.

As proof of their interest, H. G. Otis, acting in concert with other collectors in Boston, commissioned Allston to purchase several "old master" paintings on his trip to Paris in 1817.[23] The works acquired by Boston merchants would eventually form the nucleus of pictures shown at the Boston Athenaeum. At about the same time, the Commonwealth of Massachusetts commissioned Allston to find a qualified sculptor for erecting a monument to George Washington. After conferring with Benjamin West, Allston recommended Francis Chantrey for the $10,000 commission.[24] The outlay of such a sum for a public monument must have been further evidence to the painter that the Boston community was financially capable of patronizing the arts.

It was apparently through exhibition of his large painting to the public outside the halls of an established art academy that Allston hoped to make a profit from *Belshazzar's Feast*. Even if he could not immediately find an institutional buyer, he could, in the tradition of West and John Singleton Copley, earn a return from admission tickets and the sale of engraved reproductions. Allston confirmed that this had been his original intent in a letter that he wrote to Henry Pickering in the spring of 1820:

The experience I had in Europe determined me against painting many small pictures, as I found the highest prices I could obtain for them bore no proportion to the time they cost. My only hope then of making my art profitable beyond a mere and precarious support seemed to be by devoting myself principally to large works and exhibiting them. This indeed was both Mr. West's opinion and advice; and the success of his picture at the Hospital in Philadelphia [Christ Healing the Sick] encouraged me to hope that the exhibition of large pictures would be as profitable to me in this country, as in England; and for this purpose I began the picture before alluded to, which is sixteen feet by twelve, the subject Belshazzar's Feast. . . . [25]

Apparently convinced of the subject's widespread popularity in Boston and other cities, Allston, from the beginning, had intended *Belshazzar's Feast* for an American audience. American literary interest in the theme was as old as the poetry of Anne Bradstreet.[26] In the visual arts, Belshazzar's feast was known through illustrated Bibles. Engraved reproductions by Valentine Greene, Alexander Anderson, and others of Benjamin West's version of the subject were widely available.[27]

The Connecticut portrait painter Joseph Steward (1755–1822) executed a picture with the same title as West's and an identical number of figures covering some ninety feet of wall space in the Hartford Museum.[28] It is interesting to note that Steward was a semi-retired Congregationalist clergyman who continued to preach in Hartford upon occasion. One can imagine that he considered his painting of the *Daniel* and other religious pictures, such as *The Death of Abel*, as a natural extension of his ministry.

The *Belshazzar's Feast* of the English painter John Martin became extremely popular in America even as Allston continued to labor upon his *Belshazzar* during the 1820s. Known through individual mezzotints and illustrated Bibles, painted copies of Martin's work also appeared in this country. Early in his career, the landscape painter Thomas Cole painted a *Belshazzar's Feast*. Elwood C. Parry suggests that Cole had been inspired either by reports of Allston's work or by the news of Martin's success at the British Institution.[29] Finally, Hugh Reinagle, a scene painter for a New York theater, painted *Daniel Interpreting the Handwriting on the Wall* that measured eighteen feet by twelve, exhibiting it at Rubens Peale's museum in New York during September 1830.[30]

The theme of Belshazzar's feast and the fall of the Babylonian empire seemed to possess particular relevance for Americans during the War of 1812 and the Napoleonic wars, when two rival world empires threatened the integrity of the United States. Clergymen in America pointed to the handwriting on the wall in condemnation of Britain's imperious behavior. From the New England perspective, however, the Napoleonic empire had seemed far more threatening. Even after the British invasion of America, the War of 1812 appeared to be more a familial dispute between two states still united by ties of kinship and culture. The revolutionary French, however, had the image of an alien ideological force. Their irreligious, materialist philosophy made them the embodiment of evil to New England Federalists.

For many years after the collapse of the French empire, Napoleon's meteoric career remained vivid in the American consciousness. The fall of Babylon appeared in public discourse as a metaphorical warning to future Napoleonic despots. Since the United States was still a fledgling, vulnerable republic, the danger of Napoleonic tyranny loomed as an even more imminent threat than in Great Britain, where Coleridge, Byron, and John Martin were warning of its dire consequences. In the mind of Boston critic Alexander Hill Everett, American audiences had much to learn from Allston's and Martin's versions of Belshazzar's feast. Speaking before a society of scholars at Amherst College in 1833, Everett made an analogy between the recent revolutionary past and the period of the Babylonian empire:

. . . many of my hearers doubtless recollect how universally and how aptly the fourteenth chapter of Isaiah, which describes the fall of Babylon, was applied in our public religious ceremonies to that of Napoleon. So deep and lasting were the impressions left by this catastrophe, that two of the most celebrated painters of our day,— one of whom we are proud to claim as our countryman,—have selected it as a subject for the pencil. Mr. Allston is now engaged on a picture intended to represent the wonderful events that occurred in the interior of the Palace at Babylon, on that memorable night, when Belshazzar held his last feast. . . . [31]

An examination of sermons and orations celebrating the fall of Napoleon in America testifies to the accuracy of Everett's memory.[32] In Newburyport, Massachusetts, the Reverend John Snelling Popkin celebrated a day of national thanksgiving by comparing the Napoleonic wars and America's war with England to the history of cataclysmic wars during the Assyrian and Babylonian empires.[33]

Alexander Everett personally participated in Boston's religious and civic ceremonies celebrating Napoleon's defeat in Russia.[34] The *Columbian Centinel* reported that the highlight of the religious services was the reading of Scripture by the Reverend James Freeman, who liberally quoted, paraphrased, and juxtaposed a wide variety of biblical passages to construct a prophetic narrative of the recent past. Freeman succeeded in creating the illusion that all of the latest events had been prophesied in the Bible and that everything, therefore, was being accomplished according to God's preordained plan. Freeman reassuringly concluded his narrative by prophesying Napoleon's total defeat, based upon the words of Daniel's warning to Belshazzar:

But be not dismayed, ye that fear God. For I have read the handwriting on the wall, and thus it is written, God hath numbered thy kingdom and finished it.[35]

After the religious services, a banquet was held at the Boston Coffee Exchange. Allston's patron, Thomas H. Perkins, was chairman of the Committee of Arrangements while Harrison G. Otis was master of ceremonies. Music, poetry, toasts to Czar Alexander, and satirical broadsides against Bonaparte contributed to the festive atmosphere.

The event had domestic political meaning as well. The participants used Napoleon's defeat as a warning, akin to the handwriting on the wall, for the Republican administration of James Madison, admonishing it to end its war against Great Britain. According to the *Columbian Centinel*:

Every thing evinced the heartfelt pleasure which the succession of glorious events in Europe had inspired; and perhaps this pleasure was enhanced by the hope that these events would at least awaken our infatuated rulers to a sense of their errors, and would be considered by them as the "handwriting on the wall," intimating their approaching ruin, unless they accelerate a peace. . . .[36]

Federalists believed that America's war with Great Britain was not only bad for New England shipping and trade but was also immoral and irreligious, since England was the most powerful Christian nation in the world and, therefore, civilization's greatest hope against Jacobinism and the Napoleonic infidel. In pursuing the war, the Republicans revealed their enslavement to French influence. During one of the more partisan moments at the celebration in the Coffee Exchange, a toast was proposed to the Commonwealth of Massachusetts:

May the fire of its patriotism, like the flames of Moscow, expel what is French, and burn southward and westward, until it consumes all but native influence.[37]

Federalists urged Americans to disassociate themselves from France or "the Beast of Babylon."[38] The Reverend Freeman Parker denounced what he foresaw as "a fatal alliance of the United States with Daniel's infidel king, the tyrannical antichrist."[39]

When Napoleon finally did fall from power in April 1814, orators and clergymen repeated their warnings for Americans to avoid French philosophy's flirtation with atheism. William Ellery Channing characterized the subsequent invasion of America by British troops as God's just punishment for national transgressions. He based his sermon of 18 September 1814 upon Jeremiah 6:8 which warned against the desolation of Jerusalem through its own internal moral decay.[40] Though Channing urged resistance to the British troops, he seemed more concerned that America end its affiliation with a spiritual Babylon.

Daniel Dana told a Fourth of July audience in Newburyport, Massachusetts, to "read" the event of Napoleon's downfall as if it were a message written to them from God:

The experiment has been made. And now behold the result. Read it in that scene of blood, of devastation, of varied, accumulated misery, which Europe has exhibited for more than half an age. What loud and solemn warning is thus given to the world! And how emphatically is this warning addressed to us as a people! For we have but too readily caught the contagion of European infidelity and licentiousness. . . .[41]

The Reverend James Flint told the Massachusetts legislature in an Election Day sermon that the fall of Napoleon and America's sinful collaboration with the French emperor were events "so astonishing, so important in their consequences," that they "merit to be indelibly engraven upon our memory by frequent recollection." Likening the Napoleonic empire to the Tower of Babel, its destruction proved that the "triumph of the wicked is short" and that God is sovereign of the universe.[42]

Peace with Great Britain and the fall of Napoleon did not bring peace of mind to New England Federalists. They had always regarded the dangers that threatened America as being internal or moral in origin. Surprised by the sudden arrival of peace and the miraculous victory of General Andrew Jackson at the Battle of New Orleans, Federalist clergymen continued to insist that the war had been a warning and punishment from an angry Jehovah. Now that the Jeffersonian Republicans were more firmly in control of the national government, the possibility that an American Napoleon would emerge from the civil chaos engendered by democracy seemed as great as ever.[43] Napoleon was, in fact, admired by an apparent majority of Americans who saw him as an enemy of monarchy and aristocratic privilege. Furthermore, in the person of General Jackson, Americans seemed to have found their own homespun Bonaparte.

The Battle of New Orleans had transformed the general into an instant national hero. Immediately, the path to the White House opened as a future possibility. Jackson was told that "with the proper management," he "might be elected to the highest Office in the American government."[44] Jackson's supporters admired him because they perceived that, like Napoleon, he had risen from a humble social station to achieve world fame through military glory. He shared Napoleon's dynamism, energy, and personal magnetism. He also seemed inwardly driven to a position of political power.

A portrait of Jackson, painted shortly after his great military triumph, represented the general with a distinctly Napoleonic hair style, a style that in reality was quite different from his own. The portrait was engraved as the frontispiece to a widely popular biography of Jackson, written by John Reid and John Henry Eaton and published in 1817, the same year that Allston began *Belshazzar's Feast* commemorating Napoleon's defeat.[45]

Well before his election as president, less enthusiastic Americans compared Jackson to Napoleon because of the despotic way he had governed the city of New Orleans in 1815 under the terms of martial law. Several years later Henry Clay denounced Jackson in the House of Representatives for his arbitrary actions in Florida in the wars against the Seminole Indians. Clay ominously warned his colleagues:

Remember that Greece had her Alexander, Rome her Caesar, England her Cromwell, France her Bonaparte, and that if we would escape the rock on which they split, we must avoid their errors.[46]

Although Jackson's political views were never entirely clear until he became president, the accusation that he was nothing more than a military chieftain in the mold of Napoleon Bonaparte did nothing to comfort New England conservatives who feared that any despot would only be a tool for mob rule. After he became president, the charge that he was a Napoleonic tyrant was repeated *ad infinitum* by his political foes. Opposition was especially strong among the New England elite where Jackson's democratizing policies were perceived as a form of Jacobinism. Jackson seemed to be appealing directly to the mass of voters ''over the heads of those who considered themselves the natural leaders.''[47]

Alexander Hill Everett must have recognized that Allston's *Belshazzar's Feast* could be used as a specific warning against the Napoleonic personality of Andrew Jackson. The year before his discussion of the picture at Amherst, Everett, once a protege of John Quincy Adams, attacked Jackson as a military chieftain in the mold of Napoleon Bonaparte:

Napoleon at the height of his greatness did not receive more abject adulation than is daily lavished upon the imbecile automaton who is now the nominal head of our Government.[48]

According to early biographers of Allston, many Bostonians believed that the artist was actually modifying the figure of Daniel in his picture so that it would become a portrait of Daniel Webster, New England's law-abiding answer to the Napoleonic personality of Andrew Jackson.[49] When the unfinished painting finally was exhibited to the public after Allston's death, some critics compared the figures of Belshazzar and even the Queen to that of Napoleon.[50]

In 1828, the year that Jackson was first elected President, Allston's friend William Ellery Channing published an *Analysis of the Character of Napoleon Bonaparte* in which he criticized the emperor's ''spirit of self-exaggeration,'' his susceptibility to the flattery of courtiers and his lack of social affections.[51] Channing insisted that the Napoleonic personality had no place in the American republic. It was alien to everything that America stood for. Channing called upon men of letters, artists and poets to:

. . . teach that great truth, which is the seminal principle of a virtuous freedom, and the very foundation of morals and religion; we mean the doctrine, that conscience, the voice of God in every heart, is to be listened to above all other guides and lords; that there is a

131

sovereign within us, clothed with more awful powers and rights than any outward king.[52]

It was precisely the message that Allston hoped to convey to the American public with his great picture.

Knowing and sharing the New England elite's anxieties regarding the enervating effects of pride and luxury and their fears of a Napoleonic-style tyranny, Allston could have had little doubt that *Belshazzar's Feast* would be warmly welcomed in Boston. He probably had received assurances from Thomas H. Perkins, who had orchestrated Boston's celebration of Napoleon's defeat, that the merchant community would assist him in the public exhibition and eventual purchase of his masterpiece. In August 1818, Allston left England for Boston, accompanied by Perkins, full of high expectations as to his position within the New England clerisy.

Allston's departure for America was not sudden but had been contemplated since at least 1816 when he sold *Dead Man Restored* to the Pennsylvania Academy.[53] His subsequent success in England in 1818, when he sold *Jacob's Dream* and *Uriel in the Sun* and won a cash prize from the British Institution, did not deter him and may even have encouraged him in the idea that the moment was ripe to return to his native land. In leaving Great Britain at the very time that he was beginning to receive public accolades and the patronage of the English aristocracy, Allston could strike the pose of a Daniel, as one who ignored the gifts and rewards distributed by the prideful empire that had invaded his native land. William Dunlap summarized the love-hate relationship with the mother country that Allston seems to have shared with many other Americans, being critical of her as the metropolis of an overweening empire while craving her approval as the culture capital of Protestant civilization:

. . . insult, opprobrium, and injury were heaped upon his country by the government and writers of the United Kingdoms; and he remained until the character of the United States had been vindicated, and the pride of England mortified, both on the land and sea. He was among men who felt irritated by the defeat of their vessels of war (hitherto triumphant in every encounter) by the despised Yankee seamen, and of their invincible soldiers before the militia of America; yet he was beloved and his talents appreciated as though he were a native of Britain.[54]

Achieving the approval of English critics and patrons for his professional ability had been crucial to Allston for establishing his reputation in America. Equally important, however, was the American public's perception of the artist's moral character. The sacrifice of his material well-being in an

132

Old World ruled by aristocratic wealth and privilege for a relatively spartan life in the new republic would gratify the many American skeptics who often associated art with luxury and decadence. Allston, in effect, was reenacting the Puritan myth of fleeing to the New World for a higher spiritual purpose.[55] The artist entertained the belief held by most Americans that the course of empire and God's providential plan for mankind were moving westward to a new land.

His rather self-interested and exaggerated autobiographical comments to William Dunlap, the first chronicler of American painting, suggest that this image of Puritan self-sacrifice was precisely the one he intended to project to the public. In describing the final days before his departure in 1818, he emphasized the "generosity" of his aristocratic patrons in England, thereby suggesting the material ease he would have enjoyed had he remained. He quoted Lord Egremont, who had purchased *Jacob's Dream*, as telling him that he was sorry to see him leave and that "if you do not meet with the encouragement you deserve, in your own country, we shall all be very glad to see you back again."[56] Allston furthermore informed Dunlap that:

My friends wrote me that I should have been made an academician some years ago had I been in London, on the occurrence of a certain vacancy; but by the original laws of the academy (for which the present members are not accountable) no one is eligible as an academician who is not a resident of the United Kingdom. This law is peculiar to the English academy, and I cannot but think it a narrow one.[57]

He had thus sacrificed the generous patronage of Lord Egremont, the marquis of Stafford and Sir George Beaumont and a position of influence in the Royal Academy for the love of his native land: "A home-sickness which (in spite of some of the best and kindest friends, and every encouragement that I could wish as an artist) I could not overcome, brought me back to my own country in 1818."[58] The artist described the return to Boston Harbor as if it had been sanctioned by the Creator Himself since all the elements of Nature, earth, wind, water and fire, joined together in celebration:

We made Boston Harbour on a clear evening in October. It was an evening to remember! The wind fell and left our ship almost stationary on a long low swell, as smoothe as glass and undulating under one of our gorgeous autumnal skies like a prairie of amber. The moon looked down upon us like a living thing, as if to bid us welcome, and the fanciful thought is still in my memory that she broke her image on the water to make partners for a dance of fire-flies— and they *did* dance, if I ever saw dancing.

133

In concluding the recollection of his return he even invoked the memory of the great Puritan divine Cotton Mather and praised America as history's newest empire:

Another thought recurs: that I had returned to a mighty empire— that I was in the very waters, which the gallant Constitution had first broken . . . and whose "slaughter-breaking brass," to use a quotation from worthy Cotton Mather's magnalia, *but now* "grew hot and spoke" *her name* among the nations!

There is no reason to question the sincerity of Allston's ardent nationalism. However, pride in America's victory of arms did not prevent him from criticizing the moral and religious failures of his fellow countrymen. Overcoming these shortcomings would require the revitalized use of Puritan imagery and forms, particularly the admonishments of the jeremiad. In the tradition of the American jeremiad, Allston's *Belshazzar's Feast* called public attention to human depravity and sin, while, at the same time, offering the millennial hope of spiritual progress.

It was precisely this element of hope that distinguished the American jeremiad from the European political sermon.[59] Allston's picture was therefore eminently American in spirit if not in form. While the European jeremiad instilled a sense of resignation toward the repeated rise and fall of earthly empires, the American jeremiad, like Allston's *Belshazzar*, was designed to create a feeling of spiritual unfulfillment, a desire to correct and even perfect the current state of affairs. Americans' cultural tendency to compare their sacred national trust with ancient Israel's holy covenant formed the basis for the artist's evolving conception of his masterpiece and for conservatives' hopes to break the fateful cycles of history.

CHAPTER 7

The Old Testament
as a Source for National Symbols

Allston was not initially disappointed by a lack of patronage upon his return to Boston. He immediately received commissions for a number of smaller pictures that he undertook so that he would have sufficient money to finish *Belshazzar's Feast.* Furthermore, he had been offered a commission from the Boston Hospital for a large picture, which he agreed to paint after he had completed *Belshazzar.* Allston wrote his friend William Collins that Boston Hospital had agreed to pay him five thousand dollars for a subject from Scripture and that he would be allowed the privilege of exhibiting it "for my own benefit in three of our principal cities."[1] He estimated that its exhibition could "produce from six to eight thousand dollars," a sum he termed "substantial."

Two years later, Allston summarized for Collins the activity of his three years since returning to Boston, explaining that the first three months had been consumed "in visiting my friends, but since then I have not been a week idle."[2] Though disappointed that he had not been able to finish *Belshazzar* for a lack of funds, he listed a series of pictures that he had sold as soon as he had completed them, including three major works from Scripture, *Jeremiah Dictating His Prophecy of the Destruction of Jerusalem to Baruch the Scribe, Saul and the Witch of Endor,* and *Miriam the Prophetess.* All three of these pictures are thematically related to *Belshazzar's Feast* as manifestations of God's unremitting justice against sinful nations and rulers. As Horatio Greenough wrote after Allston's death, "whether in *Jeremiah,* in *Miriam,* in *Saul,* or in *Belshazzar,* we have the same dreadful words, 'I will repay.' "[3]

The *Jeremiah* could be considered a chronological companion to *Belshazzar* (fig. 34). While Daniel pronounces sentence against the Babylonian empire, liberating the Jews from their captivity, Jeremiah prophesies the beginning of the Jews' Babylonian Captivity. Based upon the thirty-sixth chapter of the Book of Jeremiah, Allston shows the prophet dictating to Baruch, his amanuensis, the words that God had spoken against the sins of Israel and Judah. By showing them

Figure 34
Washington Allston, *Jeremiah Dictating His Prophecy of the Destruction of Jerusalem to Baruch the Scribe,* 1820, oil on canvas, 84 × 98½ in. Yale University Art Gallery, New Haven, Connecticut; Gift of S.F.B. Morse, B.A., 1810.

their sin, God hoped that His people would repent and reform their errant ways. But when Jeremiah sent Baruch to read the scroll before the other prophets, they advised Jeremiah and Baruch to hide from King Jehoiakim, who decided to burn the scroll. Jeremiah then dictated a second scroll to Baruch that prophesied the destruction of Jerusalem at the hands of the Babylonian king.

Allston specifies this second dictation as the central moment of the picture. Jeremiah, enthroned majestically in a stone niche, by his Michelangelesque appearance also bears a close resemblance to that of Allston's Daniel.[4] When Allston visited Rome in 1805, he expressed a profound admiration for Michelangelo's prophets:

As I stood beneath his colossal prophets and sybils, still more colossal in spirit, I felt as if in the presence of messengers from the other world, with the destiny of man in their breath, in repose even terrible. . . . no one could mistake the prophets of Michael Angelo for inhabitants of our world; yet they are true to the imagination, as the beings about us are to the senses.[5]

136

In his *Jeremiah*, Allston wished to emulate Michelangelo, encouraging the public's belief in an invisible world of spirit. Contemporaries observed the glazed, trance-like eyes of the prophet, which seemed to be "looking beyond all earthly things, into the infinite distance."[6] They saw Jeremiah's gigantic size as an appropriate metaphor for his spiritual mission and viewed the repose of the figure and the calm of the picture as a whole to be in character with the nature of divine inspiration.

In painting *Jeremiah* Allston acquired compositional ideas and motifs that he would later use when he returned to work on *Belshazzar's Feast*. The artist created a spatial division in the composition of *Jeremiah* between foreground and background, symbolizing the opposing apocalyptic forces of good and evil. The foreground is illuminated by a source of spiritual light emanating from the upper right-hand corner of the picture. This light makes contact with Jeremiah's wide-eyed gaze and establishes the painting's golden brown and greyish-green harmony of color. Meanwhile, the background space is visible only through a doorway in the upper right quadrant. It is dimly lit by a separate source of light to reveal a Piranesi-like prison courtyard. To suggest the vastness of the space, Allston painted a tiny sentinel ascending a grand flight of steps toward a dark, indefinite space beyond.

Instead of a unified pictorial space in *Jeremiah*, Allston juxtaposed foreground and background as a narrative and symbolic device to indicate the consequences of the prophet's admonitions and the dark power of sin within the soul of man. So depraved had God's favored people become that they imprisoned Jeremiah, refusing to heed his warning that Jerusalem would be destroyed.

The dark prison space, its compressed vastness suggesting a kind of spiritual claustrophobia, contrasts sharply with the expansive openness and glowing color harmonies of the foreground. The awestruck reverence of the young Baruch was precisely the attitude that Allston desired the beholder to assume toward the prophet of God, the spiritual self-portrait of the artist. Contemporaries, who saw the picture in exhibitions at the Boston Athenaeum, were unable to separate Jeremiah's image from their respect for Allston as a minister of God. In the words of one spectator, ". . . I wish I felt at liberty to tell Mr. Allston how grateful I am to him for having shown me one of the prophets of old, and for having sent me away a more thoughtful and religious man."[7]

Jeremiah belonged to Mary Channing Gibbs, the mother-in-law of the Reverend William Ellery Channing. Significantly, Allston painted the picture specifically for the dining room of his patron's Beacon Hill residence. When Elizabeth Palmer Peabody told Reverend Channing that she thought it "an inappropriate adornment" for a dining room, the clergyman replied "yet Allston painted it for this place. Mrs. Gibbs said to him one day that she would give him one thousand dollars to paint a picture to hang between these two windows; and he painted this one."[8]

Far from being inappropriate, Allston may have considered the dining room itself as an instructive counterpoint to his painted image. *Jeremiah* would become a kind of *memento mori* surrounded by the material wealth of a dining room table laden with wine, food, silver, and fine china. *Belshazzar's Feast* contained a contrast between luxury and spiritual beauty within the picture space. In its original setting, *Jeremiah* evoked a similar contrast through the incorporation of real space.

Considered together, *Belshazzar's Feast* and *Jeremiah* would have conveyed to a Boston audience the conviction that God punishes as well as protects his chosen people. Divine retribution ought to be expected when a nation pursues its material welfare at the expense of its infinitely more important spiritual objectives. The perfectly shaped vessel in the lower left corner of *Jeremiah* symbolized the harmony and unity that a nation could achieve if it agreed to obey the laws of God. The beautiful piece of pottery was surely intended as a reference to Jeremiah 18:3–6 in which Jehovah draws an analogy between a flawed vessel and a disobedient Israel. Just as the potter breaks an imperfect vessel to make a better one, so the Lord asks, "O house of Israel, cannot I do with you as this potter?" The analogy is repeated again in Jeremiah 19:11. "Thus saith the Lord of hosts; Even so will I break this people and this city [Jerusalem], as one breaketh a potter's vessel, that cannot be made whole again. . . ."

Saul and the Witch of Endor continued Allston's interest in the relationship between God and a disobedient Israel (fig. 35). Threatened by the armed forces of the Philistines, Saul sought the advice of the Lord (I Samuel 28). But God refused to answer him because he had disobeyed an earlier commandment to utterly destroy the Amalekites. In desperation, Saul sought out a witch, demanding that she raise the ghost of Samuel. By doing so, he disobeyed one of his own decrees that had outlawed the practice of witchcraft and wizardry. When Samuel's spirit does appear, it tells Saul that "the Lord is departed from thee . . . because thou obeyedst not the voice of the Lord, nor executedst his fierce wrath upon Amalek" (vv. 16, 18). Samuel prophesies that Israel will fall to the Philistines and that Saul and his sons shall die.

Unlike earlier versions of the subject by Benjamin West

and Henry Fuseli, Allston's *Saul and the Witch of Endor* is more didactic than horrific.[9] Rather than the supernatural appearance of Samuel, Allston chose to focus upon Saul's guilty conscience and the fateful consequences that his disobedience had for Israel. Allston was less influenced than either West or Fuseli by the Burkean sublime.[10] He was far more concerned with the "moral sublime" espoused by the Scottish Common Sense philosopher Dugald Stewart and others. Advocates of the moral sublime wished that artists would appeal to the conscience more than the emotions of the viewer. They therefore de-emphasized horrific pictorial effects for the clear representation of the distinction between good and evil. As William Ellery Channing wrote in the *Monthly Anthology,* "The moral sublime is the most essentially and universally sublime of all species of sublimity," because it is "founded on the distinctions which exist between moral good and moral evil, distinctions as eternal, immutable and important as the Deity himself."[11] For Channing the stories of the Old Testament were a treasure-house for the moral sublime, since nowhere is there a greater contrast between the infirmity and finitude of human nature and "the moral nature of God's omnipotence."[12]

Allston sought to indicate Saul's moral weakness rather than his physical collapse. Like Belshazzar, Saul recoils in fear from the agency of doom. With his right hand, he draws attention to his sword that has ominously fallen within the magic circle being circumscribed by the witch. Both Samuel and the witch glare accusingly at Saul, whose awkward demeanor bears testimony to his moral guilt. In the background, terrified soldiers begin to flee from the scene, thereby foreshadowing Israel's devastating military defeat on the following day. Lest Americans should have forgotten their dependence upon God after their second victory over the British, *Saul and the Witch of Endor* would remind them that a nation's military was helpless without its people and rulers adhering to the will of God. Furthermore, the pathetic figure of Saul, like that of Belshazzar, could be interpreted as Allston's ridicule for the pretensions and delusions of Bonapartism.

By choosing this particular moment of spiritual recognition rather than Saul's dramatic fainting or prostration before Samuel's ghost, Allston satisfied the demands of his Boston audience who regarded art as an instrument for moral instruction. *Saul* was purchased by Thomas H. Perkins, who lent it frequently for public exhibition. Perkins also allowed it to be engraved under the aegis of the New England Art Union, which distributed pictures to the public that were "calculated to elevate and purify, rather than to startle by dramatic incongruities."[13] Edward Everett, speaking for the directors of the Art Union, indicated that Allston's clear, classical style was suited to their moral purpose.

The other painting from Scripture that Allston finished during the first three years of his return was *Miriam the Prophetess* (fig. 36). It was painted for a wealthy Boston businessman and philanthropist, David Sears, whose wife happened to be named Miriam. Sears was one of the most important founding members of Saint Paul's Episcopal Church, the church that Allston chose to join.[14] He was also, like T. H. Perkins and most other members of the Boston elite, a die-hard Federalist who distrusted the growth of democracy in the United States.

Allston's *Miriam* is based upon the text of Exodus 15:20–21. With a timbrel in her left hand, the prophetess looks upward toward heaven in gratitude for Pharaoh's defeat: "Sing ye to the Lord, for he hath triumphed gloriously; the horse and the rider hath he thrown into the sea." The triumphant figure of Miriam dominates Allston's canvas while in the distant background tiny Egyptian soldiers are overwhelmed in the Red Sea. Oliver Wendell Holmes praised *Miriam* as possessing both the moral grandeur of a history painting and the immediacy of a portrait.[15] Theodore Stebbins, Jr., believes that Allston used a portrait sketch of Mrs.

140

Figure 36
Washington Allston, *Miriam the Prophetess*, 1821, oil on canvas, 72 × 48 in. William A. Farnsworth Library and Art Museum, Rockland, Maine.

Sears as his starting point for the picture.[16] Yet, for Elizabeth Palmer Peabody, who praised the picture in Allston's retrospective exhibition of 1839, *Miriam* possessed the timeless beauty and truth of history painting:

The inspired songstress seems to start out of hoar antiquity in all the flush of life; and her voice sounds over the dark sea of *time*, in which so many kings and warlike hosts have sunk under many waters, even as it sounded over the Red Sea and its victims,—loud, clear, triumphant.[17]

Like *Belshazzar's Feast*, this image of death and destruction is also a representation of Jewish liberation and, therefore, an emblem or type for America's millennial promise and desire. Together with *Saul and the Witch of Endor, Miriam the Prophetess* demonstrated the powerlessness of military arms when confronted by the hand of divine providence. The artist's pacific temperament was highly praised by Federalists and Whigs, who associated the celebration of military aggressive-

141

ness and the toleration of violence with the crudity and belligerance of Jacksonian Democracy.[18]

After completing *Jeremiah, Saul and the Witch of Endor, Miriam the Prophetess,* and a number of other smaller pictures, Allston had accumulated enough money to return to work on *Belshazzar's Feast* in September 1820. He asked Gilbert Stuart to look at the work. It is said that Stuart's criticism of the picture's perspective motivated the sensitive young artist to make the compositional changes previously discussed. He thus spent the first few months working to correct his composition according to the laws of perspective.

Far from being discouraged at the necessity of the changes, Allston believed that the expansion of the background space enhanced the imaginative effect of the picture and that he had gained "a deeper knowledge of perspective than I ever had before."[19] He urged Charles R. Leslie to join him by working on some great history painting: "I cannot help thinking it a duty which you owe to yourself, and to Posterity, to devote occasionally some portion of your life to the highest department of art." News of John Martin's success with his *Belshazzar* at the British Institution seemed to encourage Allston's spirits. He instructed Leslie to "Tell Martin I would get up before sunrise and walk twenty miles to see his picture, which is saying a great deal of me, who have seen the sunrise about as often as Falstaff saw his knees."[20] Allston added that he was still hard at work on *Belshazzar.*

However, in a letter that he wrote to Francis B. Winthrop in November 1821, Allston reported that his work on *Belshazzar* had been interrupted for six months since the previous September "by an exhausted purse."[21] Impatient to get on with his great picture, he reported that he had decided to borrow money "(which I must soon do) than thus fritter away my time for a base daily subsistance." The patrimony which he had lived on for many years had been exhausted in England. Now that he was forced to live from the sale of his own paintings, the otherworldly Allston seemed incapable and even unwilling to manage his affairs according to the limitations of the American art market. If he suffered from a lack of money, then it was not so much his fault as it was an American society that failed to appreciate the nature and value of art. It was society that would have to change. Art and the living conditions of artists were standards by which societies ought to be judged.

Residing in a young, unrefined nation, Allston felt that America was still an environment hostile to the needs of artists and men of letters. Despite the number of pictures he had painted and sold since returning to America, the prices were rather low.[22] Conflicts with patrons often disrupted the serenity of the artist's studio. For Allston, no one could have represented the vulgar materialism of American society more than the "patron" to whom he wrote in late November 1821. More than a decade earlier, Francis Winthrop had purchased an Allston landscape for $500 only to sell it later at a $300 loss. Winthrop indignantly wrote to Allston insisting that the artist make up his financial loss by painting him another picture.[23] Allston did not dispute Winthrop's right to a compensatory picture, sending him a study for *The Angel Releasing St. Peter from Prison*, but his letter describing his own disregard for profit could be interpreted as a veiled criticism of Winthrop's ungenerous demand. With a firm sense of his own spiritual superiority, Allston told Winthrop:

I can produce nothing approaching to excellence, large or small, without labour; my pictures therefore for the most part cost a length of time very disproportioned to the prices I have charged for them. But I cannot paint for mere profit, or leave a picture when I know that I can still improve it. Could I have done so I might have been rich before this.[24]

A decade later Allston wrote another impatient patron:

I never suffer a picture to go out of my hands until it is as good as I can make it; and to make it such, I must work *con amore,* in other words, I must be pleased with my work. This method, I am aware, is not the most profitable in a pecuniary sense; but I know it to be so in reputation.[25]

In Allston's view, the great artist, by definition, did not live for remuneration in the present. Artistic fame was posthumous in origin while "the love of gain," he claimed, had "marred" many a painter.[26] Allston sacrificed his own earthly well-being for the posterity of mankind, its salvation and his. He even refused to marry again until he had finished *Belshazzar's Feast.* Just as he had delayed his marriage to Ann Channing for the sake of his artistic mission, so did he now prolong the engagement to Martha R. Dana, which he announced in 1821. Not until 1830 did he relent in his sacrifice of domestic bliss, finally marrying this sister of his closest friend, the poet and critic, Richard Henry Dana, Sr.

In the meantime, he expended most of his energy attempting to perfect *Belshazzar's Feast,* making more compositional changes and falling deeper and deeper into debt until he wrote John Cogdell in December 1825 that he had become "Belshazzar's *slave.*"[27] He began to see his task as an arduous, seemingly infinite path toward artistic excellence in which he was acquiring an ever "larger apprehension" of his subject. Moved by Allston's difficulties and the promised greatness of his picture, Cogdell, a part-time sculptor from

143

Charleston, soon joined a group of Boston businessmen to alleviate the artist's financial stress. Thomas H. Perkins, James Perkins, David Sears, Samuel Eliot, Samuel Appleton, Nathaniel Emory, Timothy Williams, William S. Rogers, Loammi Baldwin, Benjamin Welles, and George Ticknor, all bought shares in the picture at $500 a share.[28] The sum of $10,000 was held in trust by a third party. By 1827, when the agreement was officially reformulated, Allston had already consumed $5000 of the total and, at that time, he received only an additional $1500. The remaining money would not be paid until the picture's completion.

As Joy S. Kasson has effectively argued, far from relieving the pressure of indebtedness, the "tripartite agreement" that Allston formally signed in 1827 only increased his feeling that he had "lost control of his own life."[29] For lack of money, he had been forced to mortgage his intended masterpiece, agreeing to surrender its ownership. Upon completion of the picture, he would not be able to exhibit it independently as he had originally planned. Once finished, the painting would immediately pass into public, corporate hands. Allston's fellow artists commiserated with his plight and blamed American materialism for forcing him to waste his time upon moneymaking "parlor pieces" rather than "the mighty task" that would "vindicate his fame."[30]

Allston's legendary, sacrificial labor upon *Belshazzar's Feast* elevated the role of the painter in America to new spiritual heights. In his monastic dedication to the picture, he refused to live or behave as a mere craftsman or portrait painter who possessed only a certain manual dexterity. He insisted that his labor was primarily intellectual in nature. His slow, deliberate technique of glazing which transformed color into something ethereal, his obsession with "correct" drawing and perspective, learned only after years of study, his insistence that he had to be inspired by the subject of his pictures were factors that made his financial martyrdom all but inevitable. His refusal to compromise the artistic principles he had gleaned from his education in Europe was implicit criticism of American anti-intellectualism and common sense materialism.

While working on *Belshazzar's Feast*, Allston complained that the "spirit of enterprise," which enabled Americans "to dash through every known and unknown sea," seemed to inhibit the development of an introspective, contemplative life in the United States.[31] Americans were preoccupied with the exploration and conquest of a new continent to the detriment of examining their own minds and the collective soul of the nation to which they belonged. In his *Lectures on Art*, composed during the 1830s, Allston insisted that man no longer needed to be obsessed with the fulfillment of material needs.[32] The civilized state was now able to provide for all physical requirements. The most important priority had become the development of man's spiritual state, his never-ending quest for moral and intellectual perfection. By insisting upon the perfection of his greatest masterpiece, Allston hoped to set a moral example for his fellow countrymen. Like the potter's vessel in the Book of Jeremiah, his great painting would be a metaphor for the soul of the artist and of the nation to which he belonged.

The nation had to follow the lead of its artists and men of letters in perfecting a life of the spirit. Economic and geographic expansion had to serve some ulterior, providential destiny in order to justify the confident pride witnessed in American newspapers and journals. The four paintings of Old Testament prophecy that preoccupied Allston during the 1820s, *Belshazzar, Jeremiah, Saul,* and *Miriam,* were symbolic images intended to reveal the law of conscience that resides within every individual and to define America's sense of purpose as a nation chosen by God to lead the world to Christ.

Following the divisive atmosphere created by the War of 1812, a new sense of patriotism and national unity had emerged in America. Politically devastated by the successful outcome of the war they had stubbornly opposed, Federalists rallied to support the Republican presidency of James Monroe. Monroe, in turn, adopted many of the policies of the old Federalist party and was warmly welcomed to Boston by such conservative stalwarts as Thomas H. Perkins and Harrison Gray Otis. The Monroe administration witnessed the passage of economic policies designed to satisfy the needs of New England's merchants and growing industrial elite: improvement of the nation's transportation and communication through the building of roads and canals, the protection of industry through the adoption of a tariff, and the establishment of a uniform currency through the chartering of a national bank.

Yet, even as a triumphant United States declared its independence from the decaying ruins of Europe and began to build its economic infrastructure, conservatives remained uneasy with the nation's youth and anti-authoritarian disrespect for tradition. With the elimination of property restrictions for voting and officeholding, the propertied classes were rapidly losing their political control of government. The notion that the man of wealth had a natural right and duty to hold public office fell with the development of democratic institutions. To compensate for this loss of public authority, the New England elite turned increasingly to the establishment of private corporations or societies as a means for pre-

serving its socio-economic status. Through lyceums, athenae-
ums, colleges, religious, moral, and philanthropic societies,
wealthy New England merchants and industrialists, in alliance with clergymen, intellectuals, artists, and lawyers,
mounted a cultural counteroffensive against the radical tendencies of political democracy.

As enunciated by the old Anthology Society established
at the beginning of the century in Boston, the New England
elite hoped to mold the national character through the control of culture and education. Given wide support by members of the business community, Society intellectuals, their
progeny, and allies in other cities would socialize individual
Americans to behave in "dependable and predictable" patterns according to the law of conscience.[33]

Because of the missionary zeal of its clergymen and educators, and the overwhelming predominance of its educational institutions, New England hoped to acculturate the
rest of the nation to its values and ideological viewpoint. In
the final analysis, party affiliation, whether one was a Federalist, Republican, Democrat, or Whig, mattered little.

According to Peter Dobkin Hall:

Although character education might have come into being under
the auspices of men with particularist religious and political goals, it
produced men who, while retaining the universalistic forms of self-
discipline and self-control, easily shed the Federalist and Congregationalist association of character if it proved convenient for them to
do so. Indeed, the character educators had resocialized men to
behave in certain ways without providing them with the concrete
information that would have made them Congregationalists and
Whigs. The failing was, at the same time, the greatest strength of
character education, for it made it a mode of organizing behavior
that was sufficiently universal in character to be useful, applicable,
and acceptable in virtually any setting.[34]

The Boston Athenaeum, founded by the members of the
Anthology Society, was one of the private corporations
designed to educate the American character through propagation of the arts and letters. As the Anthologists argued,
"In proportion as we increase in wealth, . . . the more we
ought to perceive and urge the importance of maintaining
the laws by manners, manners by opinion, and opinion by
work, in which genius and taste unite to embellish the
truth."[35]

Having been closely affiliated with the Anthology Society since its inception, Washington Allston had been a leading voice in arguing the efficacious nature of painting in
raising man to higher levels of spiritual development. Athenaeum members apparently accepted the promise of *Belshaz-*

zar's Feast as being a work of taste and genius, a sermon in paint, which would help to discipline public behavior.

Of the eleven Boston subscribers to the great picture all but two (William S. Rogers and Loammi Baldwin) were listed as proprietors or subscribers of the Anthenaeum.[36] The subscribers planned that *Belshazzar* would be the principal attraction in the inaugural exhibition of fine arts at the Athenaeum. After Allston had returned to his labors upon the picture, the institution formed a committee to raise funds for a lecture room and art gallery. Contributions amounting to more than $4,000 were made in 1823.[37] When this amount was deemed inadequate, Allston's patron, Thomas H. Perkins, and the son of Perkins' deceased brother, James, who had also been a subscriber to *Belshazzar's Feast*, gave $8,000 toward the building of a museum. After the Athenaeum Gallery was opened in 1826, Allston was allowed studio space so that he could finish *Belshazzar's Feast* in time for the inaugural exhibition in 1827. Unfortunately, he was unable or unwilling to complete the picture for this important event in Boston's cultural history. Allston apparently told the disappointed subscribers, who had assumed that the painting was virtually finished, that the perspective was still defective so that the foreground figures would have to be further enlarged.[38] Then, in the winter of 1828–29, Allston's studio was sold and the artist was forced to roll up the large canvas. Though repeatedly expressing his intention to return to the work, he waited until 1839 before he finally did so.

Allston's other Old Testament prophecy paintings, *Jeremiah, Miriam the Prophetess,* and *Saul and the Witch of Endor,* were shown at the 1827 exhibition and were the most highly praised of all the artist's pictures. The critic for the *North American Review* claimed that *Jeremiah* "has a grandeur of design worthy of Michelangelo" and that it brought "back the great age of painting."[39] *Miriam* and *Saul* both were said to possess "something of the same character with the *Jeremiah.*" Interestingly, the critic disliked Allston's landscapes for being too labored, an opinion that was not shared by later critics who preferred the landscapes to the religious pictures.[40]

Athenaeum members and Boston's critics eagerly sought to encourage the painting of scriptural subjects. In his review of the 1830 Athenaeum exhibition, Alexander Everett chiefly commented upon the religious paintings of the old masters and even copies thereof, expressing regret that native American artists were not better represented in this highest of genres: "The artists of the age of Leo X rarely employed their pencils upon any other than scriptural scenes; and this very circumstance is doubtless one among the causes of their extraordinary success."[41] Everett praised Allston for confining "himself to historical, scriptural and poetical subjects," but he expressed the impatience of the artist's patrons when he criticized the artist for his "extreme fastidiousness" that results in his "correcting, maturing and repainting a single piece, not always perhaps with any real accession of effect, the time and labor which would have been sufficient for completing a dozen."[42] In the New England clerisy's campaign to discipline the anarchic forces of democracy and materialism, questions of "correct" perspective seemed trifling when compared with the urgent need to disseminate moralizing pictures from the Scripture:

In a community like ours, where the disposition to active pursuits, and their selfish views and angry controversies that are naturally connected with them, is perhaps too strong—where the form of government keeps up an almost uninterrupted war of political parties—it is highly important that every principle of a soothing and civilizing tendency should be brought as much as possible into vigorous action. The cultivation of the arts, if not the most effectual of these principles,—and we are not disposed to exaggerate its influence—nevertheless has its value. It comes in aid of the great and essential elements of civilization, which are found in a judicious system of political and religious institutions, and gives the last polish to the character of men and nations.[43]

Paintings were thus viewed as an "aid" to the "system of political and religious institutions" and Allston's work was considered part of a much broader cultural and social movement. Critics in Boston, New York, and elsewhere lamented that Allston's paintings did not receive enough public exposure, that they could not be seen by citizens from all sections of the country.[44] Engravings by inferior hands were no substitute for the experience, bordering upon religious ecstacy, of the real thing. Allston, himself, had hoped that he would be able to exhibit *Belshazzar's Feast* in cities outside of Boston, just as John Trumbull, William Dunlap, and Rembrandt Peale had been able to do. Indeed, after its initial showing at the Boston Athenaeum, the picture was to have traveled to Philadelphia where it would have been exhibited at the Pennsylvania Academy.[45]

Allston's supporters hoped that his paintings would help win souls for Christ. Elizabeth Palmer Peabody, a Unitarian Sunday-school teacher, believed that the artist's pictorialization of Scripture could function in the same direct manner as the handwriting on the wall or some other biblical miracle. Allston's divinely inspired paintings were reminders that God was still present as a living reality, just as he had been for the ancient Jews. In reviewing *Dead Man Restored*, Peabody wrote in 1839:

The sight of it will show the value of a miracle in arousing nature from its animal indolence and gross materiality. In the sympathetic stir of our souls we shall appreciate and worship the wisdom of that dispensation of wonders which revealed an ever-present God to men before the Word was made flesh. Not a few amongst us require this preparation for the more spiritual revelation of Christ, not less than the Jews did of that early day.[46]

When Rembrandt Peale exhibited his *Court of Death* in 1820–21, 32,000 people viewed it, while a number of clergymen preached upon it as a warning to those spiritually unprepared for death. Allston's patriotic, evangelical friends could have entertained hopes that *Belshazzar's Feast* would be an even greater instrument for the creation of an America united under the banner of Christ. The sudden, unexpected arrival of death was one of the most pervasive revivalist themes during the Second Great Awakening that spanned the first half of the nineteenth century.[47] In the tradition of colonial gravestone motifs, macabre subjects like the Court of Death, or Belshazzar's feast (painted by several other American artists besides Allston, including an orthodox Congregational clergyman) reminded their audiences that the things of this world were transitory and unreliable. Wealth and imperial power were meaningless unless one was prepared to meet God's judgment. In reviewing Robert Pollock's poem "The Course of Time," for an evangelical journal, *The Spirit of the Pilgrims*, Allston's brother-in-law, Richard Dana, described "the vain efforts of man to escape death," quoting a passage from Pollock's work inspired by Belshazzar's feast and the handwriting on the wall:

Still, on his halls of mirth, and banqueting,
And revelry, thy shadowy hand was seen
Writing thy name of—Death.[48]

Evangelical scholars sought to inculcate an awareness of death's power even among the youngest of America's citizens. The nation's schoolbooks during the early part of the century were full of scenes "set at the bedside of the dying infidel whose sufferings are horrible to contemplate as he realizes too late for redemption."[49]

A host of religious journals, missionary, Sunday school, temperance, and Bible societies were founded in New England during the Second Great Awakening. Together they formed a national organizational network spreading to the South and West. Unlike the revivalism of the First Great Awakening in the 1740s, nineteenth-century revivals did not disrupt church life but actually increased local church membership while stimulating the growth of lay religious societies.

149

More than anything else, the Second Great Awakening "began as an organizing movement" designed to unify the nation into a cultural whole.[50] According to Lyman Beecher, the most influential revivalist of the 1820s, religion, in alliance with the country's colleges and schools, would be able to overcome the atomizing effects of political factionalism:

The integrity of the Union demands special exertions to produce in the nation a more homogenous character and bind us together with firmer bonds. . . . The prevalence of pious, intelligent, enterprising ministers through the nation, at the ratio of one of a thousand, would establish schools, and academies, and colleges, and habits, and institutions of homogenous influence.

These would produce a sameness of views, and feelings, and interests, which would lay the foundation of our empire upon a rock. Religion is the central attraction which must supply the deficiency of political affinity and interest.[51]

Under Beecher's careful orchestration, revivals were controlled and restrained.[52] Discouraging ecstatic emotional outbursts, he took time to ascertain whether converts were genuine and sincere in proclaiming their spiritual rebirth. True believers were soon enrolled in established churches and particular stress was placed upon rigorous moral behavior according to the laws of God. After years of organizing revivals in Boston and the New England area, Beecher moved West to become President of Lane Seminary in Cincinnati.

A graduate of Yale, Beecher was merely one conspicuous example of many New England college graduates who moved South and West to found and staff the nation's educational institutions, religious and secular alike. Thanks to their control of higher education, New England graduates were also able to dominate the content of America's textbooks for elementary and secondary schools.

Allston followed the cultural and religious developments of the Awakening with great interest. He received issues of the *Christian Spectator,* which reported the activities of the various tract, Bible, and missionary societies.[53] With Richard Dana, he watched the progress of Lyman Beecher's revivals in New England. Beecher had helped to found the *Christian Spectator* in New Haven as a means to combat the newly forming Unitarian denomination. He and Nathaniel W. Taylor halted their attacks upon the Episcopal church to form an evangelical alliance against the heresy. In 1828, in collaboration with the orthodox clergymen remaining in the city of Boston, Beecher established the *Spirit of the Pilgrims,* a journal to which Allston gave at least his indirect support and his friend Dana contributed several important articles.

Accompanied by the Danas, the artist often attended

services at the Congregational First Church of Cambridge.[54] When the parish and church were split by the Unitarians in the late 1820s, he remained loyal to the moderate Calvinist theology of the Reverend Abiel Holmes, whose sermons he had listened to while an undergraduate at Harvard and who now assisted Beecher in publishing the *Spirit of the Pilgrims*.[55] Allston even designed the meetinghouse for the Shepard Congregational Society in Cambridge, Holmes's reorganized church following the schism.[56]

Meanwhile, in the pages of Holmes's and Beecher's *Spirit of the Pilgrims*, Richard Dana, who closely monitored the progress of Allston's *Belshazzar's Feast*, set the evangelical context within which he hoped the painting would be viewed. Besides his review of Pollock's *Course of Time*, Dana attacked the antirevivalist rationalism of the Unitarians' overly confident faith in man and nature. Unitarians drained all the mystery from life and religion when they argued that God merely works through man and natural law. They denigrated the work of the Holy Spirit when they deified the spirit of man. For Dana, the revivalism of the present was a supernatural phenomenon, inexplicable unless one took into account the active influence of God's light and grace in the act of conversion. According to Dana, no story illustrated so vividly the living, unequal relationship between God and man better than Daniel's story of Belshazzar's feast. The story of the handwriting on the wall, though full of supernatural mystery, blends with the natural, "common actions" of life to become "a rule and a help in our daily concerns." The vision demonstrates the palpable reality of spiritual truth as God, through the light of the Holy Spirit, "lifts the eyes of the groveller to Himself."[57]

Both Dana and Allston accepted the prescription for religious conversion commonly advised by evangelical clergymen. Before one could be saved or be born again, one's own sinful being and unworthiness had to be acknowledged. After the death of his first wife, Allston expressed the truth of this tenet in the propitiating verses of "The Atonement" (see chapter 4). Now, Dana restated the belief in man's depraved nature, arguing that in the fifth chapter of the Book of Daniel "God has mercifully considered us, not only as we should be, but also as we are," with "our spiritual vision being darkened." The handwriting on the wall, to be sure, is the warning of an angry God, but it is also evidence that God cares enough for man to provide him with visible signs and teachers as a means for bringing him to the light of saving grace. In nineteenth-century America, signs and teachers could include artists and their paintings.

An important dimension of the story of Belshazzar's

feast was that it manifested the inseparable nature of individual salvation (the covenant of grace) from the idea of a national covenant. In prophesying the fall of Babylon, Jeremiah established the basis for the dual covenant, sacred and secular, with the children of Israel.[58] While European nations tended to maintain the two covenants as separate and distinct, Americans tended to fuse them, so that individual sin could mean the captivity or fall of an entire state, while the private acceptance of God's will (the covenant of grace) contributed to national destiny. The individual conversions of the Second Great Awakening were grounded upon the notion of America as an elect nation where the millennium, the turning of the world to Christ, would have its beginning. Much of the public interest in Allston's painting and other versions of Belshazzar's feast may be attributed to the fact that the theme of Babylon's fall and the Jews' restoration to Jerusalem often appeared in jeremiads as a type, foreshadowing the coming millennial rule of Christ.

In a sermon delivered in 1823 before the Foreign Mission Society at Old South Church in Boston, the Reverend James Sabine declared:

The subject [the second coming of Christ] has excited much attention of late. As the time advances for the fulfillment of God's purposes . . . there is generally an impression upon the minds of his people corresponding with that design. When the time for delivering Israel from Babylon was approaching, there was a great excitement upon the minds of God's people; and upon the minds of Daniel and his companions this excitement was exceedingly powerful and operative. Cyrus, the Persian King, their victor sovereign, was deeply wrought upon, hence his decree and proclamation for their release and return to Jerusalem.[59]

Considering that the historical records of so many great empires had been lost forever, the Reverend Abiel Holmes argued that God must have had good reason to preserve the Hebrew Scriptures. The stories of Old Testament Israel ought to be interpreted typologically as applicable to this nation, which was also founded upon a covenant with God. At the two hundredth anniversary of the Pilgrims' landing at Plymouth, Holmes cited I Corinthians X:11 as proof that all the events in Hebrew history happened as "ensamples" or "types" for "our admonition, upon whom the ends of the world are come."[60]

Thanks to their acceptance of a dual, sacred, and secular covenant, the Jews in Babylon had survived yet another adversity so that they could bring the true word of God to the Gentiles. As the new nation chosen to spread the Gospel to the four corners of the earth, America, likewise, had survived physical and spiritual trials at the hands of "Babylon-ish" forces. During the course of the Second Great Awakening, evangelical Americans sought to develop national unity upon the strength of America's special role in Christian eschatology.

The vast network of Christian educators, religious and moral societies, and evangelical journals, designed to create a homogenous national spirit, could not have been organized without a simultaneous revitalization of America's traditional religious symbolism derived in part from the heritage of Puritan New England. The Puritans' typological metaphors from the Old Testament and their millennial eschatology became powerful motivating forces for the creation of a spiritually dynamic form of nationalism. Simple residency within the geographic boundaries of the United States did not make every citizen an American, just as mere church attendance did not mean an individual was one of God's elect. In the words of one clergyman:

. . . he is not an American who is one outwardly . . . but he is an American, who is one inwardly; and citizenship is that of the heart, in the spirit, and not in the letter. As they were not all Israel, who were of Israel; so neither are they all American, who are of America. . . . Our designation as a people imports a moral, rather than a physical idea; a political rather than a geographic position. "Our country," says Burke, "is not a thing of mere physical locality. It consists in a great measure, in the ancient order into which we are born. . . ."[61]

Nationalism in America, like membership in the Christian elect, was not an established, certain fact but rather an evolving process and a persistent cause for enormous anxiety. Just as Christians could never be completely sure that they and their loved ones would all be saved, so Americans perpetually worried that some of their number were unfaithful to the principles upon which the nation had been founded. Based upon the implicit acceptance of the dual covenant, the private morality and loyalty of one was regarded as the public responsibility of all. Those who subverted the nation's principles were deemed un-American or in the pay of foreign interests. The problem, however, was to identify and agree upon those principles and symbols which constituted the essence of the American spirit. Particularly during the period of the early republic, there was bitter disagreement as to the nature of the American mission.

According to the cultural anthropologist Clifford Geertz, in modern post-revolutionary societies, there tend to be at least two competing groups that attempt to answer the question of "what cultural forms—what systems of meaningful

153

symbols—to employ to give value and significance to the activities of the state, and by extension to the civil life of its citizens."[62] One group, the "epochalist," tends to look to contemporary, dynamic social and political movements, the future generations, and the popular media for a nation's collective definition. The other, "essentialist," grouping seeks continuity with the past. Its national ideology is based upon loyalty to ancestors and respect for "traditional authority figures, to custom and legend."[63] Geertz cautions that "rarely is such an ideology anywhere purely essentialist or purely epochalist. All are mixed and one can speak at best only of a bias in one direction or other, and often not even of that."[64]

Many Jeffersonian Republicans and, later, Jacksonian Democrats viewed the American Revolution in epochalist terms as marking a discontinuous break with the past. The Revolution had actually meant a liberation from history. The United States was a kind of tabula rasa upon which mankind could begin itself anew. George Bancroft, one of the few Democratic historians of the period, defined "American nationhood in terms of popular will, not in terms of tradition or the acceptance of historic limitations."[65]

Allston and his Boston patrons clearly tended toward an "essentialist" national ideology. The fact that there seemed to be no genuine historical precedent for America's national experiment was a cause for concern among conservatives. The ancient republics had never encompassed such a vast territory of land as the United States nor had they permitted so much liberty to so many. Even with their more homogenous and less democratic political structures, these republics had still fallen into disarray and tyranny.

Most Federalists, however, eventually felt compelled to adapt to the new political realities and at least pay lip service to democratic government. This became easier once the Federalist-Whig moral revolution showed signs of progress. As the religious societies, schools, and journals did their work, spreading to the South and the West, disciplining American behavior, territorial expansion and the popular will gradually became less worrisome.

William Tudor, the editor of the *North American Review* who had sought to lure Allston back to Boston through the founding of an institution of fine art, actually found reason for optimism in America's historical uniqueness. Though he had been worried about attracting "the right sort of people" to Boston, he publicly asserted his confidence that the ancient republics had never known a people so virtuous or a system of government that allowed such a degree of freedom.[66] The nation's uniqueness would serve to discredit the validity of cyclical theories of government. At the same time, however, Tudor believed that American history since the Revolution lacked a sacred quality. The meaning of recent events was not clear, since they were still the subject of partisan debate. Revolutionary and post-revolutionary history was too unstable a source from which to draw the nation's unifying symbols. America's pre-revolutionary history was a more certain period for discovering the principles upon which the nation ought to be founded.

For the New England clerisy, the "ancient order" into which Americans had been born was the system of civil and religious relations and set of cultural symbols that the Puritans had brought with them from Protestant England. New England historians traced the origins of American nationalism back to the Protestant Reformation when the first blow had been struck against the Roman Catholic antichrist.[67] While Jeffersonian Republicans and Jacksonian Democrats railed against England and America's colonial past, New England Federalists and Whigs urged Americans to remember the history of English Puritanism as a struggle for civil and religious liberty and the source of ideas for the American Revolution.

Ruth Miller Elson has called Allston's poem "America to Great Britain" the "most complete expression of this fusion of American nationalism" with Britain's cultural heritage.[68] During the 1830s the poem was published numerous times in various American schoolbooks or readers. In the poem Allston emphasized the value of England's art, manners, and religion, which had protected its people from the forces of tyranny:

While the language free and bold
Which the Bard of Avon sung,
In which our Milton told
How the vault of heaven rung
When Satan, blasted, fell with his host;—
While this, with reverence meet,
Ten thousand echoes greet,
From rock to rock repeat
Round our coast;—[69]

In the tradition of Milton and English Puritanism, New England intellectuals, from Cotton Mather to Washington Allston, taught successive generations of Americans to think of their history in providential terms as a spiritual antitype for events described in the Old Testament. During the post-revolutionary period, Federalists had to overcome the prejudices of Enlightenment rationalism in order to establish the Old Testament as a vital motivating force for American nationalism.

Thomas Paine's *Age of Reason*, which ridiculed the history of ancient Israel, had been something of a best seller in the late 1790s. Indeed, many influential Bostonians remained wary of the Old Testament because of its violence and stories of immorality. Elizabeth Palmer Peabody, one of Allston's most articulate advocates, lamented that Unitarian Sunday-school teachers had collectively decided not to teach the Old Testament to children because in the view of most it violated "the moral sentiment and conscience of childhood."[70]

Articles in the *Spirit of the Pilgrims* written by Richard Dana and others criticized Unitarian biblical criticism that questioned the authenticity and divine inspiration of the Old Testament texts.[71] Other Bostonians, like the Episcopalian William Tudor, believed that the Puritans had relied too heavily upon the Old Testament as a political guide.[72] The theocratic authoritarianism of the Hebrews' system of government frightened Americans who had come to accept the disestablishment of church from state.

Peabody argued, however, that if the Old Testament was not interpreted literally but spiritually or symbolically then it retained its usefulness as a moral guide for both the individual and the nation. Evangelicals and moral educators in New England did not wish to reestablish formal governmental ties to the church, particularly when the government itself was in the hands of their Democratic opponents. They did wish, however, to make religion the foundation upon which the national spirit was based and, for this purpose, the model of Old Testament Israel was still relevant. According to Peabody, William Ellery Channing, Boston's leading Unitarian minister, attributed the welfare of the nation to the individual morality of each citizen and this fundamental principle he derived from the Old Testament: "This is patriotism of the true pattern, such as Moses suggested, in referring all public calamities to some sin of omission or commission of perhaps but one citizen."[73]

Furthermore, in the disinterested character of the Old Testament patriarchs and prophets, Federalists and Whigs saw an ideal model of statesmanship that they believed was sorely lacking in Washington, D.C. Perhaps due to the popularity of Daniel Webster, New Englanders seemed especially to admire the prophet Daniel as an example of citizenship and public service. Daniel rose above selfish, factional interest to render justice to the will of God. His refusal of Belshazzar's gifts and honors proved his integrity and devotion to duty.[74] According to one moral educator:

In whatever way religion is dragged from its lofty and controlling sphere, and made to gild the claims of a party or of a sect, then and there we have a repetition of Belshazzar's profanation.[75]

By contrast, the prophet Daniel and his American counterpart or antitype (a Daniel Webster or a George Washington) sought to rise above party to enunciate essential, universal principles upon which nations ought to be ruled.[76] The austere demeanor and the rhetorical gesture of Daniel in Allston's picture was designed to appeal to a nation where political oratory and the sermon were the most popular forms of public entertainment and persuasion.

The Hebraic paradigm was attractive to citizens of the new republic because it reconciled pride in American uniqueness with the desire for continuity with a sacred, antique past. The "Second War for Independence" and the Second Great Awakening removed many of the doubts from the minds of Republicans and Federalists alike that the United States was a new Israel. According to Perry Miller, Americans during the early national period "grew to regard themselves as so like the Jews that every anecdote of tribal history seemed like a part of their own recollection."[77]

Though some Federalists like William Tudor doubted the value of Old Testament typological associations, most believed that the concept of a new Israel would continue to be an important incentive to virtue and piety. The Puritans had taught that their history would lead the way to the second coming of Christ just as surely as the history of the ancient Jews had led to the birth of Christ. Thanks to the energetic revivals of the Second Great Awakening and the growth of voluntary religious societies, this belief in the country's special mission within Christian eschatology gave nationalist ideology in the United States powerful religious overtones.

That Allston's *Belshazzar's Feast* was interpreted within the Hebraic spirit generated by millennial expectations is evident by a review of the picture in the *Christian Examiner,* the Boston Unitarian journal that orthodox critics so often charged as being hostile to Old Testament history. For the Reverend William P. Lunt, Allston's painting was "an impressive illustration of a people who had been humbled in every possible way."[78] Lunt's concern was not with the fate of Belshazzar or even so much the commanding presence of Daniel. Allston's *Belshazzar* was a monument to the children of Israel and a pledge "that the acts and experience of that peculiar people, shall continue in the memory of all periods of time, to verify the august Providence of God."[79] Lunt admired Daniel "not merely as a man" but as being representative of the Jewish nation and faith.

Exhibition of Allston's Old Testament paintings became occasions when Boston's writers could assess the nature of the Hebraic character and decide whether it was worthy of

157

national emulation. There were those who dissented from Allston's idealized vision of Jewry. Ralph Waldo Emerson, after seeing Allston's portraits of Polish Jews in the artist's retrospective of 1839, wrote in a journal entry that they "are an offense to me; they degrade and animalize."[80] It seems that for Emerson, it was better to paint beardless angels rather than the whiskers of Jews. Emerson rebelled against the adoption of traditional, timeworn symbols, as being external to the soul of man:

. . . never need we ask Moses or the prophets, if we are in danger or what God will do. There is God in you.[81]

Emerson was of the opinion that because Allston relied upon traditional Old Testament subjects, his pictures lacked individuality and soul. They were empty symbols in which it was left to the spectator to impute their meaning. By glorifying the past, Allston essentially impoverished the present.

Other Transcendentalist thinkers like Peabody and Margaret Fuller approved of Old Testament subjects, even though they sometimes criticized the deficiency of Allston's pictorial conception. Thus, in her review of *Miriam the Prophetess*, Fuller praised the Jewish national character as an inspiration for the artist.[82]

To those patrician critics who argued that the ancient Jews had been a barbaric tribe of nomads, Allston and his friends in the New England intellectual community sought to demonstrate the greatness of the Bible as literature and as a record of a nation's unity under the law of God. Horatio Greenough wrote in 1844 that "Allston's unwavering adherence to the neglected poetry of the Bible" had been especially heroic because of the art public's prejudice in favor of classical literature.[83] In 1826, James Marsh, president of the University of Vermont (who visited Allston whenever he was in the Boston–Cambridge area) translated J. G. Herder's *Spirit of the Hebrews*.[84] Herder interpreted Hebrew poetry as the first real expression of national patriotic feeling. The patriarchs and prophets of the Old Testament had been the first to speak to a unified national public.[85] Old Testament language and metaphor had awoken a national consciousness in Israel, an accomplishment Herder hoped to emulate in contemporary Germany. Similarly, Marsh, by translating Herder for an American audience, wished to strengthen the national character and government through the contemplation of Old Testament principles.[86]

In 1830, a new edition of Bishop Robert Lowth's eighteenth-century classic, *Lectures on the Sacred Poetry of the Hebrews*, was glowingly reviewed in the *North American Review*, a journal which normally preferred the more

reserved diction of classical authors. Yet, in contrasting
Hebrew Scriptures with Greek and Roman literature, G. B.
Cheever agreed with Lowth that Hebrew poetry "goes
deeper into the human soul and breathes a finer harmony of
feeling." The reason for this superiority was the organic
national community within which the Hebrews lived. That
"the Sovereign of the Universe" was also "the Supreme
Administrator of their State" was the central inspiration for
their art and poetry.[87]

For Dana, Allston, and others, Americans seemed forever in danger of forgetting their providential mission as a
chosen people and of falling into the sins of luxury, sensuality, and intemperance. Like the ancient Israelites, they lived a
relatively uncivilized primitive existence. In the accumulation
of wealth, the clearing and cultivation of virgin land, and the
construction of roads westward, Americans had found little
time for the "mental pleasures" that would elevate their
souls beyond the earthly realm. Richard Dana believed that
Americans were "blinded by the dust that is raised in the
clutter of material things." Railroads were a fine invention,
but "the almost exclusive pursuit of the physical" was
detrimental if the "higher order" of the mind was "left
to sleep."[88]

American artists and poets found it useful to argue
before a public skeptical of the value of art that the so-called
primitive authors and prophets of the Bible had themselves
been artists. They had been the first to demonstrate the value
of art in elevating the spirit to God and in creating a unified
national consciousness. The song that Moses and Miriam
sang after the crossing of the Red Sea was praised as a "trea-
sure in the annals of the nation, whose worth in the formation of the national spirit we cannot adequately appreciate."[89] For Fuller, Miriam was a prototype for the poet who
exalted the national soul by memorializing a great event in its
history.

Unlike the biblical poets, Allston did not believe he could
justifiably memorialize an event in America's national history. America was a promise as yet unfulfilled. The artist was
more interested in its future than its recent past. Only by
turning to the prophetic prefiguration of America in the Old
Testament could he suggest and encourage its central role in
the fulfillment of history.

Allston intended that his Old Testament paintings, fus-
ing art, religion, and national feeling, would foster a selfless,
disinterested state of mind in his audience. By elevating their
spirit beyond the earthly realm, he hoped to unite Americans
for the accomplishment of the single "great purpose of life,"
which is to prepare for the world beyond.[90] American nation-

alism, like economic success, could never be an end in itself. In order to prosper it had to subordinate itself to a transcendent reality.

Allston most explicitly stated his belief that Christianity was the bulwark of American national unity when he suggested the Three Marys at the Tomb as a subject for one of the panels in the Capitol Rotunda in Washington. In a letter to his old friend Gulian C. Verplanck, who had become chairman of the Committee on Public Buildings for the House of Representatives, Allston wrote that he would eagerly accept a Rotunda commission if he would be allowed to choose a subject from Scripture:

With such a source of inspiration and the glory of painting for my country, if there be anything in me, it must come out. Would it might be so! . . . supposing such a commission given, there's a subject already composed *in petto*, which I have long intended to paint as soon as I am at liberty—the three Marys at the tomb of the Saviour, the angel sitting on a stone before the mouth of the sepulchre. I consider this one of my happiest conceptions. The terrible beauty of the angel, his preternatural brightness, the varied emotions of wonder, awe, and bewilderment of the three women, the streak of distant daybreak, lighting the city of Jerusalem out of the darkness, and the deep-toned spell of the chiaroscuro mingling as it were the night with the day, I see now before me; I wish I could see them on the walls at Washington.[91]

Two years after halting work on *Belshazzar's Feast*, Allston hoped that a Rotunda commission would rescue him from his financial indebtedness. He thus told Verplanck:

I should not indeed refuse ten thousand, should Uncle Sam take the generous fit upon him to offer it; but eight is my price for that particular composition, which would consist of four figures, seven feet high; the picture itself (an upright) twelve or thirteen feet high and ten or twelve wide.

Allston's remarkable suggestion for a painting drawn from the story of Christ's Resurrection to decorate America's national temple was entirely in keeping with the theocratic ideology of New England's evangelical clergy. The daylight breaking over the horizon of the city of Jerusalem would have symbolized America as the new Jerusalem bringing the world to the dawn of the millennial age.

Allston told Verplanck that he saw no good reason why his proposed subject should be refused, since "This is a Christian land, and the Scriptures belong to no country, but to man. The facts they record come home to all men, to the high and the low, the wise and simple. . . ."

Though he did not say it, Allston also wished to imply that the Scriptures did not belong to any one political party.

Unlike the battles and events recorded in recent American history, biblical symbols and images were not divisive but unifying. Surely even Jacksonian Democrats like his friend Verplanck, a former professor of Revealed Religion, could agree upon a subject from Scripture. Yet Allston's letter indicates that he realized his proposal would be poorly received by the Democratic representatives. He referred to it as "a forlorn hope" and a "dream," because he knew that the Jacksonian Democrats favored a complete separation of church and state in opposition to the theocratic tendencies of New England conservatives. Indeed, in his reply to Allston, Verplanck dismissed the artist's proposal out of hand: "To Scripture I fear we cannot go in the present state of public opinion and taste."[92]

In the year following Jackson's election, evangelicals had intensified their efforts to Christianize the nation. The campaign crystallized around the issue of Sunday mail service. Conservatives insisted that the service be stopped to keep the Sabbath pure as a day of rest and contemplation. John Quincy Adams, Josiah Quincy, the mayor of Boston, and the Reverend Lyman Beecher were among the New England leaders of the Sabbatarian movement. In a vigorous counterattack, Jacksonian Democrats joined with political radicals in lashing out at the clergy and the "ecclesiastical hierarchy." In 1829, the House of Representatives firmly rejected the petitions of the Sabbatarians. Lyman Beecher warned in the *Spirit of the Pilgrims* that Americans faced "national chastisement" for scorning the sacredness of the Lord's day.[93]

Allston attempted to add his voice to the apocalyptic chorus sounding from New England's pulpits. That year, he began a study for *The Angel Pouring Out the Vial of Wrath over Jerusalem* from the Book of Revelation (fig. 37). There is no firm evidence to prove that Allston began the picture as a rebuke to the decision of the House of Representatives on the purity of the Sabbath. But, in the following year, the artist's pessimistic assessment of the chances for Congress approving the Three Marys at the Tomb for the Capitol Rotunda shows that he disapproved of the growing secularization in government.

Never had Allston begun a painting whose subject and conception was so menacing and apocalyptic in nature. Despite its threatening theme of the destruction of Jerusalem, the *Jeremiah* still possessed an atmosphere of quiet, dignified grandeur. In the unfinished sketch of 1829, however, a muscular angel floats belligerently in the air, pouring out the plague of wrath over the city below.

While Allston's more liberal religious friends believed that progress toward Christ's second coming would be the

Figure 37
Washington Allston, *The Angel Pouring out the Vial of Wrath over Jerusalem,* begun 1829, chalk study on canvas, 36³/8 × 29¹/2 in. From the collections of the Boston University Libraries, Massachusetts.

result of man's gradual moral improvement, Allston's study from Revelation and his Old Testament images of prophetic doom warned that progress against the forces of evil could be less smooth than commonly imagined. Divine punishments would, perhaps, be required periodically just as God had chastized the ancient Hebrews.

Allston's increasing indebtedness, chronic illness, and growing sense of isolation from the secularizing policies of the American government contributed to a spiritually depressed state of mind. He had begun *Angel Pouring Out the Vial* during a severe illness and was unable to finish it.

Seemingly at the point of mental and physical exhaustion, Allston decided to relent. With *Belshazzar's Feast* rolled up and in storage and his suggestion for the Three Marys at the Tomb rejected for the Capitol Rotunda, he finally decided to postpone no longer his marriage to Martha R. Dana. The couple moved to Cambridgeport where the artist could live in relative isolation from the rest of society. Allston wrote to his friend John Cogdell, one of the subscribers to *Belshazzar's*

Feast, that a quiet domestic home life "with the woman of my choice, must have no ordinary value in my eyes, after the restless, wandering Arab life which I have led for the last ten years."[94] Allston had decided that he needed a respite from his heroic labors upon *Belshazzar's Feast* but he never, for a moment, intended to abandon it entirely. As he explained to a patron in 1831:

... sometimes I get what the artists call, "stuck," that is, I come to a part with which I cannot please myself, and which becomes worse and worse the more I work on it; my only remedy then is to lay it aside, and return to it after a time with a fresh eye, when I am generally able to hit at once what I might else have laboured for in vain. In the meantime, as I have neither the leisure nor inclination to be idle, I proceed with some other picture till I either finish that, or am "brought up" by it in a similar way.[95]

For more than a decade, Allston did not unroll *Belshazzar's Feast* but he never lost his passionate interest in the picture. When he returned to it in 1839, he did so with the same missionary zeal as when he had begun it in 1817. If anything, social and religious changes in Boston and America intensified the artist's commitment to the picture.

CHAPTER 8

Allston Interpreting to Americans the Handwriting on the Wall

Art historians have interpreted Allston's decision to move to the sleepy village of Cambridgeport, just outside Boston, as an indication that he was becoming more introspective and less interested in that most public of genres, history painting. As Allston had conceived *Belshazzar's Feast* in the aftermath of war and social revolution, it has been argued that the artist lost his original inspiration for the picture because by 1830

. . . a more tranquil spirit had emerged, particularly in an America witnessing great political and territorial growth and conceiving of itself as a new Eden. The spirit of confrontation embodied in *Belshazzar's Feast* had given way to one of reconciliation. . . . The wrathful God of the Old Testament had little place in a new land on which the Deity seemed to be bestowing his blessing.[1]

Yet, for an unregenerate Federalist like Allston, the 1830s and '40s in America were scarcely years of reconciliation. Nor were they lacking in social, political, and intellectual confrontation. Allston dreaded the progress of democracy, ridiculed the American form of government, and looked askance at the public's taste and intelligence.

Peter Dobkin Hall has argued that Federalists tended to view the universe in Manichaean terms as a struggle between the forces of good and evil, order and chaos.[2] This outlook did not disappear with the collapse of the Federalist party after the War of 1812:

The Federalist vision of the dangers posed by democracy and popularly defined authority, the threat of society's collapsing into either chaos or dictatorship, remained a basic theme of their rhetoric until the Civil War. Events constantly kept the theme alive: the association of Jeffersonianism with slavery, the virtual dictatorship of Andrew Jackson, and the restive agitation of laborers and urban mobs.[3]

During the 1830s, the age of Jacksonian Democracy, Allston diagrammed his Manichaean vision of the universe (see fig. 21). The idea that man has a free moral choice between just two constellations of forces, the Deity and Sin, had informed his conception of *Belshazzar's Feast,* its division between foreground and background space. His *Lectures on Art,* written during the last decade of his life, are also intimately related to this paranoid view. Allston conceived art as an instrument delegated by God to bring man out of a life of sin and into a state of harmony with the infinite universe.

During the 1830s and '40s, Allston never lost the apocalyptic frame of mind that had originally conceived *Belshazzar's Feast.* If anything, he sensed that satanic evil was threatening the new American Eden more powerfully than ever. In 1833, he was again painting a subject from Milton's *Paradise Lost,* entitled *Gabriel Setting the Watch at the Gates of Paradise.* Though now lost, the picture represented a later moment in Milton's epic than the artist's earlier work, *Uriel in the Sun,* conceived during the same period as *Belshazzar.*[4] Satan had been able to escape the watchful eye of the archangel Uriel. The next defense against the evil one's attempt to penetrate the Gates of Paradise was Gabriel, chief of the angelic guards. Despite Gabriel's promise that "at this Gate none pass / The vigilance here plac't, but such as come / Well known from Heav'n" (Book IV: 579–81), Satan succeeds in entering Paradise, and begins to tempt Eve in a dream before being apprehended by Gabriel's guards.

For Allston, the progress of evil in *Paradise Lost,* overcoming the strongest of defenses, seemed to find its parallel in nineteenth-century America. The evil effects of democratic and equalitarian institutions steadily grew despite New England's campaign for moral improvement and religious reawakening. In fact, the evangelical movement experienced a series of external and internal crises during the 1830s that actually contributed to democracy's progress.

Externally, the ideal of a homogenous Christian America was threatened by the increasing tide of Catholic immigrants from Europe. Just as William Tudor had predicted to Harrison G. Otis (see chapter 6) foreign immigration on a large scale began soon after the Napoleonic Wars. The Industrial Revolution in Europe caused severe population dislocations and unemployment. Many European governments encouraged their excess population to migrate to the New World, relieving themselves of the burden of pauperism.

With the steady increase of Catholics from Ireland and the European continent, the Catholic church in America grew rapidly during the 1820s. A new militance developed in Rome, as the Church began to envision the day when the United States would be converted to Catholicism.[5] In 1829, the passage of the Catholic Emancipation Bill in England gave the Vatican cause for hope that Protestantism was waning in strength.

The English campaign for Catholic emancipation created an enormous storm of controversy. Evangelicals like Henry Drummond and the Presbyterian clergyman Edward Irving made dire, apocalyptic predictions against its passage. They charged that the Anglican church was forging an alliance with the papal Babylon and that England, once an elect nation, had become apostate.[6] In 1829, the year that Catholic emancipation passed Parliament, Drummond and Irving were joined by a number of Anglican evangelicals in issuing a statement from a series of meetings called the Albury Conferences. They concluded that the vials of wrath, described in Revelation, chapter 16, were now being poured out and that the final day of judgment and the second advent of Christ were imminent.[7]

The wealth of apocalyptic literature during the period of 1825–30 encouraged English artists to continue painting scenes of deluge and catastrophe. Following in the footsteps of John Martin, Francis Danby may have been influenced by Edward Irving's sermons and prophecies to paint such pictures as *Babylon and Infidelity Foredoomed* and the *Sixth Seal*.[8] Meanwhile, Robert Southey, Poet Laureate of England, who had praised Allston in his poem, "A Vision of Judgment," loudly denounced popery, defending the Church of England, in a series of articles in the Tory Journal, the *Quarterly Review*.[9]

Since events in England were closely followed by evangelicals and particularly Episcopalians in America, one might speculate that Allston's *Angel Pouring out the Vial of Wrath over Jerusalem* was inspired by the apocalyptic warnings voiced by defenders of the Anglican faith. Allston's precise view on the Catholic Emancipation Bill is not known, nor is it likely that he was inclined to believe in the literal prophecies made by the radical participants of the Albury Conferences. Yet, one might assume that the artist saw a disturbing trend in the secularization of the state in the two national pillars of the Protestant faith, England and America.

At the very time that Catholicism was becoming more militant, Protestantism seemed to be disarming itself. In America, the House of Representatives, far from supporting any particular sect, had gone on to declare that government had nothing whatever to do with religion. Such a view could only have infuriated a man like Allston who used apocalyptic imagery as a means for moral admonishment. As Ernest R. Sandeen and other scholars have argued, the distinction between fanatical millenialists who predict the precise moment of doom, like the Millerites in America, and evangelical Episcopalians ought not to be drawn too sharply.[10] Episcopalians were equally adept in warning of dire, apocalyptic catastrophes if only as an instrument to enforce the law of conscience.

High-church and low-church Episcopalians were important contributors to the growing anti-Catholic sentiment in America. Not only were they critical of developments in England but they feared the acceleration of Catholic immigration into this country. In 1829, the bishops of the Episcopal church issued a pastoral letter warning of the dangers of popery.[11] Bishop Alexander Griswold of the Eastern Diocese urged church members to reject the principles of Catholicism.

Allston, an Episcopalian, had spent several years in Rome and had admired the Catholic church's patronage of the arts. In *Monaldi*, written in 1822, he had portrayed the kindness of monks in an Italian convent, compelling the narrator of the story to forget all his "prejudices against monks and monasteries."[12] Yet, in the 1830s, there is evidence that the artist shared the growing fear that the Catholic church intended to subvert the American continent, forcing it to submit to Rome.

In 1831, Allston produced his first major dramatic painting in ten years, *Spalatro's Vision of the Bloody Hand*, from Ann Radcliffe's Gothic romance *The Italian*, written in 1797. The picture, destroyed by fire and known only through an engraving, was commissioned by an art collector from Charleston, South Carolina, Hugh Swinton Ball (fig. 38). Ball apparently discussed the novel with Allston, who had been a great admirer of Radcliffe's since his school days at Harvard.

The chief villain of Radcliffe's novel is a Catholic priest of almost superhuman, satanic powers named Schedoni. Schedoni is the confessor and secret advisor of the marchesa di Vivaldi, an extremely wealthy woman whose husband had great power and influence in the kingdom of Naples. The marchesa promises to promote Schedoni's career if only he will prevent her son, Vicentio, from marrying a girl of inferior social rank, the beautiful and virtuous Ellena. To this end, Schedoni has Ellena kidnapped with the hope of forcing her to join a nunnery in some distant mountain retreat. Ellena escapes with the help of Vicentio but they are apprehended by the Inquisition just as they are about to make their marriage vows. Schedoni then decides that Ellena must be murdered. He hires the assassin Spalatro and together one night they go to Ellena's prison room, Spalatro being armed with a dagger. Suddenly, however, the hired assassin sees

Figure 38
Spalatro's Vision of the Bloody Hand, engraved frontispiece after a lost painting of 1831 by Washington Allston, for Mrs. Clara Erskine Waters, *A Handbook of Legendary and Mythological Art* (New York: Hurd and Houghton, 1871). Courtesy, Princeton University Library, New Jersey.

the apparition of a bloody hand, guiding and beckoning him to the accomplishment of the evil deed.

This is the moment of the novel that Allston chose to represent. The artist did not actually paint the bloody hand since he wished to suggest that it was really Spalatro's inner vision or conscience addressing him. The assassin thus points to empty space and Schedoni, who fails to see what is bothering Spalatro, sternly urges him forward, taking the dagger into his own hand. Seized by the terror of a guilty conscience, Spalatro instinctively backs away clutching onto the hand of Schedoni. His fearful action recalls Belshazzar's guilt-ridden movement away from the handwriting on the wall in the artist's frustrated masterpiece. Critics noted with admiration the sharp contrast between this contorted face of Spalatro, "produced by a terror-stricken conscience," and "the stern unpitying fixedness of the man who grasps the dagger, and points the way to his sleeping victim."[13]

The glacial, inhuman countenance of the Catholic priest seems the very epitome of evil. Directly behind Schedoni are chains and instruments of torture, emblems or reminders of the Inquisition. To the right, leaning against a pair of steps, are a pick and shovel, tools for Ellena's burial. The gloomy dungeon space is illuminated by the lamp that Schedoni holds aloft, though the priest's piercing deep-set eyes, as described by Radcliffe and faithfully rendered by Allston, seem able to penetrate the darkness without its assistance. Yet, seemingly bereft of a conscience, Schedoni is incapable of feeling the guilt and horror over his own moral degradation. While the viewer could, perhaps, feel a degree of pity for the guilt-ridden Spalatro, no such empathy was possible for the remorseless Schedoni. As Mario Praz has argued, Mrs. Radcliffe appealed to the anti-Catholic prejudices of her English audience who believed that the primary sources of "mysterious crimes" in the world could be found in the Inquisition and the Society of Jesus.[14]

Ann Radcliffe's Gothic tales of horror were avidly read in the United States. In 1827, Allston's friend Richard H. Dana praised her novels, referring to the scene of the bloody hand as one of the most sublime passages in her oeuvre.[15] Soon after he had painted *Spalatro,* Allston began to write his *Lectures on Art* where in discussing the concept of the moral sublime he seems to have recalled Radcliffe's novel. He wrote that the Inquisition was one of the most profound examples of evil in the world, causing us to become "lost in wonder at the excess of human wickedness."[16] Primary moral blame was not upon the actual executioner or hired assassin but upon the evil mastermind of a Schedoni or "presiding Inquisitor." It is the latter that we curse as being beyond the pale of human feeling or sympathy. Toward the presiding Inquisitor "we award a hatred commensurate with the sin, so indefinite and monstrous that we stand aghast at our judgment."[17]

In his unpublished essay on religion, Allston continued his discussion of the Inquisition. He puzzled over the question of how reputed Christians could disguise such an evil institution to give it the appearance of being good, or how they could delude themselves that they were serving God by breaking His commandments:

For no one can doubt that among the numberless members of that atrocious tribunal, there have been many self-supposed pious inquisitors, who have immolated their victims without a twinge, nay even with the sanction of their consciences.[18]

Allston concludes that such a misinterpretation of Christianity or the "Religion of Love" could not have occurred "without a previous perversion of the mind, under the indurating process of pride, ambition, and other sinful affections that throng the human atmosphere ever ready to drop their devilish seeds into the selfish heart—waiting only a wink from the consenting will."

Schedoni's character would have been a case in point for Allston because, like Milton's Satan, Schedoni could easily assume an appearance of piety, thereby fooling the critical judgment of the most skeptical observer. Furthermore, through complex, "artificial" arguments and the "wily cunning of his nature," he could twist the truth to his own selfish purposes.[19] In this way, says Mario Praz, Schedoni was "reminiscent of the Machiavellians and Jesuits who had been among the abiding features of the English Theatre of the seventeenth century."

Before it went to South Carolina, *Spalatro's Vision* was exhibited in Boston and New York in 1832. In both cities, anti-Catholic sentiment was surfacing as a socially volatile phenomenon. While Bostonians continued to practice a liberal tolerance in matters of theology, after 1830, Irish immigrants began to be feared as a hostile, alien force that threatened national spiritual unity. The loyalties of new immigrants were held in suspicion. Many believed that their primary loyalty was not to America but to the pope in Rome. While theological liberals and even the orthodox could tolerate differences in spiritual doctrine, the perception grew that the Catholic church desired temporal power as well.

In 1830, Lyman Beecher began a series of anti-Catholic sermons, in which he argued that Catholicism was the natural ally of political despotism while Protestantism was inherently sympathetic to republican principles. With visions of the Inquisition in their heads, American anti-Catholics or nativists contended that Roman Catholics were opposed to freedom of conscience. The Catholic hierarchy disallowed the individual's right to read the Bible in the privacy of his own home. The papacy controlled it subjects by keeping them in ignorance from the true faith, making them superstitiously dependent upon the authority of priests and monks.

Allston's *Spalatro* suggested the horrible fate awaiting victims of Catholic authoritarianism. Spalatro, a mere outsider to the machinations of the Church, is overcome by the warnings of his conscience. His horror is the moral response with which the beholder identifies. Schedoni's conscience, by contrast, can scarcely be said to exist. So remorseless and depraved had he become that he lived entirely outside the laws of God. Thanks to his personal ambition, the church had become a law unto itself.

Anti-Catholic literature in the United States focused upon the image of the priest as sadist, as one who controverted all known standards of conscience and morality. According to one historian, American nativists had a kind of perverse fascination in the lives of Catholic monks:

What was it like to be a member of a cohesive brotherhood that casually abrogated the laws of God and man, enforcing unity and obedience with dark and mysterious powers? As nativists speculated on this question, they projected their own fears and desires into a fantasy of licentious orgies and fearful punishments.
Such a projection of forbidden desires can be seen in the exaggeration of the stereotyped enemy's powers, which made him appear at times as a virtual superman.[20]

171

In 1834, anti-Catholic violence finally erupted in Charlestown, Massachusetts, just outside of Boston. About forty or fifty brickmakers led a mob in the burning of the Ursuline convent school. Fear of competition from Irish Catholic laborers and bizarre stories of dungeons and torture chambers deep within the convent walls motivated the mob action.

Boston's leading citizens loudly condemned the violence and vowed to punish the perpetrators. But revulsion from this notorious act of violence failed to arrest anti-Catholic sentiment even among perfectly respectable members of American society.

During the same year as the Charlestown convent fire, Allston's old friend Samuel F. B. Morse wrote a series of letters to the nativist newspaper, the *New York Observer*, warning that the papacy and the Catholic monarchies of Europe were conspiring to subvert the United States by encouraging the emigration of their pauper population.[21] Insisting that he was not writing against the Catholic religion but rather against the Catholic quest for political power, Morse repeated Lyman Beecher's charge that Catholicism was in alliance with despotism. Popery was the enemy of general education and free conscience and, therefore, it was essentially anti-American. By flooding the American West with Catholic immigrants, the papacy hoped to gain control of the U.S. government. Morse carefully rejected violence as a weapon to combat the enemy. He instead called upon Americans to educate the immigrants, freeing them from their ignorance and their enslavement to foreign tyrants. Through the organization and influence of the various evangelical missionary and Bible societies, Morse hoped that the immigrants' conscience could be freed from the yoke of Catholic oppression.

Morse's letters received widespread national attention, were critically praised and published in book form in 1835. Allston possessed a copy of the book.[22] Probably, Morse had sent it to him as a gift in recognition of their long friendship. Although we do not know what the older artist thought of the specific conspiracy charges in the letters, *Spalatro's Vision* and his writings on the Inquisition demonstrate that he harbored a genuine fear of the Catholic church. Nor can it be doubted that the exhibition of *Spalatro's Vision* contributed in its own limited way to the revival of anti-Catholic prejudice.

Furthermore, in 1837, Allston began to paint another subject with anti-Catholic overtones, *The Death of King John*, from Shakespeare's play *King John* (see fig. 39). He never completed the work, but it was exhibited after his death and was praised by William Ware as one of his finest conceptions.[23] Like *Spalatro's Vision*, *The Death of King John* is related to *Belshazzar's Feast* in that it represents the law of conscience

working within the mind of an unregenerate sinner. Shakespeare based his play upon an earlier anonymous work entitled *The Troublesome Reign of John King of England* which was popular for its vehemently anti-Catholic bias.[24] In the older play, King John was portrayed as a kind of national hero who attempted to stand up to the authority of the pope as Henry VIII was to do several centuries later. Ultimately, however, John submitted to the Church, which had urged the French monarch, King Philip, to invade England. At the end of the play, John is poisoned by a monk and dies in Swinstead Abbey.

Shakespeare toned down the anti-Catholic elements in his own play by making the character of John unattractive and weak. He implies that John had essentially usurped the English crown from Arthur, the son of his brother who had been the previous king. John goes so far as to order that the young Arthur be murdered. Far from being a national hero, John, Shakespeare suggests, opposed the Church merely out of personal ambition. After his excommunication, he orders the looting and seizing of monastic property. Finally, Shakespeare deemphasized the questionable tale of a monk poisoning John, moving the actual poisoning offstage.

Nevertheless, since at least the middle of the eighteenth

century, Shakespeare's *King John* had become popularized and presented as an anti-Catholic play. King John's reply to Pandulph, the papal legate, in Act III, Scene I, "that no Italian priest shall tithe or toll in our dominions" fueled Protestant prejudice and nationalist feeling. Critics in the nineteenth century overwhelming interpreted the play as either anti-Catholic or anti-papal in attitude, protesting not so much the Catholic religion as its interference in the political affairs of sovereign nations.

Faithful to Shakespeare's interpretation, Allston represents King John's death as that of a sinner and not as a national hero. Yet, while Shakespeare downplayed the role of Catholic monks in John's death and called for none in the final scene, Allston represented four of them around the King's deathbed. He did not caricature the three at the right as evil beings, but the monk at the left, earnestly leaning over John's body, reveals no grief or human sympathy as he frowns and furrows his brow. His anxious, but pitiless, concern suggests a collaborative role in the poisoning. His bald head and piercing, deep-set eyes, connoting a dark personality, bear an unmistakable resemblance to the malevolent features of Schedoni in *Spalatro's Vision*. The Gothic gloom of the abbey setting and the mysterious cowled monk at the far right certainly expressed the popular image of the monastic orders as a dark and secretive brotherhood existing outside the familiar realm of society and normal domestic relations. By stressing the role of an evil-appearing monk in John's death, in contradiction to Shakespeare's minimizing intent, Allston continued to show his distrust of Catholicism.

However, in portraying John as a guilty, lost sinner, another Belshazzar, Allston condemned a persecutor of the Catholic church. Just as Belshazzar had violated the sacred by using holy vessels from the Jewish Temple for his impious feast, so had King John desecrated religion by vandalizing the abbeys. Allston furthermore repeated the theme of profanation during the 1830s in a chalk sketch, *Heliodorous Driven from the Temple*, based upon Raphael's famous painting in the Vatican.[25] Although the *Heliodorus* sketch is not precisely dated, it is tempting to believe that Allston thought of the subject after the infamous fire at the Ursuline convent in 1834. *The Death of King John* could also be interpreted as the artist's condemnation of anti-Catholic violence, a position that every respectable Protestant assumed, including nativists like Samuel Morse.

Rejecting mob rioting did not simultaneously mean relinquishing anti-Catholic prejudice. Denouncing the violation of their religious property did not entail an endorsement of the Catholic church's political designs nor their clergy's unnatural, celibate lifestyle. Allston's friend, Gulian C. Verplanck, published a new edition of Shakespeare's works in which he quoted a critic of *King John,* arguing that just because Shakespeare refused "to pander to popular prejudice," avoiding "coarse abuse of the Roman Catholics," it did *not* mean that the playwright felt "direct sympathy with the enemies of the Reformation."[26]

Allston may have been attracted to the final scene of *King John* because it contained a plea for national unity and reconciliation. The dark, melancholic figure who stands in the foreground, aside from the central scene, in Allston's painting is surely Faulconbridge, the bastard son of Richard the Lion-Hearted. Faulconbridge served as a kind of chorus or commentator upon the events in the play and seems to have expressed Shakespeare's actual point of view.[27] In his famous final speech after observing the death of John, Faulconbridge stated that England had never and would never submit to a foreign conquerer unless it had become internally divided or "did help to wound itself" (act V, scene VII, line 120). England need only remain true to itself to survive.

The woman who kneels in grief before John's deathbed was, like the monks' presence, not called for by Shakespeare's text. Allston may have intended her as a symbol of benevolence and the process of national healing called for by Faulconbridge. She and the evil Schedoni-like monk seem, in fact, to be moral opposites contending for the body of the king, who, as head of state, personifies the nation. Once again, as in *Belshazzar* and the *Jeremiah,* Allston portrays the Manichaean conflict between the forces of discord and harmony as each side holds onto one of the king's arms.

While the Catholic immigrants and their priestly confessors were perceived by many Protestants as an unassimilable group and a dangerous threat to America's unity and favored role in converting the world to Christ, these same Protestants continued to be seriously divided amongst themselves. The schism within Congregationalism between theological liberals and the orthodox became official as each side increasingly refused fellowship with the other and each began to organize their own churches separately. Subsequently, there were further divisions within both orthodoxy and Unitarianism that caused considerable controversy, fragmenting the evangelical movement and even calling into question the validity of Christian revelation altogether.

Within the ranks of the orthodox, the so-called New School or New Divinity Presbyterian and Congregationalist preachers, like Lyman Beecher and Nathaniel W. Taylor, began to argue more insistently that man had a natural ability to obey God's law and to begin the process of regeneration independently of God's grace.[28] Influenced by the Scottish Common Sense philosophers, Taylor argued that man had an innate moral sense that allowed him to choose between good and evil without supernatural assistance. The Holy Ghost only influenced, but did not alter the heart, since man was fundamentally a free agent. According to Taylor, the workings of the Holy Spirit were no more effectual than "the solicitations of a friend."[29] New School Calvinists furthermore denied that all mankind shared in Adam's guilt. Sin was associated only with one's own voluntary actions. Rejecting the idea of innate depravity, the revivalist preacher, Charles G. Finney argued that man actually had the ability to attain moral perfection in the present world. Perfect obedience to God's "absolute" law was adjusted to coincide with each individual's circumstances and capacity for understanding.

The Common Sense rationalism inherent in New School revivalist thought did not surface into public controversy until 1828 when conservative "Old School" Calvinists finally decided that Nathaniel Taylor's views were heretical. During the 1820s, Unitarians had, in fact, been arguing that both Beecher and Taylor diverged significantly from traditional Calvinist doctrine, which had stressed man's depravity and his inability to initiate the process of regeneration, much less to attain moral perfection.[30] Unitarian critics claimed that Beecher and Taylor, their nominal opponents, were closer to Unitarian theology than they might like to think.

Allston and his brother-in-law Richard H. Dana were uncomfortable with New School ideas. They could agree that God's grace was not absolutely determining in the process of regeneration, but they insisted that it was vital nonetheless. Only the power of the Holy Spirit could sustain man, protecting him from temptation.[31] Nathaniel Taylor and Charles Finney seemed to be steering the revivalist movement in a dangerously democratic direction. By watering down the absolute nature of God's law to suit the individual circumstances and nature of man, New School revivalists unjustifiably exalted the pride and confidence of the common man. Dana insisted that the law is supra-individual and universal in nature, a divine standard that exists outside the will of man. Such law, based upon a heavenly, and not an earthly order, could not possibly be obeyed perfectly and equally by all men. God's law teaches humility rather than pride and is, therefore, qualitatively different from democratic ideology.

In his correspondence with the Reverend James Marsh, the leading Coleridgean scholar in America, Dana attacked "the brawling, shallow, rambling stream of Taylorism."[32]

Marsh, in turn, harshly criticized the methods of revivalist preachers like Jedidiah Burchard:

> . . . the substance of his doctrinal views . . . is *Taylorism*. . . . He takes a perfectly empirical and notional view of the *free-will*, and maintained through a considerable part of his sermon the perfect ability of the sinner to repent, and do all God required of him without any conditions and limitation. . . . He ridiculed the notion, that God would require of the sinner any thing that he had not a natural ability to perform.[33]

By an "empirical and notional view" of free will, Marsh meant that the Taylorites regarded man's will as determined by the laws of cause and effect that ruled material life. Marsh believed that if man's will rests upon the same ontological plane as external nature, then it cannot be free. Basing his arguments upon those of Coleridge, Marsh believed that free will can only exist in a philosophy that distinguishes between the understanding, whose objects are the phenomena of this world, and a higher reason that intuits the truth of a heavenly, noumenal existence. Through the process of regeneration, God's grace transforms man's vision, enabling him to rise above "the demands of appetite" and "the law of nature" and to perceive those objects of the spiritual world.[34] To assume with the Taylorite revivalists that man could achieve this transformation simply through his own effort smacked of democratic demagoguery:

> Consider the mode in which ignorant and inexperienced persons are first literally dragged into those seats, taught to expect immediate conversion by a mere act of their own will. . . .
>
> Does it not tend to awaken in the church a spirit of fanatical self confidence in their own power? Does it not tend to depreciate the regular and patient, and humble use of the ordinary duties and charities of the Christian life? . . . Does it not *set us afloat* upon a boundless sea of *novel and untried experiments* . . .?[35]

As one who had assisted Marsh in understanding the ideas and personality of his old friend Samuel Taylor Coleridge, Allston shared Marsh's position that man's understanding had little to do with a religion of the heart. In opposition to the rationalism of Scottish Common Sense philosophy, which was the basis for Unitarian and New School optimism, Allston repeatedly stressed the incommensurability of earthly and spiritual phenomena. Thus fallen man is struck dumb whenever he confronts "a holy spiritual presence." The so-called natural sublime discussed by Burke and others was not nearly so powerful or affecting as the religious or moral sublime. Allston posed the rhetorical question:

"What of the Sublime in this lower world would so shake us" as an encounter with an angel, whose sinless being was immeasureably distant from our own?

Though his beauty were such as never mortal dreamed of, it would be as nothing,—swallowed up as darkness—in the awful, spiritual brightness of the messenger of God. Even as the soldiers in Scripture, at the sepulchre of the Saviour, we should fall before him—we should 'become' like them, 'as dead men.'[36]

While it may have seemed to him that Unitarians and New School Calvinists were in collusion, when they minimized the importance of man's dual nature, Allston believed that man's moral and physical being were in a constant state of war and conflict. He warned:

Let no man trust to the gentleness, the generosity, or seeming goodness of his heart, in the hope that they alone can safely bear him through the temptations of this world. This is a state of probation, and a perilous passage to the true beginning of life, where even the best natures need continually to be reminded of their weakness. . . .[37]

Given Americans' lack of spiritual humility, the nation's prosperity and expansion westward could only have seemed an illusory, superficial phenomenon to a man of Allston's political and religious persuasion. Historians have challenged the traditional notion that optimism reigned supreme during the era of Jacksonian Democracy. Prosperity was always viewed as something of a mixed blessing because it encouraged immoderate behavior, impiety, pride, and excessive luxury, thereby inviting divine retribution. In such a context, the imagery and themes of *Belshazzar's Feast* scarcely would have lost their potency. As Fred Somkin has said of the period:

To those who profited most from the spectacular growth of the American economy the possibility of violent revolution always remained a grinning death's head at the rich feast.[38]

Catastrophe literature flourished in the 1830s and '40s partly because economic development and irreligion seemed to go hand in hand.[39] Industrial and urban growth was outstripping the ability of the revivalist movement to organize Americans into a national network of churches and religious societies. Fears of infidelity increased as clergymen became aware that population growth was almost exceeding the rate at which new churches were being founded.[40] In 1829, Abner Kneeland, a former carpenter and Baptist preacher, began to publish a newspaper, the *Boston Investigator,* in which he attacked the Christian religion in the name of a homespun enlightenment rationalism. In 1833, the Commonwealth of

Massachusetts indicted Kneeland for publishing a "scandal-ous, impious, obscene, blasphemous and profane libel" upon the existence of God.[41] Kneeland was found guilty by Chief Justice Lemuel Shaw (a close friend of Allston's), who argued that the Christian religion was actually incorporated within the fabric of the Common Law. By impairing or destroying the reverence due to God, Kneeland had broken the law and, therefore, merited punishment.

Kneeland was deemed especially dangerous because he appealed to the socially volatile "mechanics" and artisans in Boston. The French Revolution had taught that irreligion and social revolution went hand in hand. Thus when a record number of labor strikes occurred in 1835 and 1836, Boston merchants and industrialists braced themselves for the worst. Indeed, when an economic crisis did strike with severe force in 1837, Orestes Brownson turned to the apocalyptic texts of Revelation and Daniel to proclaim that "Baby-lon is falling." The privileged and wealthy had finally been forced "to see the hand-writing on the walls of their palaces, and to feel everything giving way beneath them."[42] Brown-son condemned the "spirit of gain" or the "commercial spirit," equating it with the city of Babylon.[43]

Although Babylon did not fall at the hands of the labor-ing classes, the fear of a social revolution did not dissipate. Economic depression with widespread bankruptcies and a high rate of unemployment lasted until 1843, the year of Allston's death. According to Larzer Ziff, the panic of 1837 jolted Americans' faith in the Common Sense materialism of Scottish philosophy, opening the door for Transcendentalist idealism:

The panic of 1837 silenced the shouts of national confidence and in the hush Emerson's voice was heard. In the 1840s, the economy recovered. . . . But 1837 was remembered, and ever thereafter there were listeners for Emerson's message.[44]

But for Allston and other conservative Bostonians, the panic of 1837 was far less perturbing than Emerson's mes-sage. The latter's egotistical, pantheistic apostasy threatened to cause further division within the ranks of the New England clerisy, the self-appointed spiritual guides of Ameri-can culture. Allston, Dana, and Marsh observed with grow-ing pessimism the evolution of Transcendentalist thought from its origins in the optimistic humanism of Unitarian belief and Taylorite revivalism.

In finally adopting the evangelical methods of the ortho-dox clergy during the 1830s, radical Unitarian ministers, like Emerson, had found that their emotional pleas to the hearts of their audience were hindered by the excess intellectual baggage of Christian tradition. Taking the Coleridgean distinction between understanding and an intuitive, "higher" reason to its extreme but logical conclusion, they decided that it was unnecessary to introduce God's supernatural grace or the Holy Spirit into the formula of religious conversion. Man's feeling or higher reason was independent of God's grace, Scripture, and all external authority. Emerson and his disciples ultimately rejected not only Unitarianism but organized religion altogether because it was too intellectually complex, too dependent upon man's understanding.

Orthodox Bostonians and more conservative Unitarians recoiled from the Transcendentalists' prideful dismissal of Scripture and their insistence that God resides entirely within nature and the soul of every man. In a letter to James Marsh following Emerson's lectures of 1837–38, Richard Dana charged that Emerson had deprived the religious instinct of its proper object, God. Without an object, man's "*highest* Instinct" becomes abstract and meaningless.[45] In response, Marsh acknowledged that while "the personality of God cannot be proved by speculative reasoning yet conscience commands us to recognize his personal being."[46]

Unitarian attacks upon Emerson's Divinity School Address of 1838 also reaffirmed the notion of a personal God. In his sermon, *The Personality of the Deity,* Henry Ware, Jr., expressed alarm over the harmful moral effects of an abstract conception of God.[47] Without a God who acts as a judge and personally rules the universe, Ware feared that morality would lose its authority. Social anarchy loomed as the ultimate danger. Even Orestes Brownson initially had strong reservations over Emerson's deification of the soul:

. . . The soul's conception of God is not God, and if there be no God out of the soul, out of the *me*, to answer to one's conception, then there is no God.[48]

Allston's feverish activity during the last few years of his life, his return to *Belshazzar's Feast,* his long-overdue publication of *Monaldi* in 1841, and his intention to deliver publicly a series of lectures on art, ought to be interpreted as his profound disapproval of a non-Christian transcendentalism. The arguments of his *Lectures on Art,* written while the Transcendentalist crisis raged, particularly seem to be addressed to the claims of Emerson and his followers.

In outlining the epistemological and ontological grounds for his theory of art, Allston argued that the traditional concept of God was demanded by man's conscience. If, as he repeatedly stated throughout the *Lectures,* man's spiritual desire is infinite, it must have an infinite object. Since man's dual nature, *physical* as well as moral, relegates him to a state

180

of finitude, the self cannot be the object of spiritual desire, at least, not in this present earthly realm:

We have said that man cannot to himself become the object of Harmony,—that is, find its proper correlative in himself; and we have seen that, in his present state, the position is true. How is it, then, in the world of spirit? . . . as a finite creature, having no centre in himself on which to revolve, may it not be that his true correlative will there be revealed (if, indeed, it be not before) to the disembodied man, in the Being that made him?[49]

Thus, not until after his death when man had shed his physical being and become "disembodied," can he be completely united with the harmony of God's universe. If this religious truth is revealed to man while he yet lives on earth, then he can at least live in a state of perpetual hope. That man does, indeed, live in hope and longing for an "unapproachable Infinite" is the clearest evidence that an "Infinite Creator" actually exists.

Employing a logic similar to that used by his friends Dana and Marsh, Allston contended that every idea had to have an object or "assimilant." This was true whether the object was physical or spiritual. An idea was not merely a representation of reality but was completely objective. Essentially an emanation from God and only partially comprehended by man, the very existence of an idea guaranteed the existence of its object or assimilant. Allston thus concluded:

. . . in the *conscious presence* of any *spiritual* idea, we have the surest proof of a spiritual object; nor is this the less certain, though we perceive not the assimilant. Nay, a spiritual assimilant cannot be perceived, but, to use the words of St. Paul, is "spiritually discerned," that is, by a sense, so to speak, of our own spirit.[50]

Allston proceeded in the next few sentences to prove the existence of God, arguing from "the law of Conscience" that we could not have "the idea of a moral law without a moral lawgiver . . . without an objective, personal God."

Allston tempered his art theory with Christian humility and a certain measure of Scottish Common Sense realism.[51] While relying heavily upon Coleridgean theory in *Lectures on Art*, he was unwilling to accept some of the poet's more radical ideas. Allston toyed with the distinction between reason and understanding so insisted upon by Emerson, but he failed to develop and incorporate it into his theory. As Doreen Hunter has observed, Allston's notion of a higher intuitive power within man is "akin to Coleridge's Reason," yet it was not conceived of as "an organic expression of our nature but comes from beyond us."[52] The "higher power" discussed by Allston seems closer to the conversionary light of the Holy Spirit, praised by the American revivalist Jonathan Edwards, than it does to Coleridge's higher reason. Allston probably shared Dana's opinion that Coleridge, "in his fondness for speculating and refining . . . sometimes runs off upon a course that leads him away from the simple meaning of the Bible, though he makes that book his starting-point."[53]

Lacking Coleridge's reverence for the Word of God, Emerson and his disciples had seemingly wandered into a spiritual desert from which the English poet had already returned. While Emerson argued that every artist is a god because he reenacts the creation, Coleridge had grown conservative with age, hesitating to attribute too much power to the imagination. He ultimately believed that the poet, through his symbolic language, "could only approximate a God who is ineffable and whose being is incommunicable."[54] He often associated the creative act with evil. The artist was guilty of both ingratitude and hubris since his work showed a dissatisfaction with the present world and a desire to create a reality independent of God.

Sharing Coleridge's Christian anxiety, Allston often hesitated to use the word imagination in his *Lectures*, preferring the term "delegated power," as if to indicate that the artist's source of inspiration is external and divine.[55] Allston also refused to state that the artist actually created anything. He merely "constructs" from what God has already created.[56] Though he wished to defend the spiritual value of art from its skeptical American detractors, Allston often added qualifying and limiting remarks, noting, for instance, that art is but "a part (small though it be) of that mighty plan which the Infinite Wisdom has ordained for the evolution of the human spirit. . . ."[57] Probably responding to Emerson's unrestrained enthusiasm for the inspired miracle of artistic creation, he also emphasized that art was a collegial, cooperative endeavor, dependent upon a respect for tradition and requiring an enormous expenditure of intellectual labor. A great work of art did not appear suddenly from a flash of inspiration. Allston, instead, argued that art progressed gradually over time. Even the best of painters studied the work of the old masters, "for the experience of one man must necessarily be limited . . . so that in one short life, and with but one set of senses, the greatest genius can learn but little."[58] The work of art perfectly realized the "secondary" ideas of the artist but, "as a whole," it had no actual reference to objective reality, except insofar as the artist could partially perceive the archetypal "primary" ideas of the Creator.[59]

Though Emerson never formally reviewed Allston's work, he was surely one of the artist's most hostile critics. Dissatisfied with both his derivative European style and his refusal to paint explicitly American subject matter, Emerson argued that Allston's pictures were empty shells, lacking all individuality and character. His imagination was passive, "feminine or receptive and not masculine or creative." Allston's paintings, like Greenough's classical sculptures, failed to express the present age and failed to excite the "Universal Yankee Nation" beyond "a few prosperous gentlemen and ladies."[60] It was meaningless to continue painting scenes from the Old Testament if God did, in fact, live completely within the soul of every man.

Emerson's audaciously irreverent dismissal of Scripture must have horrified the pious Allston. The egalitarian tendencies of American democracy had now been taken to their ultimate limit. The Transcendentalists' higher reason did not recognize distinctions in education, taste, or social class. All were blessed with the power to become one with the infinite universe. Everyone and anyone would be able to prophesy like Daniel, Isaiah, or Jeremiah.

Whereas Emerson gloried in the power of the self to become one with its infinite object, Allston saw the individual self as an insurmountable obstacle to objective truth. Not even the greatest artist could entirely overcome the limitations of his "secondary" ideas. How much more difficult then for lesser beings to overcome the burden of material self-interest and physical desire, to perceive that selfless spiritual harmony of God's universe. Allston argued that even if man were sinless, "still would these sinless acts be of themselves insufficient to his perfect happiness—inasmuch as the paramount law of his spirit, grounded on his infinite desires, is necessarily of a never-ceasing activity, implying a never-ceasing object. . . ."[61]

The artist's move to Cambridgeport was a strategic retreat from the distracting social life and everyday business affairs of a growing commercial city. Located in a relatively isolated, rural setting, his new studio became a temple of art, where he could pursue the never-ceasing spiritual object and better play the role of oracle or prophet.[62] Hidden within, the unfinished *Belshazzar* remained protected from its would-be proprietors.

According to Allston's brother-in-law, America needed more Daniels or Jeremiahs who were willing to counteract the self-satisfied optimism generated by the Taylorites and Unitarians. Richard Dana, Sr., wrote that instead of "hearing eulogies upon human nature . . . we should be listening to admonitions upon our faults, and warnings against our dangers." Thanks to Unitarianism, there had been "a growing disposition among men to overrate their good qualities, to lower the standard by which they should measure themselves, to lessen the requisitions of the Deity."[63] In letter after letter, Dana promoted Allston as the greatest artist-prophet in America. In 1839, he wrote a friend describing the spiritual impact which the artist's retrospective exhibition was having in the Boston area:

Oh that you could see the glorious show that Allston's paintings make! . . . you can hardly imagine the Power with which they break upon everyone when first standing in their midst. . . . Cannot our people be roused up to come from East and West and North and South to see this great creation, the like of which may not be seen here again for centuries? Surely Allston stands in this age alone.[64]

Allston's retrospective exhibition of 1839 finally extricated him from nearly a decade of indebtedness that had prevented him from returning to *Belshazzar's Feast.* His financial problems had persistently intruded upon the tranquil state of mind so necessary for the accomplishment of his sublime masterpiece. As he wrote John Cogdell in 1832:

With an honest heart yearning to give everyone his due, and an empty purse, I know from bitter experience that the fairest visions of the imagination vanish like dreams never to be recalled, before the daylight reality of such a visitor [debt]. Poverty is no doubt a stimulus to general industry, and to many kinds of mental effort, but not to the imagination; for the imagination must be abortive—is a non-entity—if it have not peace as its immediate condition. Pictures that would have otherwise brought me hundreds, not to say thousands, have crumbled into nothing under its pressure, and been thrown aside as nothing worth.[65]

Like his misanthropic brother-in-law, Richard Dana, Allston was not impressed by the age of industrial and economic improvement. America was too obsessed by material gain and commercial enterprise leaving little time for the cultivation of the mind. At the beginning of the Panic of 1837, Allston complained to James McMurtrie:

The *power* of our art . . . cannot be known out of Italy. It is there only where you will find the existence of invisible Truths proved palpably. . . . Why we have so little of this ideal revelation *now* is, perhaps, explained in the matter of fact character of the present age. Men are too busy with the palpable useful to open their minds to those higher influences which in other times were considered as the natural cravings of an immortal spirit.[66]

Nineteenth-century American artists still lacked the patronage and taste of a Cosimo or Lorenzo de Medici. While merchants and industrialists accumulated more and more wealth, Allston bitterly felt the nation's misconceived priorities which had permitted his great masterpiece to remain unfinished because he could not extricate himself from debt.

His escape from debt and the critical success of the 1839 retrospective encouraged him to return to *Belshazzar's Feast*, but his success cannot explain the intense enthusiasm he seems to have felt in resuming work upon the picture. In ill health much of the time, Allston's overwhelming compulsion was to identify his career and reputation with this one painting's fate. The public had long found it impossible to discuss the artist without also speculating about the status of the great canvas. Certainly, Allston did nothing to discourage this habit. Thus on 5 December 1839 he excitedly wrote to John Cogdell:

... the "King of Babylon" is at last liberated from his imprisonment, and now holding his court in my painting-room. . . . I feel that in returning to my labors upon it as if I had returned to my proper element.[67]

Speaking of the painting as if it possessed some kind of living force or magical power over his being scarcely connotes lack of interest or inspiration. One could better argue that Allston suffered from too much inspiration, an argument that he had once made to Cogdell, claiming that his conception of the painting was constantly expanding, outstripping the limited technical means for transforming the ideas adequately into paint.[68] Gilbert Stuart merely repeated Allston's own convenient, but undoubtedly sincere, philosophical excuse, when he told Walter Channing that *Belshazzar's Feast* would never be finished:

Mr. Allston's mind grows by, and beyond his work. What he does in one month, becomes imperfect to the next, by the very growth of his mind; so sir, it must be altered. He can never be satisfied with what is best done in one part of the picture, for it will cease to be so when he has finished another. The picture will never be finished, sir.[69]

After Allston finally did resume the painting, Oliver Wendell Holmes attributed this reluctance to finish the work to the fastidious habits and ideas of Coleridge. He compared the English poet's inability to complete "Christabel" with the fate of the "great unseen" *Belshazzar's Feast*.[70] Taking the cue from Holmes, Elizabeth Johns has discussed the parallels between the careers and ambitions of the two friends and between their two unfinished masterpieces:

For years Coleridge worried about his longest poetic work, the unfinished "Christabel." He talked about it obsessively, claimed occasionally that he had had the completing part of the narrative in his head since he began it and need only put it to paper, and then finally admitted to a friend that he did not dare complete the poem because it could never live up to his own or anyone else's expectations. Is not this the burden of over-expectation that also haunted Allston?[71]

If Oliver Wendell Holmes saw a parallel between Coleridge's "Christabel" and *Belshazzar's Feast*, perhaps Allston was aware of one as well. Like his own great work, "Christabel" addressed the cosmological struggle between the forces of good and evil. Just as the shining pagan idol and the richness of an oriental court were intended to beguile the eye of the viewer, so too in "Christabel" does evil treacherously conceal its true nature behind the appearance of physical beauty. "Christabel" was a warning to the complacent that evil's force was often independent of moral choice.[72] Sin was not merely the result of a conscious act but had infected the very being of man since the Fall.

Emerson and his disciples were, however, the more immediate inspiration for Allston's work upon *Belshazzar's Feast* beginning again in 1839. They were the serpent in the Garden, present also at the throne of King Belshazzar, assuring man that "ye shall be as gods" (Genesis 3:5). In their celebration of man's "higher reason," The Transcendentalists committed the primal sin of hubris. *Belshazzar's Feast* urged the beholder to adopt an attitude of humility in recognition of the sublime distance between earthly human glory and divine omnipotence. While the spiritual kingdom of God knows no beginning or end, earthly kingdoms, like those envisioned by the prophet Daniel, rise and fall "in fearful alternation." "Mid falling empires," Allston insistently warned against "that dark fount of Pride, of which to drink / Is but to swallow madness, ..."[73]

In *Lectures on Art*, *Belshazzar's Feast*, and *Monaldi*, the artist or prophet is nothing more than a divine instrument. The ultimate source of his magical powers lies beyond him in a personal Creator and Lawgiver. *Belshazzar's Feast* was a lesson in virtue for those men of letters who, like the Chaldean soothsayers, flatter themselves and their audience with reassuring promises of self-reliance, natural ability, and individual power. An artist's duty was not to please or flatter but rather to instruct and admonish according to the still-valid spirit of Old Testament law. The changes that Allston continued to work on in his picture, lowering the point of sight, increasing the sense of infinite space, and further monumentalizing the scale of his figures, were all designed to put the beholding public into a state of reverential awe. The painting's epic proportions, elevated high above eye level, proclaimed the existence of an ideal world of being that was yet distinct and qualitatively superior to that which presently existed in the American "paradise."

In *Lectures on Art,* Allston argued that art's purpose was directed toward realizing some distant potential within man or projecting a future realm of spiritual being. Art is not fulfilling its proper function if it merely celebrates and, thereby, reifies, that which already exists. The imagination expresses man's infinite desire and longing. It takes him out of the imperfect surroundings of his present world because it is based upon the memory of an archaic past when body and spirit were perfectly united and because it harbors the undying hope for the future recovery of that which once existed.

Allston could not have followed Emerson's advice to celebrate the American present because it would have implied a sense of individual self-satisfaction and national fulfillment. He did not feel the former and he knew that the Christian millennium, the raison d'être of American nationalism, had not been achieved. Allston perceived that the times were even more "out of joint" during this "age of the common man" than when he had first been inspired to begin his great picture in 1817. The growing number of impoverished European immigrants, many of them Catholic, only strengthened the hand of democratic demagoguery. Industrialization and urbanization were not only destroying gentility of manners but were also contributing to irreligion at the very time that the evangelical movement was splintering into disunity. The betrayal of religious principle by those men of letters who gave philosophic sanction to the anarchic leveling process struck at the very heart of conservatives' longing for a Christian millennium. While heresy may have inspired his return to *Belshazzar,* America's worsening spiritual state obviously contributed to an enervating pessimism, which scarcely enhanced the chances that the artist would complete the picture.

Working almost daily upon *Belshazzar's Feast,* the spiritual mirror which reflected his own dual being, Allston could not help but feel his inadequacy. His physical self, aging and plagued by sickness, severely limited his capacious imagination. His inability to "correct" the picture's perspective and to satisfy his epic conception of the subject was a constant reminder of his weakness both as an artist and as a finite human being. Yet, he was surely comforted with the knowledge that if perfection was beyond his grasp, it was beyond that of all mankind. The lesson of *Belshazzar* was essentially identical to that of his poem "The Atonement," which he had composed in a trancelike state after his first wife's death in 1815. As a result of man's fallen condition, *Belshazzar's Feast* could never be perfectly realized no matter how great the artist's skills.

Ultimately, it probably mattered little to Allston whether he actually did finish the painting. In fact, he may have seen a positive value in never finishing it. It would become an emblem of the aching void within the heart which never could be filled on earth:

> O, rather let me, in the void I feel,
> With no misgiving seek my lasting weal;
> Things blank and imageless in human speech
> Have oft a truth imperative in might.[74]

By sacrificing himself upon the altar of artistic and moral perfection, he set a powerful example for Americans who had a tendency either to settle for far less or to presume that they could readily achieve perfection while yet on earth.

It was more important to be seen laboring after perfection, thereby revealing a moral yearning for the infinite, than actually to finish the labor. Actually to finish the labor could even be interpreted as an act of hubris and deceit, since it would imply that one had, indeed, successfully transcended the finite while yet on earth. This conclusion was something that Allston consciously and emphatically wished to deny. Far better would it be if his vision of man's liberation from Babylon were forever arrested in a state of unfulfillment. Death would bestow the final spiritual harmony, the stasis, for which he longed.

Notes

Preface

1. For a recent psychological study of Allston, see Phoebe Lloyd, "Washington Allston: American Martyr?," *Art in America* 72 (March 1984), 145–55, 177.

2. Clifford Geertz, "Art as a Cultural System," *MLN* (*Modern Language Notes*) 91 (1976), 1478.

3. W. H. Oliver, *Prophets and Millennialists: The Uses of Biblical Prophecy in England from the 1790s to the 1840s* (Oxford: Oxford University Press, 1978), p. 192.

Chapter 1

1. Quoted in Jared B. Flagg, *The Life and Letters of Washington Allston* (1892; reprint, New York: Benjamin Blom, 1969), p. 347.

2. Fisher to Durand, 16 October 1828, New York Public Library.

3. "The Athenaeum Gallery and the Allston Collection," *Bulletin of the American Art-Union* (October 1850), p. 110.

4. As recalled by Walter Channing, "Reminiscences of Washington Allston," *Christian Register and Boston Observer*, 5 August 1843, p. 124.

5. "Exhibition of Pictures Painted by W. Allston at Harding's Gallery, School Street," *North American Review* 50 (April 1840), p. 374.

6. Ibid.

7. Quoted in H. W. L. Dana "Allston in Cambridgeport 1830–1843," *Cambridge Historical Society Publications* 29, Proceedings for the Year 1943 (Cambridge, Mass., 1948), p. 66.

8. H. A. S. Dearborn, "Allston's Feast of Belshazzar," *Knickerbocker* 24 (September 1844), pp. 214–5.

9. Story, "Athenaeum Gallery—Allston's Belshazzar," *Harbinger*, 5 July 1845, p. 57.

10. Ibid.

11. "Note," *North American Review* 51 (October 1840), p. 520.

12. Ibid., p. 519.

13. Holmes, p. 372.

14. Dugald Stewart, *Philosophical Essays*, 2d ed. (Edinburgh: 1816), pp. 394–96.

15. Quoted in David B. Morris, *The Religious Sublime: Christian Poetry and Critical Tradition in 18th Century England* (Lexington: University of Kentucky Press, 1972), pp. 53–54. See also Laurence S. Lockridge, *Coleridge the Moralist* (Ithaca, N.Y.: Cornell University Press, 1977), pp. 165–67.

16. Henry Greenough, "Allston's Feast of Belshazzar—No. 2," *Boston Post*, 25 July 1844, p. 1. For the first part of Greenough's review, see "Remarks on Allston's Belshazzar," *Boston Post*, 10 June 1844, p. 1.

17. Story, p. 57.

18. William Ware, *Lectures on the Works and Genius of Washington Allston* (Boston, 1852), pp. 133–35.

19. Though he did not really analyze Allston's oeuvre in detail, one must credit J. F. C. Harrison for recognizing its apocalyptic as well as millennialist fervor. See Harrison's *The Second Coming: Popular Millenarianism, 1780–1850* (New Brunswick, N.J.: Rutgers University Press, 1979), pp. 131–32. Bryan Jay Wolf has also analyzed the significant spatial dualism in several compositions by Allston, though Wolf's ahistorical, deconstructive methodology and the conclusions he draws are very different from my own. See *Romantic Re-Vision: Culture and Consciousness in Nineteenth Century American Painting and Literature* (Chicago: University of Chicago Press, 1981), pp. 9–16; 43–44.

20. *Boston Post*, 25 July 1844, p. 1.

21. Story, p. 57.

22. William H. Gerdts, "The Paintings of Washington Allston," in *A Man of Genius: The*

Art of Washington Allston, 1779–1843, by William H. Gerdts and Theodore E. Stebbins, Jr. (Boston: Museum of Fine Arts, 1979), p. 109.

23. On the importance of caricature for allegory, see Angus Fletcher, *Allegory: The Theory of a Symbolic Mode* (Ithaca and London: Cornell University Press, 1964), pp. 33–34.

24. Theodore E. Stebbins, Jr., "The Drawings of Washington Allston," in *A Man of Genius: The Art of Washington Allston, 1779–1843*, by William H Gerdts and Theodore E. Stebbins, Jr., p. 235.

25. Quoted in Patricia A. Anderson, *Promoted to Glory: The Apotheosis of George Washington* (Northampton, Mass.: Smith College Museum of Art, 1980), p. 11.

26. Washington Allston, *Lectures on Art and Poems, and Monaldi*, vol. 1, *Lectures on Art and Poems*, ed. Richard Henry Dana, Jr. (1850; reprint, Gainesville, Florida: Scholars' Facsimiles and Reprints, 1967), pp. 13–17.

27. David Carew Huntington, *Art and the Excited Spirit: America in the Romantic Period* (Ann Arbor: University of Michigan Museum of Art, 1972), p. 1.

28. J. C. Lavater, *Essays on Physiognomy: for the Promotion of the Knowledge and the Love of Mankind*, translated by Thomas Holcroft, vol. 1 (London: G. G. J. and J. Robinson, 1789), p. 15.

29. Ibid., p. 198.

30. Charles Colbert, "'Each Little Hillock Hath a Tongue'—Phrenology and the Art of Hiram Powers," *Art Bulletin* 68 (June 1986), p. 298.

31. John Stephens Crawford, "The Classical Orator in Nineteenth Century American Sculpture," *American Art Journal* 6 (November 1974), pp. 59–60.

32. E. L. Magoon, *Living Orators in America* (New York: Charles Scribner, 1851), p. 57.

33. Story, p. 57.

34. Thus, according to Sarah Clarke, ". . . it [Belshazzar] could be only a puzzling wonder to those who go to an exhibition to see finished pictures. . . ." Clarke, "Our First Great Painter, and His Works," *Atlantic Monthly* 15 (February 1865), p. 139.

35. Carol Troyen, *The Boston Tradition: American Paintings from the Museum of Fine Arts, Boston* (New York: The American Federation of Arts, 1980), pp. 10–11 and Frederic Alan Scharf, "Art and Life in Boston, 1837 to 1850: A Study of the Painter and Sculptor in American Society," *Archives of American Art*, pp. 120–24.

36. Story, p. 58.

37. Lunt, "Belshazzar's Feast," *Christian Examiner* 37 (July 1844), p. 56.

38. Ibid., p. 57.

39. Ibid., pp. 56–57.

40. Dearborn, p. 211.

41. Ware, p. 129. See also M. F. Sweetser, *Allston* (Boston: Houghton, Osgood and Co., 1879), p. 128.

42. Dearborn, p. 206. Actually, as I shall suggest in chapter five, George Washington was a more likely spiritual model for Daniel than Webster. Washington had become a kind of universal symbol for statesmanship, while Webster was still alive and well and steeped in divisive political controversy.

43. Ibid., p. 208.

44. Joy S. Kasson, *Artistic Voyagers: Europe and the American Imagination in the Works of Irving, Allston, Cole, Cooper, and Hawthorne* (Westport, Conn.: Greenwood Press, 1982), p. 71.

45. Dearborn, p. 209.

46. Gerdts, p. 159.

47. The full title of Spear's exhibition catalogue, published in Boston in 1846 by Eastburn's Press, read *Description of the Grand Historical Picture of Belshazzar's Feast by Washington Allston, Painted on Another Canvass of the Same Size, and Finished With a View to Carry Out the Design of the Author*. See Gerdts, p. 160.

48. Quoted in Gerdts, p. 162.

49. Editor's preface to Story's "Athenaeum Gallery—Allston's Belshazzar," p. 55.

50. Quoted in the review of *Discourses on the Christian Spirit and Life* by C. A. Bartol in *Literary World* 17 November 1847, p. 421.

51. C. A. Bartol, "Perfection," in *Discourses on the Christian Spirit and Life* (Boston, 1850), pp. 402–8.

52. Quoted in Angus Fletcher, p. 250.

53. "The Athenaeum Gallery and the Allston Collection," *Bulletin of the American Art-Union* (October 1850), p. 111.

54. Quoted in Barbara Novak, *Nature and Culture: American Landscape and Painting, 1825–1875* (New York: Oxford University Press, 1980), p. 207.

55. Quoted in H. W. L. Dana, p. 64.

56. Alan Wallach, "Thomas Cole and the Aristocracy," *Arts Magazine* 56 (November 1981), pp. 94–106.

57. Dawn Glanz, *How the West Was Drawn: American Art and the Settling of the Frontier* (Ann Arbor, Mich.: UMI Research Press, 1982), pp. 77–80.

58. C. Edwards Lester, *The Artists of Amer-*

ica: A Series of Biographical Sketches . . . (New York: Baker and Scribner, 1846), pp. 25–26.

59. "Monaldi," *American Review: A Whig Journal* 7 (April 1848), pp. 352, 354.

60. Quoted in Gerdts, p. 162.

61. Allston to James McMurtrie, 2 March 1837, Pennsylvania Historical Society.

Chapter 2

1. Isaiah 65:17; 66:22; Revelation 21:1–2; 3:12.

2. Sacvan Bercovitch, *The American Jeremiad* (Madison: University of Wisconsin Press, 1978), p. 54.

3. *The Interpreter's Dictionary of the Bible,* vol. 1 (Nashville and New York: Abingdon Press, 1962), s.v. "Daniel." Bernhard W. Anderson, *Understanding the Old Testament,* 3d ed. (Englewood Cliffs, N.J.: Prentice-Hall, 1975), pp. 576–91.

4. Ernest Lee Tuveson, *Redeemer Nation: The Idea of America's Millennial Role* (London and Chicago: University of Chicago Press, 1968), pp. 31–32.

5. Chapter 5. See *Interpreter's Dictionary of the Bible,* vol. 2, s.v. "Exile."

6. Millard Meiss, "An Illuminated Inferno and Trecento Painting in Pisa," *Art Bulletin* 47 (March 1965), p. 22.

7. C. R. Dodwell, *Painting in Europe: 800 to 1200,* The Pelican History of Art, ed. Nikolaus Pevsner (Baltimore: Penguin Books, 1971), pp. 102–113. Meyer Schapiro, "The Beatus Apocalypse of Gerona," *Art News* 61 (January 1963), pp. 36, 49–50.

8. Craig Felton and William B. Jordon, eds., *Jusepe de Ribera, lo Spagnoletto: 1591–1652* (Fort Worth, Tex.: Kimbell Art Museum, 1982), pp. 146–47.

9. E. von der Bercken, "Unbekannte Werke des Jacopo Tintoretto in der Sammlung Italico Brass in Venedit," *Pantheon* 15 (January 1935), pp. 24–30; *Venetian Seventeenth Century Painting* (London: National Gallery, 1979), pp. 124–25; Andor Pigler, *Barockthemen* (Budapest: Verlag der Ungarischen Akademie der Wissenschaften, 1956), 1:213–16; Photographic Archive, Frick Art Reference Library, New York.

10. Johannes Müller of Amsterdam (1571–1628) painted a Belshazzar's feast that was similar to that of the Wadsworth Atheneum's painting. Müller's painting was engraved by his brother Herman, and versions of the work appeared in various Dutch Bibles, some of which found their way to America. The Müller composition has been suggested as the probable prototype for a mid-eighteenth-century American limmer painting from Albany, New York. See Ruth Piwonka and Roderic H. Blackburn, *A Remnant in the Wilderness: New York Dutch Scripture History Paintings of the Early Eighteenth Century* (Albany: Institute of History and Art, 1980), p. 48, no. 22. See also the Photographic Archive, Frick Art Reference Library, for reproduction of works by Northern, as well as Italian, painters of Belshazzar's feast.

11. Christian Tümpel, "Religious History Painting," in *Gods, Saints and Heroes: Dutch Painting in the Age of Rembrandt* by Albert Blankert et al. (Washington, D.C.: National Gallery of Art, 1980), p. 50. The National Gallery catalogue also illustrated a *Belshazzar* by Pieter de Grebber, p. 184, fig. 3.

12. J. Wayne Baker, *Heinrich Bullinger and the Covenant: The Other Reformed Tradition* (Athens: Ohio University Press, 1980), pp. 4–5.

13. H. G. Koenigsberger and George L. Mosse, *Europe in the Sixteenth Century,* A General History of Europe, ed. Denis Hay (London: Longman Paperback, 1971), pp. 278–80; see also George L. Mosse, *The Culture of Western Europe: The Nineteenth and Twentieth Centuries,* Rand McNally History Series, ed. Fred Harvey Harrington (New York: Rand McNally, 1961), pp. 53–54.

14. Perry Miller, "From the Covenant to the Revival," in *The Shaping of American Religion,* ed. James Ward Smith and A. Leland Jamison (Princeton: Princeton University Press, 1961), pp. 322–68. See also Bercovitch, p. XIV.

15. Calvin, *Commentaries on the Book of the Prophet Daniel,* trans. and ed. Thomas Myers (Grand Rapids, Michigan: Wm. B. Eerdmans, 1948), 1:320. See Michael Walzer, *The Revolution of the Saints: A Study in the Origin of Radical Politics* (New York: Athenaeum, 1968), pp. 63–64.

16. *Eikonoklastes,* ed. William Haller, in *The Works of John Milton,* Frank Allen Patterson, ed. (New York: Columbia University Press, 1932), 5:109.

17. *Bible and Sword: England and Palestine from the Bronze Age to Balfour* (New York: New York University Press, 1956), p. 80.

18. "Of Reformation Touching Church Discipline in England," ed. Harry Morgan Ayres, in *The Works of John Milton,* Frank Allen Patterson, ed. (New York: Columbia University Press, 1931), 3, pt. 1, p. 55.

19. Margaret C. Jacob, *The Newtonians and the English Revolution, 1689–1720* (Ithaca, N.Y.: Cornell University Press, 1976), p. 107.

20. Ibid., p. 127. See also Mel Scult, *Millennial Expectations and Jewish Liberties: A Study of the Efforts to Convert the Jews in Britain, up to the Mid-Nineteenth Century* (Leiden: E.J. Brill, 1978), pp. 67–68.

21. Winton Dean, *Handel's Dramatic Oratories and Masques* (London: Oxford University Press, 1959), p. 441.

22. *Belshazzar: An Oratorio* (London: J. Watts, 1745), pp. 3–5. In the end, Cyrus promises that "I will build thy city, God of Israel / . . . Be free, ye captives, / And to your native land in peace return. / Thou, O Jerusalem, shalt be rebuilt; / O Temple, thy foundation shall be laid." Sacred Harmonic Society, ed. *Belshazzar* (London, 1885), p. 16.

23. Virginia Larkin Redway, "Handel in Colonial and Post-Colonial America (to 1820)," *The Musical Quarterly* 21 (1935), 190–207. Late in his life, Allston wrote a song for the famous Handelian singer, John Braham. See *Programme of Mr. Braham's Farewell Concert at the Melodeon, Wednesday Evening, February 17, 1841* (Boston: Clapp and Son's Press, 1841). A copy is in the Massachusetts Historical Society.

24. *The Captivity: An Oratorio* (New York: G. Schirmer, 1890), pp. 145–46. On Goldsmith's enthusiasm for Handel, see Mollie Sands, "Oliver Goldsmith and Music," *Music and Letters* 32 (April 1951), 147–53. That Goldsmith's and Handel's oratorios represented England's growing sense of identification with the ancient Hebrews is noted in Murray Roston, *Prophet and Poet: The Bible and the Growth of Romanticism* (Evanston: Northwestern University Press, 1965), p. 88.

25. Roston, p. 87. Lowth's *Lectures on the Sacred Poetry of the Hebrews* was originally published in Latin in 1753, and translated into English in 1787.

26. Herbert M. Atherton, *Political Prints in the Age of Hogarth: A Study of the Ideographic Representation of Politics* (Oxford: Clarendon Press, 1974), pp. 145, 172, 252, 254.

27. Merle Curti, *The Growth of American Thought*, 3d ed. (New York: Harper and Row, 1964), p. 261.

28. James Thomas Flexner, *America's Old Masters*, rev. ed. (Garden City, N.Y.: Doubleday and Co., 1980), p. 319; Peter S. Walch, "Charles Rollin and Early Neoclassicism," *Art Bulletin* 49 (June 1967), 123–26.

29. Helmut von Erffa and Allen Staley, *The Paintings of Benjamin West* (New Haven and London: Yale University Press, 1986), p. 446.

30. Paulson, *Hogarth; His Life, Art and Times* (New Haven: Yale University Press, 1971), 2:51–52.

31. Bromley, *A Philosophical and Critical History of the Fine Arts* (London, 1793), 1:15–16.

32. The collection of the Earl of Derby, Knowsley House. Edgar Preston Richardson, *Washington Allston: A Study of the Romantic Artist in America* (Chicago: University of Chicago Press, 1948), p. 122.

33. M. G. Jones, *Hannah More* (Cambridge, England: Cambridge University Press, 1952), p. 217.

34. *The Works of Hannah More* (London: T. Cadell, Strand, 1830), 1:110.

35. Von Erffa and Staley, p. 319.

36. Jane Dillenberger, *The Hand and the Spirit: Religious Art in America, 1700–1900* (Berkeley, Calif.: University Art Museum, 1972), p. 28.

37. Bernard Bailyn, *The Ideological Origins of the American Revolution* (Cambridge, Mass.: Belknap Press of Harvard University Press, 1967), p. 135.

38. Patience Wright, who designed *The Invisible Junto,* was a friend of West's and, like West, took pride in her identity as an American Quaker in exile. Wright's *Invisible Junto*, like many earlier English political cartoons, features a large balance weighing the merits of a political issue. See note 26. In this case the scales are tipped in favor of a Bible, liberty cap, and a copy of Algernon Sidney's treatise on government against all the weight of George III and his ministers, who are in alliance with the devil himself. The balance is held by a hand which has emerged from a cloud and is connected to a word bubble, quoting Daniel's message of doom for Belshazzar. See Charles Coleman Sellers, *Patience Wright: American Artist and Spy in George III's London* (Middletown, Conn.: Wesleyan University Press, 1976), pp. 142–43.

39. Waterhouse, *An Essay on Junius and His Letters* (Boston: Gray and Brown, 1831), p. 77.

40. Ibid., p. 104.

41. Ibid., p. 189.

42. The actual identity of Junius is still not certain. T. H. Bowyer, *A Bibliographical Examination of the Earliest Editions of the Letters of Junius* (Charlottesville: University of Virginia Press, 1957), p. XIX.

43. Roy Strong, *Recreating the Past: British History and the Victorian Painter* (New York: The Pierpont Morgan Library, 1978), pp. 17–18.

44. Von Erffa and Staley, pp. 90, 97–108.

45. Allston to Charles Fraser, 25 August 1801, quoted in Jared B. Flagg, *The Life and Letters of Washington Allston* (1892; reprint, New York: Benjamin Blom 1969), pp. 43–44.

46. Based upon John Galt's hagiography, the miraculous birth of Benjamin West has been recounted many times. For an analysis of West's mythic origins, see Ann Uhry Abrams, *The Valiant Hero: Benjamin West and Grand-Style History Painting*, New Directions in American Art (Washington, D.C.: Smithsonian Institution Press, 1985), pp. 32–39.

Chapter 3

1. Patricia A. Anderson, *Promoted to Glory: The Apotheosis of George Washinton* (Northampton, Mass.: Smith College Museum of Art, 1980), p. 1.

2. Quoted in Joseph A. Groves, *The Alstons and Allstons of North and South Carolina* (Atlanta: Franklin Printing and Publishing Co., 1901), p. 53.

3. Quoted in Jared B. Flagg, *The Life and Letters of Washington Allston* (1892; reprint, New York: Benjamin Blom, 1969), p. 4.

4. Ibid.

5. Ibid., pp. 4–5.

6. Susan Lowndes Allston, *Brookgreen Waccamaw in the South Carolina Low Country* (Charleston, S.C., 1956), p. 19.

7. Quoted in Flagg, pp. 26–27.

8. Sacvan Bercovitch, *The American Jeremiad* (Madison: University of Wisconsin Press, 1978), p. 124.

9. Kenneth Silverman, *A Cultural History of the American Revolution* (New York: Thomas Y. Crowell, 1976), p. 503; Helen Cooper, *John Trumbull: The Hand and Spirit of a Painter* (New Haven: Yale University Press, 1982), cat. nos. 159–60, pp. 256–58.

10. Flagg, p. 6.

11. Silverman, pp. 396–97.

12. Ibid., pp. 474–75.

13. Ibid., p. 33.

14. No social libertarian himself, Richard H. Dana, Jr., wrote in his journal on 22 April 1843 that Allston "is less of a Republican than ever. . . . He says that the manners of gentility, its courtesies, deferences, and graces are passing away from among us." Quoted in Charles Francis Adams, *Richard Henry Dana* (Boston and New York: Houghton, Mifflin and Co., 1891), 1:72.

15. Groves, p. 51.

16. Flagg, p. 2.

17. Ibid., p. 6.

18. Ibid., p. 34.

19. William H. Gerdts briefly describes Allston's efforts to assist his family's slaves in "The Paintings of Washington Allston," in *A Man of Genius: The Art of Washington Allston (1779–1843)*, by William H Gerdts and Theodore E. Stebbins, Jr. (Boston: Museum of Fine Arts, 1979), p. 157.

20. Washington Allston, *Lectures on Art and Poems, and Monaldi*, vol. 1, *Lectures on Art and Poems*, ed. Richard Henry Dana, Jr. (1850; reprint, Gainesville, Florida: Scholars Facsimiles and Reprints, 1967), p. 54.

21. Flagg, p. 5.

22. David Hackett Fischer, *The Revolution of American Conservatism: The Federalist Party in the Era of Jeffersonian Democracy* (N.Y.: Harper and Row, 1967), p. 49.

23. Carol Troyen, *The Boston Tradition: American Paintings from the Museum of Fine Arts, Boston* (N.Y.: The American Federation of Arts, 1980), pp. 82–84, cat. no. 20.

24. Flagg, p. 8.

25. Ralph E. Carpenter, Jr., *The Arts and Crafts of Newport Rhode Island, 1640–1820* (Newport: The Preservation Society of Newport County, 1954), p. 127.

26. Ibid., p. 121.

27. George Gibbs Channing, *Early Recollections of Newport* (Newport, 1868), p. 51.

28. Flagg, p. 17.

29. Ibid., p. 20.

30. George Gibbs Channing, p. 202.

31. See Hannah R. London, *Portraits of Jews by Gilbert Stuart and Other Early American Artists* (N.Y.: William Edwin Rudge, 1927) and Hannah R. London, *Miniatures of Early American Jews* (Rutland, Vermont: Charles E. Tuttle Co., 1970).

32. Edmund S. Morgan, *The Gentle Puritan: A Life of Ezra Stiles, 1727–1795* (New Haven: Yale University Press, 1962), p. 142.

33. Quoted in Paul F. Boller, Jr., *George Washington and Religion* (Dallas: Southern Methodist University Press, 1963), p. 186.

34. From an address written by the Beth Elohim congregation, Charleston, South Carolina, quoted in Boller, Jr., pp. 154–55.

35. *The New Oxford Book of American Verse*, ed. Richard Ellman (New York: Oxford University Press, 1976), pp. 91–92.

36. William Dunlap, *History of the Rise and Progress of the Arts of Design in the United States*,

ed. Rita Weiss (1834; reprint, New York: Dover Publications, 1969), 1:166–67.

37. Quoted in Flagg, p. 16.

38. H. W. L. Dana, "Allston at Harvard, 1796–1800," *Cambridge Historical Society Publications,* no. 29, Proceedings for the Year 1943 (Cambridge, Mass., 1948), 14–15. See also William Roscow Thayer, ed., "Journal of Benjamin Waterhouse," *Cambridge Historical Society Publications,* no. 4, Proceedings January 26–October 26, 1909 (Cambridge, Mass., 1909), 22–37.

39. Oscar Kraines, "The Holmes Tradition," *Publication of the American Jewish Society,* no. 42 (June 1953), 344–45; Conrad Wright, *The Beginnings of Unitarianism in America* (Boston: Starr King Press, 1955), p. 258.

40. Abiel Holmes explained the basis for his typological interpretation of the Old Testament in his *Two Discourses on the Completion of the Second Century From the Landing of the Forefathers of New England at Plymouth, 22 Dec. 1620, Delivered at Cambridge 24 Dec. 1820* (Cambridge, Mass.: Hilliard and Metcalf, 1821), p. 3. Allston's fondness for Holmes' preaching will be discussed further in Chapter 7.

41. David Tappan, *Lectures on Jewish Antiquities* (Boston: W. Hilliard and E. Lincoln, 1807), p. 31.

42. George H. Williams, *Wilderness and Paradise in Christian Thought* (New York: Harper and Brothers, 1962), pp. 201–2.

43. *A Sermon Delivered at Cambridge 30 September 1804, . . .* (Cambridge, Mass.: University Press, 1804), pp. 22–23.

44. *Age of Reason* (New York: Willey Book Co., n.d.), p. 139. See also Gary B. Nash, "The American Clergy and the French Revolution," *William and Mary Quarterly* 22 (July 1965), 402.

45. Samuel Eliot Morison, *Three Centuries of Harvard, 1636–1936* (Cambridge: Harvard University Press, 1936), p. 185.

46. *Memoir of William Ellery Channing,* ed. William Henry Channing (Boston: Wm. Crosby and H. P. Nichols, 1848), 1:60.

47. Quoted in Nash, p. 403.

48. Quoted in Vernon Stauffer, *New England and the Bavarian Illuminati* (New York: Columbia University Press, 1918), p. 85.

49. Diana Strazdes, "Washington Allston's Early Career, 1796–1811," Ph.D. Diss., Yale University, 1982, p. 24.

50. Strazdes argues that the central figure in the first scene, the buck who raises his glass in a toast, is really the principal character in the series and not the country bumpkin, as previous historians have assumed. Yet, the buck-toothed, straight-haired figure receiving a new hair-do, the main character in the second sketch, clearly resembles the bumpkin of the first, not a sophisticated dandy. Strazdes, pp. 22–23.

51. Quoted in Flagg, p. 113.

52. Class of 1800—Seniors, May 9, 1800. Library Charging List, Harvard University Archives, Pusey Library. It is possible that the scribbled "Jennings' evidences" charged out to Allston on this date refers to a treatise by the Calvinist dissenter David Jennings (1691–1762) entitled *The Scripture Testimony . . . An Appeal to Reason . . . for the Truth of the Holy Scriptures* (1755). However, I am inclined to believe that the name has been misspelled in the library records and that Allston was actually checking out Soame Jenyns' extremely popular treatise, first published in 1776. Jenyns' a London poet and writer of essays, had abandoned scepticism for religious orthodoxy. His new profession of faith was widely hailed and celebrated by evangelical authors such as Hannah More. Dr. Samuel Johnson referred to it as a "pretty book, not very theological indeed." It thus would have been more suited to Allston's taste than the sterner, Calvinist theology of David Jennings. As Diana Strazdes has argued, Allston had not yet developed a scholarly taste for theology. Strazdes, pp. 53–55. See *The Dictionary of National Biography* (Oxford: Oxford University Press, 1937–38), s.v., "Jenyns, Soame."

53. Quoted in Samuel Eliot Morison, p. 186.

54. Vernon Stauffer's book is still the most detailed account of the scare. See also Larzer Ziff, *Literary Democracy: The Declaration of Cultural Independence in America* (New York: Viking Press, 1981), p. 106.

55. Quoted in Flagg, p. 29.

56. As a Jacksonian Democrat, Jarvis may have wished to free Allston's reputation from too serious an identification with the defunct and discredited Federalist Party, which had fallen into near total disrepute thanks to its vociferous opposition to the War of 1812. See Shaw Livermore, Jr., *The Twilight of Federalism: The Disintegration of the Federalist Party, 1815–1830* (Princeton: Princeton University Press, 1962).

57. J. M. S. Tomkins, *The Popular Novel in England, 1770–1800* (1932; reprint, Lincoln: University of Nebraska Press, 1961), p. 283.

58. Quoted in William Henry Channing, ed., 1:69.

59. Allston to Knapp, 23 October 1800, the

Washington Allston Papers, Dana Collection, Massachusetts Historical Society, Boston.

60. Gerdts and Stebbins, plate 3.

61. Kenneth Hopkins, *English Poetry* (London: Phoenix House, 1962), p. 216.

62. Pusey Library, Harvard University, Cambridge, Mass.

63. Allston to Knapp, 23 October 1800.

64. Allston to Fraser, 25 August 1801, in Flagg, p. 43.

65. Ibid.

66. "Eccentricity," in *Lectures on Art and Poems, and Monaldi*, vol. 1, *Lectures on Art and Poems*, pp. 241–42.

67. Samuel F. B. Morse to his parents, Mr. and Mrs. Jedidiah Morse, 1 November 1812, The Samuel Morse Papers, Library of Congress, Washington, D.C.

68. Charles I. Foster, *An Errand of Mercy: The Evangelical United Front, 1790–1837* (Chapel Hill: University of North Carolina Press, 1960), pp. VII–VIII.

69. See Allston's description of the work in a letter to Charles Fraser, 25 August 1801, quoted in Flagg, p. 46.

70. Franz Kobler, *Napoleon and the Jews* (Jerusalem: Massada Press, 1975), pp. 55–57.

71. Ibid., p. 84.

72. Ibid., p. 86; Mel Scult, *Millennial Expectations and Jewish Liberties: A Study of the Efforts to Convert the Jews in Britain, Up to the Mid Nineteenth Century* (Leiden: E. J. Brill, 1978), pp. 79–83.

73. Quoted in Kobler, p. 87.

74. "Rappel des Juifs," *Monthly Anthology* 5 (March 1808), pp. 147–48.

75. The date of Allston's departure from Paris has been the subject of some debate. See Diana Strazdes, p. 102. But in the last of three letters that his friends had published, Allston clearly states that he had left Paris on 21 September 1804. See his letter of 5 January 1805 in *Monthly Anthology* 2 (December 1805): 634. The first letter was published in *Monthly Anthology* 2 (August 1805): 400-2 and has been attributed to Allston in *Anthology Society* (Boston: Boston Athenaeum, 1910): 319. The second letter, dated 5 March 1804 appeared in *Monthly Anthology* 2 (September 1805): 450–51. The first two letters were both written from Paris. All signed under the pseudonym "Smelfungus," the final letter, written from Siena, was actually numbered as the fourth. In the October 1805, issue of the *Anthology,* the editor was forced to explain that one of the letters from Smelfungus had been "irretrievably lost." See "Original Letters. No. 3," *Monthly Anthology* 2 (October 1805): 502. Internal evidence for Allston's authorship of all three letters is the fact that lines of verse and praise for such artists as Rubens and Pelligrino Tibaldi appear again later in the artist's published poetry.

76. Quoted in Flagg, p. 366.

77. "The Scholar, the Jurist, the Artist, the Philanthropist," in *The Works of Charles Sumner* (Boston: Lee and Shepard, 1874), 1:274.

78. William H. Gerdts, "Washington Allston and the German Romantic Classicists in Rome," *Art Quarterly* 32 (Summer 1969), p. 189; Keith Andrews, *The Nazarenes: A Brotherhood of German Painters in Rome* (Oxford: Clarendon Press, 1964), p. 19.

79. Quoted in William Vaughan, *German Romanticism and English Art* (New Haven: Yale University Press, 1979), p. 45.

80. Quoted in *Neoclassicism and Romanticism, 1750–1850*, ed. Lorenz Eitner, Sources and Documents in the History of Art Series, H. W. Janson, ed. (Englewood Cliffs, N.J.: Prentice Hall, 1970), 2:36.

81. Flagg, p. 64.

82. Quoted in Murray Roston, *Prophet and Poet: The Bible and the Growth of Romanticism* (Evanston, Ill: Northwestern University Press, 1965), p. 174.

83. Ibid., p. 125.

84. Quoted in David B. Morris, *The Religious Sublime: Christian Poetry and Critical Tradition in 18th Century England* (Lexington: University of Kentucky Press, 1972), pp. 53–54.

85. Ibid., pp. 50–53.

86. Quoted in Laurence S. Lockridge, *Coleridge the Moralist* (Ithaca, N.Y.: Cornell University Press, 1977), p. 167.

87. David P. Calleo, "Coleridge on Napoleon," *Yale French Studies* 26 (1960–61), 83–93.

88. Strazdes, p. 175.

89. *A Sermon, Delivered in Boston, Sept. 16, 1813* (Boston, 1813), p. 22.

90. Hannah Adams, *The History of the Jews, from the Destruction of Jerusalem to the Present Time* (London: A. Macintosh, 1818), p. 119. Adams' book was originally published in Boston in 1812.

Chapter 4

1. Russel Blaine Nye, *The Cultural Life of the New Nation, 1776–1830*, The New American Nation Series, ed. Henry Steele Commager

and Richard B. Morris (New York: Harper Torchbooks, 1960), pp. 33–34.

2. Alexander Wellington Crawford, *The Philosophy of F. H. Jacobi,* Cornell Studies in Philosophy, no. 6 (1905), pp. 12–13. Allston's interest in the work of Jacobi is noted in Martha Gregor T. Goethals, "A Comparative Study of the Theory and Work of Washington Allston, Thomas Cole, and Horatio Greenough," Ph.D. Diss. Harvard University 1966, p. 54.

3. Nye, p. 36.

4. David S. Reynolds, "From Doctrine to Narrative: The Rise of Pulpit Storytelling in America," *American Quarterly* 32 (Winter 1980), pp. 479–98.

5. *Elias Boudinot's Journey to Boston in 1809,* ed. Milton Halsey Thomas (Princeton: Princeton University Library, 1955), pp. 50–52.

6. *Memoirs of Rev. Joseph Buckminster, D. D., and of His Son, Rev. Joseph Stevens Buckminster,* ed. Eliza Buckminster Lee (Boston: Wm. Crosby and H. P. Nichols, 1849), pp. 336–37.

7. Quoted in Jared B. Flagg, *The Life and Letters of Washington Allston* (1892; reprint, New York: Benjamin Blom, 1969), pp. 245–46.

8. Ibid., p. 2.

9. Quoted in Flagg, p. 30.

10. *Memoir of William Ellery Channing, with Extracts from His Correspondence and Manuscripts,* ed. William Henry Channing (Boston: Wm. Crosby and H. P. Nichols, 1848), 1:60.

11. Anne C. Rose, *Transcendentalism as a Social Movement, 1830–1850* (New Haven: Yale University Press, 1981), pp. 11–12. See also Conrad Wright, *The Beginnings of Unitarianism in America* (Boston: Starr King Press, 1955).

12. Buckminster, *Memoirs,* p. 229.

13. Doreen Hunter, "America's First Romantics: Richard Henry Dana, Sr. and Washington Allston," *New England Quarterly* 45 (March 1972), 6–8.

14. "Scraps from a Correspondent," *Monthly Anthology* 1 (December 1803), p. 62.

15. Letter (27 November 1803) written from Paris in *Monthly Anthology* 2 (August 1805), pp. 400–2. See chapter 3, note 75.

16. According to the secretary who kept the minutes for the Anthology Society, on December 12, 1809, "Mr. Buckminster . . . read a fine long burlesque poem 'The Paint King' by our friend Alston [sic], which was accepted" for publication in the December issue of *Monthly Anthology.* See Boston Athenaeum, *The Anthology Society: Journal of the Proceedings of the Society which Conducts the Monthly Anthol-ogy and Boston Review* (Boston: Boston Athenaeum, 1910), pp. 216–17. See also Washington Allston, "Luca Giordano," *Monthly Anthology* 8 (April 1810), pp. 242–43; "Anibal Caracci," *Monthly Anthology* 8 (April 1810), p. 244; "Myrtilla," *Monthly Anthology* 8 (February 1810), pp. 108–11.

17. *The Anthology Society: Journal of the Proceedings,* pp. 10–12.

18. Peter Dobkin Hall, *The Organization of American Culture, 1700–1900: Private Institutions, Elites and the Organization of American Nationality* (New York: New York University Press, 1983), p. 88.

19. "Loose Paragraphs," *Monthly Anthology* 1 (February 1804), p. 176.

20. Lewis P. Simpson, "Joseph Stevens Buckminster: The Rise of the New England Clerisy," in *The Man of Letters in New England and the South: Essays on the History of the Literary Vocation in America* by Lewis P. Simpson (Baton Rouge: Louisiana State University Press, 1973), p. 29.

21. Ibid., p. 29.

22. "On the Dangers and Duties of Men of Letters," *Monthly Anthology* 7 (September 1809), pp. 156–57.

23. "The Empire of Morals and Dr. Johnson," in *The Federalist Literary Mind: Selections from the Monthly Anthology and Boston Review, 1803–1811,* ed. Lewis P. Simpson (Baton Rouge: Louisiana State University Press, 1962), pp. 84–86.

24. Josiah Quincy, "Biographical Notices," in *The History of the Boston Athenaeum with Biographical Notices of the Deceased Founders* (Cambridge: Metcalf and Co., 1851), pp. 16–17.

25. *Monthly Anthology* 2 (August 1805), pp. 399–400.

26. *Monthly Anthology* 2 (August 1805), p. 402. For the two subsequent letters see *Monthly Anthology* 2 (September 1805), pp. 450–51 and *Monthly Anthology* 2 (December 1805), pp. 633–36.

27. Allston's close friend Charles R. Leslie praised the older artist's painting of *Uriel,* comparing it to "the best pictures of Veronese," because with his "rich and glowing tone" he had "avoided *positive* colours which would have made him too material." Quoted in Richard Dilworth Rust, ed., *The Complete Works of Washington Irving,* vol. 2, *Miscellaneous Writings, 1803–1859,* ed. Wayne R. Kame (Boston: Twayne Publishers, 1981), pp. 176–77.

28. *Lectures on Art and Poems, and Monaldi,* vol. 1, *Lectures on Art and Poems,* ed. Richard

Henry Dana, Jr. (1850; reprint, Gainesville, Florida: Scholars' Facsimiles and Reprints, 1967), pp. 238–39.

29. Ibid., p. 243. Carl F. Strauch believes that the didactic subject matter and the heroic couplet form would have made "Eccentricity" the more likely choice for Allston's Phi Beta Kappa poem than "Sylphs of the Seasons." See Strauch, "Emerson's Phi Betta Kappa Poem," *New England Quarterly* 23 (March 1950), p. 66 n. 4.

30. *Lectures on Art and Poems*, p. 249.

31. Ibid., pp. 252–53.

32. Ibid., p. 250.

33. Boston Athenaeum, *Anthology Society*, p. 228.

34. "Luca Giordano," *Monthly Anthology* 8 (April 1810), p. 242. Allston's very brief note on Annibale Carracci was published in the same issue, p. 244.

35. Josiah Quincy, *The History of the Boston Athenaeum* (Cambridge, Mass.: Metcalf and Co., 1851), p. 19.

36. Letter of July 23, 1819 in "Letters of Miss Anna Cabot Lowell," ed. Josiah P. Quincy, Massachusetts Historical Society, *Proceedings* 18 (May 1904), pp. 314–15.

37. Allston to Charles Fraser, August 25, 1801, in Flagg, p. 47.

38. Leslie, *Autobiographical Recollections*, ed. Tom Taylor (London: John Murray, 1860), 1:49.

39. See Coleridge's definition of the spiritual meaning of "Israelite" in *Aids to Reflection*, 4th ed., ed. Henry Nelson Coleridge (London: William Pickering, 1839), pp. 126–29.

40. Quoted in Flagg, p. 98.

41. *Lectures on Art and Poems*, p. 280.

42. *A History of the Rise and Progress of the Arts of Design in the United States*, ed. Rita Weiss (1834; reprint, New York: Dover Publications, 1969), 2, pt. 1, p. 172.

43. *Randolph, A Novel* (n.p., 1823), 2:128.

44. Leslie, 1:51–52.

45. Quoted in Flagg, p. 111. The dark, brooding theme of the picture, briefly discussed in Gerdts, pp. 89–90, was appropriate for the artist's gloomy mood.

46. Coleridge to Allston, October 25, 1815, in *Collected Letters of Samuel Taylor Coleridge*, ed. Earl Leslie Griggs, vol. 4 (Oxford: Clarendon Press, 1959), 606–7.

47. Lewis P. Simpson, ed., *The Federalist Literary Mind*, p. 26.

48. Boston Athenaeum, *Anthology Society*, p. 303.

49. See Morse's angry reply to an *Anthology* review of his *History of New England*, which had accused him of plagiarism. *Monthly Anthology* 2 (December 1805), 670–74.

50. Mrs. Jedidiah Morse to Samuel, 13 June 1814, Samuel F. B. Morse Papers, Library of Congress, Washington, D.C.

51. Mr. Jedidiah Morse to Samuel, 13 June 1814, Library of Congress.

52. *Remarks on the Rev. Dr. Worcester's Letter to Mr. Channing, on the Review of American Unitarianism in a Late Panoplist* (Boston, 1815), pp. 14–15.

53. *A Second Letter to the Rev. William E. Channing, on the Subject of Unitarianism* (Boston, 1815), p. 7.

54. *Remarks on the Rev. Dr. Worcester's Second Letter to Mr. Channing, on American Unitarianism* (Boston, 1815), p. 17.

55. Ibid., pp. 13–14.

56. Quoted in Daniel Walker Howe, *The Unitarian Conscience: Harvard Moral Philosophy, 1805–1861* (Cambridge: Harvard University Press, 1970), p. 42.

57. *A Letter to the Rev. William E. Channing, on the Subject of His Letter to the Rev. Samuel E. Thatcher, Relating to the Review in the Panoplist of American Unitarianism* (Boston, 1815), p. 22.

58. Coleridge quoted in Leslie, 1:51–52.

59. J. B. Beer, *Coleridge the Visionary* (London: Chatto and Windus, 1959), pp. 28–29.

60. Quoted in Thomas McFarland, *Romanticism and the Forms of Ruin: Wordsworth, Coleridge and Modalities of Fragmentation* (Princeton: Princeton University Press, 1981), pp. 131–32.

61. "Coleridge and Kant's Two Worlds," in *Essays in the History of Ideas* by Arthur O. Lovejoy (Batlimore: Johns Hopkins Press, 1948), pp. 273–74.

62. Quoted in Peabody, *Last Evening with Allston, and Other Papers* (Boston: D. Lothrop and Co., 1886), pp. 7–8.

63. *Lectures on Art and Poems*, p. 320.

64. Ibid., p. 319.

65. Ibid., p. 321.

66. Ibid., p. 177.

67. "Fragments on Religion," Allston Papers, Dana Collection, Massachusetts Historical Society, Boston.

68. *Lectures on Art and Poems*, p. 39.

69. "Sonnet—The French Revolution," in *Lectures on Art and Poems*, p. 324.

70. Doreen Hunter, p. 9. Upon his return to America in 1818, Allston joined the recently founded St. Paul's Episcopal Church in Boston. Even when it reorganized itself after the

Revolution, the Episcopal church had carried the stigma of America's colonial past. It was not until after Allston had left Boston in 1811 that vigorous new leadership ignited a revival of Episcopalianism among the wealthier classes. After America's victory in the War of 1812, the Episcopal church's historical ties to the Church of England seemed less threatening. Furthermore, as the unitarian controversy became more heated and divisive, the Episcopal church was able to attract disenchanted Congregationalists who felt comfortable with neither the harsh austerity of orthodox Calvinism nor the doctrinally suspect liberalism of the unitarians. Certainly, Allston felt most comfortable with this philosophical middle ground. He was also attracted to the aesthetic beauty of the Episcopalian sacraments and liturgy. It is said that he was especially conscientious in attending St. Paul's "on saints' days and other high ecclesiastical festivals." M. F. Sweetser, *Allston* (Boston: Houghton, Osgood and Co., 1879), p. 113.

71. *Lectures on Art and Poems, and Monaldi,* vol. 2, *Monaldi* (1841; reprint, Gainesville, Florida: Scholars' Facsimiles and Reprints, 1967), p. 177.

72. Ibid., p. 227.

73. Ibid., p. 244.

74. Ibid., p. 252.

75. *Collected Letters of Samuel Taylor Coleridge,* ed. Earl Leslie Griggs, 4:607.

76. Elizabeth Johns shows that this theme of reanimation was extremely popular in England during this period. "Washington Allston's 'Dead Man Revived,'" *Art Bulletin* 61 (March 1979), p. 82.

77. *Memoirs of the Life of William Collins,* ed. William Wilkie Collins (London: Longman, 1848), 1:135.

78. Ibid., 2:242.

79. *Essays on the Nature and Uses of the Various Evidences of Revealed Religion* (New York: Charles Wiley, 1824, p. III.

80. Ibid., p. 122.

81. Ibid., pp. 57–63.

82. Ibid., p. 68.

83. "Sonnet—The French Revolution," in *Lectures on Art and Poems,* p. 324.

Chapter 5

1. Quoted in Pierre M. Irving, *The Life and Letters of Washington Irving* (1863; reprint, Detroit: Gale Research Co., 1967), 1:362–63.

2. Herder, *The Spirit of Hebrew Poetry,* trans. James Marsh (Burlington, Vt.: Edward Smith), 1:205. Besides Blake, who used the Belshazzar theme as an illustration for Edward Young's poem, "Night Thoughts," William Artaud painted a Belshazzar's feast for the Macklin Bible and Benjamin Burnell, a painter of architectural views, exhibited a version of the subject at the Royal Academy in 1809 and, again, in 1810, at the British Institution.

3. A. M. Broadly, *Napoleon in Caricature* (London and New York: John Lane, 1911), 1:188–89; 2:154–55, 159.

4. The next year, Byron also published *Hebrew Melodies,* a collection of lyric poems devoted to ancient Israel's quest for political and religious freedom. Unsurprisingly, it contained a poem based upon Belshazzar's feast, entitled "Vision of Belshazzar." See Carl Woodring, *Politics in English Poetry* (Cambridge: Harvard University Press, 1970), pp. 172–78; Thomas L. Ashton, *Byron's Hebrew Melodies* (Austin: University of Texas Press, 1972), pp. 76–79.

5. William Feaver, *The Art of John Martin* (Oxford: Clarendon Press, 1975), p. 49.

6. Quoted in *Collected Letters of Samuel Taylor Coleridge,* ed. Earl Leslie Griggs (Oxford: Clarendon Press, 1959), 3:512, no. 1.

7. Coleridge to J. J. Morgan, 29 June 1814, in *Collected Letters,* 3:512.

8. Allston to Morse, 5 July 1814, Samuel F. B. Morse Papers, Library of Congress, Washington, D.C.

9. Kathleen Coburn and Bart Winer, eds., *The Collected Works of Samuel Taylor Coleridge,* vol. 6, *The Lay Sermons,* ed. R. H. White, Bollingen Series, no. 75 (Princeton: Princeton University Press, 1972), p. 34.

10. *The Collected Works of Samuel Taylor Coleridge,* vol. 4, *The Friend,* ed. Barbara E. Rooke, Bollingen Series, no. 75 (Princeton: Princeton University Press, 1969), pt. 1, p. 126.

11. Elizabeth Johns, "Washington Allston's 'Dead Man Revived,'" *Art Bulletin* 61 (March 1979), pp. 91–95.

12. Herbert M. Atherton, *Political Prints in the Age of Hogarth: A Study of the Ideographic Representation of Politics* (Oxford: Clarendon Press, 1974), p. 200.

13. "Bernini's Elephant and Obelisk," in William S. Heckscher, *Art and Literature: Studies in Relationship* (Durham, N. C.: Duke University, 1985), p. 65, note 2.

14. Ibid., p. 75.

15. Ibid., p. 70; Arthur Henkel and

Albrecht Schöne, eds., *Emblemata* (Stuttgart: J. B. Metzlersche, Verlagsbuchhandlung, 1967), p. 1856.

16. Helmut von Erffa and Allen Staley, *The Paintings of Benjamin West* (New Haven, Conn.: Yale University Press, 1986), p. 319; William H. Gerdts, "The Paintings of Washington Allston," in *A Man of Genius: The Art of Washington Allston* by William H. Gerdts and Theodore E. Stebbins, Jr. (Boston: Museum of Fine Arts, 1979), p. 100.

17. Allston to Irving, 15 March 1818, in *The Life and Letters of Washington Irving*, 1:399.

18. Allston to Henry Pickering, 18 May 1820, Allston Papers, Dana Collection, Massachusetts Historical Society, Boston.

19. Allston to McMurtrie, 7 November 1818, in Jared B. Flagg, *The Life and Letters of Washington Allston* (1892; reprint, New York: Benjamin Blom, 1969), p. 144.

20. Allston to Leslie, 20 May 1821, in Flagg, p. 166.

21. Leslie to Allston, 20 August 1821, in Flagg, pp. 167–68.

22. Allston to Leslie, 20 May 1821, in Flagg, p. 166–67.

23. For a full discussion of Everett's comments, see chapter 6. A. H. Everett, *A Discourse on the Progress and Limits of Social Improvement . . .* (Boston: Charles Bowen, 1834), p. 29.

24. "Imperfect Sympathies," in *Charles Lamb: Selected Prose*, ed. Adam Phillips (Harmondsworth, Middlesex, England: Penguin Books, 1985), p. 117.

25. *Art and the Excited Spirit: America in the Romantic Period* (Ann Arbor: University of Michigan Museum of Art, 1972), p. 4.

26. Fogg Art Museum, Harvard University, The Washington Allston Trust, accession numbers 8.1955.164 and 8.1955.220. Joined together, these two fragments form a single drawing.

27. *Lectures on Art and Poems, and Monaldi*, vol. 1, *Lectures on Art and Poems*, ed. Richard Henry Dana, Jr. (1850; reprint, Gainesville, Florida: Scholars' Facsimiles and Reprints, 1967), p. 91.

28. In 1815, Westall illustrated a Bible with more than a hundred designs engraved by Charles Heath. Many of these same compositions were published again twenty years later with others by John Martin. See Josephine Gear, *Masters or Servants? A Study of Selected English Painters and their Patrons of the Late Eighteenth and Early Nineteenth Centuries* (New York: Garland Publishing, 1977), p. 169.

29. "Sonnet on Seeing the Picture of Aeolus by Pelligrino Tibaldi, in the Institute of Bologna," in *Lectures on Art and Poems*, p. 275.

30. Gerdts, "The Paintings of Washington Allston," p. 158.

31. Allston to Jarvis, 19 June 1834, quoted in Flagg, p. 275.

32. Channing, *Analysis of the Character of Napoleon Bonaparte* (Boston, 1828), p. 45.

Chapter 6

1. Allston to Irving, 9 May 1817, in Pierre M. Irving, *The Life and Letters of Washington Irving*, The Gale Library of Lives and Letters of American Writers Series (1863; reprint, Detroit: Gale Research Co., 1967, 1:363).

2. Irving to Allston, 21 May 1817, in Pierre M. Irving, 1:366.

3. William H. Gerdts, "The Paintings of Washington Allston," in *'The Man of Genius': The Art of Washington Allston (1779–1843)* by William H. Gerdts and Theodore E. Stebbins, Jr. (Boston: Museum of Fine Arts, 1979), p. 107.

4. Leslie to Allston, 17 February 1830, in Jared B. Flagg, *The Life and Letters of Washington Allston* (1892; reprint, New York: Benjamin Blom, 1969), pp. 226–27.

5. Elizabeth Johns, "Washington Allston's 'Dead Man Revived'," *Art Bulletin* 61 (March 1979), 93–96.

6. *Samuel F. B. Morse. His Letters and Journals*, ed. Edward Lind Morse (Boston: Houghton Mifflin Co., 1914), 1:153.

7. Joy S. Kasson, *Artistic Voyagers: Europe and the American Imagination in the Works of Irving, Allston, Cole, Cooper, and Hawthorne* (Westport, Conn.: Greenwood Press, 1982), p. 52.

8. Allston to Fraser, 25 August 1801 in Flagg, p. 43.

9. Allston to Jedidiah Morse, 4 August 1815, Pennsylvania Historical Society, Philadelphia, Pennsylvania.

10. Ben L. Bassham, "The Anglo-Americans: Americans Painters in England and at Home, 1800–1820," Ph.D. Diss. University of Wisconsin—Madison, 1972, pp. 19–21.

11. Coleridge to J. J. Morgan, 15 May 1814, in *Collected Letters of Samuel Taylor Coleridge*, ed. Earl Leslie Griggs (Oxford: Clarendon Press, 1959), 3:492.

12. Allston to Van Schaick, 13 November 1816, Houghton Library, Harvard University, Cambridge.

13. Allston to Morse, April 1816 quoted in Elizabeth Johns, "Washington Allston's 'Dead Man Revived'," p. 96.

14. Morse to Allston, 10 April 1816, in *Samuel F. B. Morse, His Letters and Journals,* 1:197.

15. Morse to parents, 14 March 1814, Samuel F. B. Morse Papers, Library of Congress, Washington, D.C.

16. Quoted in Flagg, p. 121.

17. Allston to Van Schaick, 13 November 1816, Houghton Library, Harvard University.

18. Lillian B. Miller, *Patrons and Patriotism: The Encouragement of the Fine Arts in the United States, 1790–1860* (Chicago: University of Chicago Press, 1966), p. 112.

19. Tudor to H. G. Otis, 2 September 1815, quoted in Samuel Eliot Morison, *Harrison Gray Otis, 1765–1848: The Urbane Federalist* (Boston: Houghton Mifflin Co., 1969), 234–35.

20. Ronald Story, "Class and Culture in Boston: The Athenaeum, 1807–1860," *American Quarterly* 27 (May 1975), pp. 190–99.

21. "Institution for the Fine Arts," *North American Review* 2 (January 1816), 161.

22. Gerdts, "The Paintings of Washington Allston," p. 71. See also Carl Seaburg and Stanley Paterson, *Merchant Prince of Boston: Colonel T. H. Perkins, 1764–1854* (Cambridge: Harvard University Press, 1971), p. 227 and Tanya Boyett, "Thomas Handasyd Perkins: An Essay on Material Culture," *Old Time New England* 70 (1980), 45–62.

23. Samuel Eliot Morison, p. 235.

24. Washington Monument Association Report, 15 December 1818, John Lowell, Chairman, Boston Public Library, Boston.

25. Allston to Pickering, 18 May 1820, Washington Allston Papers, Dana Collection, Massachusetts Historical Society, Boston. See also Allston's letter to Gulian Verplanck, 12 March 1819, in Flagg, p. 149, where the artist states his intention to make *Belshazzar* "profitably by exhibition."

26. Lines 566–616 of Bradstreet's poem "The Four Monarchies" relates the story of Belshazzar's feast. See *The Works of Anne Bradstreet,* ed. Jeannie Hensley (Cambridge: Belknap Press of Harvard University Press, 1967), pp. 90–91. It is interesting that Allston's close friend and brother-in-law, Richard H. Dana, Sr., claimed to be a descendent of Anne Bradstreet and that he owned a 1678 edition of her poems, which included "The Four Monarchies." See James Grant Wilson, *Bryant and His Friends: Some Reminiscences of the Knicker-*

bocker Writers (New York: Fords, Howard, and Hulbert, 1886), pp. 181, 186.

27. William H. Gerdts, "Allston's 'Belshazzar's Feast'," *Art in America* 61 (March–April, 1973) p. 62; (May–June, 1973), pp. 62, 65.

28. "Joseph Steward and the Hartford Museum," *Connecticut Historical Society Bulletin* 18 (January–April 1953), pp. 1–16.

29. "Thomas Cole and the Problem of Figure Painting," *American Art Journal* 4 (Spring 1972), pp. 67, 69.

30. George C. D. Odell, *Annals of the New York Stage* (New York: Columbia University Press, 1928), 3: p. 533; Gerdts, "The Paintings of Washington Allston," in *'The Man of Genius',* p. 127.

31. *A Discourse on the Progress and Limits of Social Improvement; Including a General Survey of the History of Civilization. Addressed to the Literary Societies of Amherst College . . . August 27, 1833* (Boston: Charles Bowen, 1834), p. 29.

32. For a general discussion of the political content of sermon literature during this period, see William Gribbin, *The Churches Militant: The War of 1812 and American Religion* (New Haven: Yale University Press, 1973).

33. *A Discourse, Delivered on the National Thanksgiving for Peace, April 13, 1815* (Newburyport: W. B. Allen and Co., 1815), p. 4.

34. Marion Mainwaring, *John Quincy Adams and Russia: A Sketch of Early Russian-American Relations as Recorded in the Papers of the Adams Family and Some of Their Contemporaries* (Quincy, Mass.: Patriot Ledger, 1965), p. 19.

35. Rev. James Freeman, *A Discourse on the Russian Victories, Given in King's Chapel, March 25, 1813,* with an Introduction by Henry Wilder Foote (Cambridge, Mass.: John Wilson and Son, 1881), p. 11.

36. Quoted in Freeman, p. 5.

37. Quoted in Freeman, p. 6.

38. Gribbin, pp. 27–28.

39. Quoted in Gribbin, p. 57.

40. *A Sermon Delivered in Boston, September 18, 1814* (Boston: Henry Channing, 1814), p. 5.

41. *A Discourse Delivered in Newburyport, July 4, 1814, in Commemoration of American Independence, and the Deliverance of Europe* (Newburyport, 1814) p. 18.

42. *A Discourse, Delivered . . . on the Anniversary Election, May 31, 1815* (Boston: Russel, Cutler and Co., 1815), pp. 3, 16–17.

43. Peter Dobkin Hall, *The Organization of American Culture, 1700–1900: Private Institutions, Elites, and the Origins of American Nationality*

(New York: New York University Press, 1982), p. 89.

44. Quoted in Robert V. Remini, *Andrew Jackson and the Course of American Empire, 1767–1821* (New York: Harper and Row, 1977), p. 320.

45. John William Ward, *Andrew Jackson: Symbol for an Age* (New York: Oxford University Press, 1962), pp. 181–86, pl. VI.

46. Quoted in Ward, p. 187.

47. Daniel Walker Howe, *The Political Culture of the American Whigs* (Chicago: University of Chicago Press, 1979), p. 89.

48. *The Conduct of the Administration* (Boston: Stimpson and Clapp, 1832), p. 77.

49. William Ware, *Lectures on the Works and Genius of Washington Allston* (Boston: Phillips, Sampson and Co., 1852), p. 129.

50. H. A. S. Dearborn, "Allston's Feast of Belshazzar," *Knickerbocker* 24 (September 1844), p. 208. Richard H. Dana, Jr., also remarked upon the Queen's "Bonaparte countenance." See Joy Kasson, *Artistic Voyagers*, p. 71.

51. (Boston, 1828), p. 32.

52. Ibid., pp. 46–47.

53. Elizabeth Johns, p. 96.

54. *A History of the Rise and Progress of the Arts of Design in the United States,* ed. Rita Weiss (1834; reprint, New York: Dover Publications, 1969), 2: pt. 1., p. 181.

55. For a historical parallel, see Fred Somkin's discussion of the Marquis de Lafayette's decision to foresake Europe for America in *Unquiet Eagle: Memory and Desire in the Idea of American Freedom, 1815–1860* (Ithaca: Cornell University Press, 1967), pp. 160–61.

56. Allston quoted in Dunlap, 2: pt. 1, p. 182.

57. Ibid., pp. 183–84.

58. Ibid., p. 183.

59. Sacvan Bercovitch, *The American Jeremiad* (Madison: University of Wisconsin Press, 1978), pp. 7–9, 23.

Chapter 7

1. Allston to Collins, 1 June 1819, Allston Papers, Dana Collection, Massachusetts Historical Society, Boston.

2. Allston to Collins, 18 May 1821, Massachusetts Historical Society.

3. Quoted in Jared B. Flagg, *The Life and Letters of Washington Allston* (1892; reprint, New York: Benjamin Blom, 1969), p. 387.

4. William H. Gerdts, "The Paintings of Washington Allston," in *'The Man of Genius': The Art of Washington Allston (1779–1843)*, by William H. Gerdts and Theodore E. Stebbins, Jr. (Boston: Museum of Fine Arts, 1979), p. 119.

5. Quoted in Flagg, p. 60.

6. *Boston Daily Advertiser,* September 1830, quoted in Flagg, p. 248.

7. *Boston Daily Advertiser,* September 1830, quoted in Flagg, p. 249.

8. Quoted in Edgar Preston Richardson, *Washington Allston: A Study of the Romantic Artist in America* (Chicago: University of Chicago Press, 1948), p. 143.

9. Gerdts, "The Paintings of Washington Allston," pp. 68, 118.

10. Charles L. Sanford discusses Americans' tendency to distrust the sublime "as an immoral and atheistic European importation," in *The Quest for Paradise: Europe and the American Moral Imagination* (Urbana: University of Illinois Press, 1961), p. 142–43. See Dugald Stewart, *Philosophical Essays,* 2d ed. (Edinburgh, 1816).

11. "Scraps from a Correspondent," *Monthly Anthology* 1 (December 1803), p. 60.

12. Elizabeth Palmer Peabody, *Reminiscences of Rev. Wm. Ellery Channing* (Boston: Roberts Brothers, 1880), p. 209.

13. Edward Everett, *Bulletin of the New England Art Union,* no. 1 (1852), p. 3.

14. Robert Charles Winthrop, Jr., *Memoir of the Honorable David Sears* (Cambridge, Mass.: John Wilson and Son, 1886), p. 10.

15. "Exhibition of Pictures Painted by W. Allston at Harding's Gallery, School Street," *North American Review* 50 (April 1840), pp. 375–76.

16. "The Drawings of Washington Allston," in *'A Man of Genius': The Art of Washington Allston (1779–1843)*, by William H. Gerdts and Theodore E. Stebbins, Jr. (Boston: Museum of Fine Arts, 1979), p. 230.

17. "The Exhibition, in Boston, of Allston's Paintings, in 1839," in *Last Evening with Allston, and Other Papers,* by Elizabeth P. Peabody (Boston: D. Lothrop and Co., 1886), p. 35.

18. Daniel Walker Howe associates the American peace movement with Federalist-Whig politics in *The Political Culture of the American Whigs* (Chicago: University of Chicago Press, 1979), pp. 140–41.

19. Allston to Leslie, 20 May 1821, Massachusetts Historical Society.

20. Allston to Leslie, 7 September 1821, in Flagg, pp. 171–72.

21. Allston to Winthrop, 23 November 1821, Massachusetts Historical Society.

22. Joy S. Kasson, *Artistic Voyagers: Europe and the American Imagination in the Works of Irving, Allston, Cole, Cooper, and Hawthorne* (Westport, Conn.: Greenwood Press, 1982), p. 68.

23. Gerdts, "The Paintings of Washington Allston," p. 115.

24. Allston to Winthrop, 23 November 1821, Massachusetts Historical Society.

25. Letter of 4 January 1831, Pennsylvania Historical Society, Philadelphia.

26. Washington Allston, *Lectures on Art and Poems, and Monaldi*, vol. 1, *Lectures on Arts and Poems*, ed. Richard H. Dana, Jr. (1850); reprint, Gainesville, Florida: Scholars' Facsimilies and Reprints, 1967), pp. 168, 173.

27. Allston to Cogdell, 27 December 1825, Massachusetts Historical Society.

28. Gerdts, "The Paintings of Washington Allston," pp. 127, 129.

29. Kasson, *Artistic Voyagers*, p. 68.

30. James G. Percival, Phi Beta Kappa poem, read before the Connecticut Alpha of the Phi Beta Kappa Society, 13 September 1825, and quoted in Gerdts, "The Paintings of Washington Allston," p. 127.

31. Allston to Verplanck, 2 July 1824 quoted in Flagg, pp. 179–80.

32. *Lectures on Art, and Poems*, pp. 9–10.

33. Peter Dobkin Hall, *The Organization of American Culture, 1700–1900: Private Institutions, Elites, and the Origins of American Nationality* (New York: New York University Press, 1982), p. 90.

34. Ibid., p. 92.

35. *Monthly Anthology* 4 (November 1807), quoted in Josiah Quincy, *The History of the Boston Athenaeum* (Cambridge, Mass: Metcalf and Co., 1851), pp. 9–10.

36. For a list of the subscribers and proprietors of the Boston Athenaeum, see Josiah Quincy, *The History of the Boston Athenaeum*, pp. 243–63; C. K. Bolton, *The Athenaeum Centenary: The Influence and the History of the Boston Athenaeum from 1807 to 1907* (Boston: Boston Athenaeum, 1907), pp. 125–213.

37. Lillian B. Miller, *Patrons and Patriotism: The Encouragement of the Fine Arts in the United States, 1790–1860* (Chicago: University of Chicago Press, 1966), p. 116.

38. Chester Harding, *My Egotistigraphy* (Cambridge, Mass.: John Wilson and Son, 1866), pp. 139–40.

39. "Exhibition of Pictures at the Boston Athenaeum," *North American Review* 25 (July 1827), p. 229.

40. Gerdts, p. 144.

41. "Exhibition of Pictures at the Boston Athenaeum," *North American Review* 31 (October 1830), p. 310.

42. Ibid., p. 334.

43. Ibid., p. 310.

44. "Allston's Monaldi," *Arcturus* 3 (December 1841), p. 50; Review of Ware's Lectures on Allston, *The Literary World*, 16 October 1852, p. 246; Richard H. Dana, Sr., to C. S. Henry on Allston's retrospective in 1839, in James Grant Wilson, *Bryant and His Friends: Some Reminiscences of the Knickerbocker Writers* (New York: Fords, Howard, and Hulbert, 1886), pp. 201–2.

45. Mabel Munson Swan quotes a statement made by William Dunlap in 1828 that he exhibited his *Calvary* at the Pennsylvania Academy of Fine Arts in "place of Allston's great picture," in *The Athenaeum Gallery, 1837–1873: The Boston Athenaeum as an Early Patron of Art* (Boston: Boston Athenaeum, 1940), p. 51.

46. "The Exhibition, in Boston, of Allston's Paintings, in 1839," in *Last Evening with Allston, and Other Papers*, p. 33.

47. Elizabeth Gilmore Holt, "Revivalist Themes in American Prints and Folksongs, 1830–50," in *American Printmaking before 1876: Fact, Fiction, and Fantasy*, Papers presented at a Symposium at the Library of Congress, June 12–13, 1972 (Washington, D.C.: Library of Congress, 1975), p. 44.

48. Quoted in Dana, *Poems and Prose Writings* (1849; reprint, Upper Saddle River, N. J.: Literature House/Gregg Press, 1970), 2:369.

49. Ruth Miller Elson, *Guardians of Tradition: American Schoolbooks of the Nineteenth Century* (Lincoln: University of Nebraska Press, 1964), p. 45.

50. Donald G. Mathews, "The Second Great Awakening as an Organizing Process, 1780–1830: An Hypothesis," *American Quarterly* 21 (Spring 1969), pp. 42–43.

51. Quoted in Peter Dobkin Hall, p. 88.

52. William G. McLoughlin, *Revivals, Awakenings, and Reform: An Essay on Religion and Social Change in America, 1607–1977* (Chicago: University of Chicago Press, 1978), pp. 111–13.

53. Elizabeth Johns, "Washington Allston's Library," *American Art Journal* 7 (November 1975), p. 36.

54. M. F. Sweetser, *Allston* (Boston: Houghton, Osgood and Co., 1879), pp. 133–34.

55. Frank Luther Mott, *A History of American Magazines*, vol. 1; *1741–1850* (Cambridge: Harvard University Press, 1938), p. 572.

56. Alexander McKenzie, *Lectures on the History of the First Church in Cambridge* (Boston: Congregational Publishing Society, 1873), p. 223.

57. "Natural History of Enthusiasm," from *The Spirit of the Pilgrims* (1830), in Richard Henry Dana, *Poems and Prose Writings*, 2:381–82.

58. Sacvan Bercovitch, *The American Jeremiad* (Madison: University of Wisconsin Press, 1978), pp. 33–4, 45.

59. *The Relation the Present State of Religion Bears to the Expected Millennium* (Boston: Crocker and Brewster, 1823), pp. 7–8.

60. *Two Discourses, on the Completion of the Second Century from the Landing of the Forefathers of New England at Plymouth, 22 December 1620, Delivered at Cambridge 24 December 1820* (Cambridge: Hilliard and Metcalf, 1821), p. 10.

61. James Arbuckle, *Mental Culture: An Address . . . Delivered Before the Reading Society, Auxiliary to the Library of the Montgomery Academy . . . December 16, 1834* (New York: D. Fanshaw, 1835), p. 7.

62. "After the Revolution: The Fate of Nationalism in the New States," in *The Interpretation of Cultures*, by Clifford Geertz (New York: Basic Books, 1973), p. 242.

63. Ibid., p. 252.

64. Ibid., p. 243.

65. Daniel Walker Howe, *The Political Culture of the American Whigs*, p. 70.

66. William Tudor, *Letters on the Eastern States*, 2d ed. (Boston: Wells and Lilly, 1821), pp. 63–73. See also Tudor's publication "An Address Delivered to the Phi Beta Kappa Society, at Their Anniversary Meeting in Cambridge," *North American Review* 2 (November 1815), p. 14.

67. Frederick Butler, *Complete History of the United States of America* (Hartford, Connecticut: 1821), 1:65.

68. Elson, p. 121.

69. *Lectures on Art and Poems*, p. 291.

70. *Reminiscences of Rev. Wm. Ellery Channing*, p. 207.

71. "Natural History of Enthusiasm," *Poems and Prose Writings*, 2:393; Review of *The Christian Examiner*, in *The Spirit of the Pilgrims* 3 (October 1830), 544–45.

72. Review of *A General History of New England From the Discovery to 1680*, by Rev. William Hubbard, *The North American Review* 2 (January 1816), pp. 222–23.

73. Peabody, *Reminiscences of Rev. Wm. Ellery Channing*, p. 103.

74. Edward W. Hooker, "Political Duties of Christians, as Exhibited in the Bible, *American Quarterly Observer* 1 (July 1833), pp. 2–4; "Biography of Daniel," *The Monitor, Designed to Improve the Taste, the Understanding, and the Heart* 1 (January 1823), pp. 13–18.

75. Rev. W. A. Scott, *Daniel, a Model for Young Men* New York: Robert Carter and Brothers, 1854), p. 232.

76. Daniel Walker Howe discusses the cult of Daniel Webster in *The Political Culture of American Whigs*, pp. 211–14.

77. "The Garden of Eden and the Deacon's Meadow," *American Heritage* 7 (December 1955), p. 60.

78. "Belshazzar's Feast," *Christian Examiner* 37 (July 1844), p. 56.

79. Ibid., p. 57.

80. Quoted in Louis Harap, *The Image of the Jew in American Literature* (Philadelphia: The Jewish Publication Society of America, 1974), p. 103.

81. *The Journals and Miscellaneous Notebooks of Ralph Waldo Emerson*, vol. 5, *(1835–1838)*, ed. Merton M. Sealts, Jr. (Cambridge: Belknap Press of Harvard University Press, 1965), p. 230.

82. "A Record of Impressions Produced by the Exhibition of Mr. Allston's Pictures in the Summer of 1839," in *Papers on Literature and Art*, by Margaret Fuller (New York: Wiley and Putnam, 1846), pt. 2, pp. 113–14.

83. Quoted in Flagg, p. 386.

84. John F. Duffy, ed., *Coleridge's American Disciples: The Selected Correspondence of James Marsh* (Amherst: University of Massachusetts Press, 1973), p. 3.

85. Hans Kohn, *The Idea of Nationalism: A Study of Its Origins and Background* (Toronto: MacMillan, 1944; Collier Books, 1967), p. 439.

86. James Marsh, *An Address Delivered in Burlington Upon the Inauguration of the Author to the Office of President of the University of Vermont, November 28, 1826* (Burlington: E. and T. Mills, 1826), pp. 15–16.

87. Review of *Lectures on the Sacred Poetry of the Hebrews*, by Robert Lowth, *North American Review* 31 (October 1830), pp. 339, 342.

88. Dana to Gulian C. Verplanck, 14 March 1828, New York Historical Society.

89. Review of *Lectures on the Sacred Poetry of the Hebrews*, p. 343.

90. Allston to George W. Flagg, 29 October 1840, Pennsylvania Historical Society.

91. Letter of 1 March 1830, quoted in Flagg, p. 233–34. Differing from most scholars, Joy Kasson argues convincingly that Allston did indeed seriously consider the Rotunda commission. Allston's enthusiastic letter of 1 March 1830 to Verplanck certainly supports her argument. See *Artistic Voyagers*, p. 81, n. 102.

92. Verplanck to Allston, 9 March 1830, quoted in Flagg, p. 235.

93. Quoted in Arthur M. Schlesinger, Jr., *The Age of Jackson* (Boston: Little, Brown and Co., 1945), p. 140.

94. Allston to Cogdell, 8 June 1830, Massachusetts Historical Society.

95. Letter of 4 January 1831, Pennsylvania Historical Society.

Chapter 8

1. William H. Gerdts, "The Paintings of Washington Allston," in *'A Man of Genius': The Art of Washington Allston (1779–1843)*, by William H. Gerdts and Theodore E. Stebbins, Jr. (Boston: Museum of Fine Arts, 1979), p. 162.

2. *The Organization of American Culture, 1700–1900: Private Institutions, Elites, and the Origins of American Nationality* (New York: New York University Press, 1982), pp. 84, 88.

3. Ibid., p. 89.

4. Gerdts, p. 152.

5. Oscar Handlin, *Boston's Immigrants: A Study in Acculturation*, rev. ed. (Cambridge: The Belknap Press of Harvard University Press, 1959), pp. 185–86.

6. W. H. Oliver, *Prophets and Millennialists: The Uses of Biblical Prophecy in England From the 1790s to the 1840s* (Oxford University Press, 1978), pp. 108–9.

7. Ernest R. Sandeen, *The Roots of Fundamentalism: British and American Millennialism, 1800–1930* (Chicago: University of Chicago Press, 1970), pp. 21–22.

8. Eric Adams, *Francis Danby: Varieties of Poetic Landscape* (New Haven: Yale University Press, 1973), p. 78.

9. Walter James Graham, *Tory Criticism in the Quarterly Review, 1809–1853* (New York: Columbia University Press, 1921), pp. 7, 13.

10. Sandeen, pp. 44–46.

11. Ray Allen Billington, *The Protestant Crusade, 1800–1860: A Study of the Origins of American Nativism* (1938; reprint, Chicago: Quadrangle Books, 1964), pp. 43, 178–79.

12. Allston, *Lectures on Art and Poems, and Monaldi*, vol. 2, *Monaldi* (1841; reprint, Gainesville, Florida: Scholars' Facsimiles and Reprints, 1967), p. 13.

13. Charles Fraser, *Magnolia*, September 1842, quoted in Flagg, p. 320.

14. *The Romantic Agony*, trans. Angus Davidson, 2d ed. (1951; reprint, Oxford: Oxford University Press paperback, 1970), pp. 60–61.

15. "Radcliffe's Gaston de Blondeville," in *Poems and Prose Writings*, by Richard Henry Dana (1850; reprint, Upper Saddle River, N. J.: Literature House/Gregg Press, 1970), 2:320.

16. *Lectures on Art and Poems, and Monaldi*, vol. 1, *Lectures on Art and Poems*, ed. Richard Henry Dana, Jr. (1850; reprint, Gainesville, Florida: Scholar's Facsimiles and Reprints, 1967), p. 66.

17. Ibid., p. 67.

18. "Fragments on Religion," Allston Papers, Dana Collection, Massachusetts Historical Society, Boston, Massachusetts.

19. Mario Praz, *The Romantic Agony*, p. 62.

20. David Brion Davis, "Some themes of Counter-Subversion: An Analysis of Anti-Masonic, Anti-Catholic, and Anti-Mormon Literature," *Mississippi Valley Historical Review* 47 (September 1960), p. 217.

21. David Brion Davis, p. 207; Billington, pp. 123–26; Samuel F. B. Morse, *Foreign Conspiracy Against the United States*, 4th ed. (New York: Van Nostrand and Dwight, 1836), pp. 69–70, 95, et passim.

22. Elizabeth Johns, "Washington Allston's Library," *American Art Journal* 7 (November 1975), p. 37.

23. William Ware, *Lectures on the Works and Genius of Washington Allston* (Boston: Phillips, Sampson and Co., 1852), pp. 43–44.

24. Gerard M. Greenewald discusses Shakespeare's attitude toward Catholicism and how he altered the message of the earlier play in *Shakespeare's Attitude Towards the Catholic Church in 'King John'* (Washington, D.C.: Catholic University of America, 1938).

25. Gerdts, "The Paintings of Washington Allston," pp. 152, 200, no. 69.

26. Introduction to *King John*, in *Shakespeare's Plays: With His Life*, ed. Gulian C. Verplanck, vol. 1, *Histories* (New York: Harper and Bros., 1847), p. 8.

27. Lily B. Campbell, *Shakespeare's 'Histo-*

ries' (San Marino, Calif.: Huntington Library, 1947), p. 166.

28. Timothy L. Smith, "Righteousness and Hope: Christian Holiness and the Millennial Vision in America, 1800–1900," *American Quarterly* 31 (Spring 1979), p. 31.

29. Quoted in George M. Marsden, *The Evangelical Mind and the New School Presbyterian Experience* (New Haven: Yale University Press, 1970), p. 51.

30. Sidney Mead, *Nathaniel William Taylor, 1786–1858: A Connecticut Liberal* (Chicago: University of Chicago Press, 1942), pp. 196–97.

31. Allston, *Lectures on Art and Poems*, p. 176. See also Richard Henry Dana, "Law as Suited to Man," in *Poems and Prose Writings* (1850; reprint, Upper Saddle River, N.J.: Literature House/Gregg Press, 1970), 2:60–61, 77–78.

32. Dana to Marsh, 31 December 1834, in *Coleridge's American Disciples: The Selected Correspondence of James Marsh*, ed. John J. Duffy (Amherst: University of Massachusetts, 1973), p. 171.

33. James Marsh to Nathan Lord, December 1835, in Ibid., pp. 179–80.

34. James Marsh, Introduction to *Aids to Reflection*, by Samuel Taylor Coleridge, ed. Henry Nelson Coleridge (London: William Pickering, 1839), p. XXXV.

35. Marsh to Nathan Lord, December 1835, in Duffy, pp. 181, 183.

36. Allston, *Lectures on Art and Poems*, pp. 62–63.

37. Ibid., p. 175.

38. *Unquiet Eagle: Memory and Desire in the Idea of American Freedom, 1815–1860* (Ithaca: Cornell University Press, 1967), p. 36.

39. Curtis Dahl, "The American School of Catastrophe," *American Quarterly* 11 (Fall 1959), 380–81.

40. Anne C. Rose, *Transcendentalism as a Social Movement, 1830–1850* (New Haven: Yale University Press, 1981), pp. 16–17.

41. Quoted in Perry Miller, *The Life of the Mind in America: From the Revolution to the Civil War* (New York: Harcourt, Brace and World; Harvest Book, 1965), p. 195.

42. Orestes Brownson, *Babylon is Falling. A Discourse Preached in the Masonic Temple, to the Society for Christian Union and Progress . . . May 28, 1837* (Boston: J. R. Butts, 1837), pp. 22–23.

43. Ibid., p. 3.

44. *Literary Democracy: The Declaration of Cultural Independence in America* (New York: Viking Press, 1981), p. 17.

45. Dana to Marsh, 24 February 1838, in John J. Duffy, ed., *Coleridge's American Disciples*, p. 214.

46. Marsh to Dana, 8 March 1838, in Ibid., p. 218.

47. William R. Hutchison, *The Transcendentalist Ministers: Church Reform in the New England Renaissance* (New Haven: Yale University Press, 1959), p. 77.

48. Quoted in Ibid., p. 81.

49. *Lectures on Art*, pp. 73–74.

50. Ibid., pp. 5–6.

51. Daniel Walker Howe describes similar arguments for the existence of God used by Scottish Common Sense philosophers and their followers in America in *The Unitarian Conscience: Harvard Moral Philosophy, 1805–1861* (Cambridge: Harvard University Press, 1970), pp. 98–99.

52. "America's First Romantics: Richard Henry Dana, Sr. and Washington Allston," *New England Quarterly* 45 (March 1972), pp. 26–27. See also George P. Winston, "Washington Allston and the Objective Correlative," *Bucknell Review* 11 (December 1962), p. 107.

53. Richard Henry Dana, "Pollock's Course of Time," in *Poems and Prose Writings*, 2:379.

54. James Engell, *The Creative Imagination: Enlightenment to Romanticism* (Cambridge: Harvard University Press, 1981), p. 363. See also Laurence S. Lockridge, *Coleridge the Moralist* (Ithaca: Cornell University Press, 1977), p. 69.

55. *Lectures on Art*, p. 132.

56. Ibid., p. 94.

57. Ibid., p. 110.

58. Ibid., p. 164.

59. Ibid., pp. 7–8.

60. Entry for September 20, 1836, in *The Journals and Miscellaneous Notebooks of Ralph Waldo Emerson*, vol. 5, *(1835–1838)*, ed. Merton M. Sealts, Jr. (Cambridge: Belknap Press of Harvard University Press, 1965), pp. 195–96.

61. "Fragments on Religion," Massachusetts Historical Society.

62. The Rev. John A. Albro, presiding at Allston's funeral, claimed that the artist had been in daily communion with God while laboring in his studio-temple. See *The Blessedness of Those Who Die in the Lord. A Sermon Occasioned by the Death of Washington Allston, Delivered in the Church of the Shepard Society, Cambridge, July 16, 1843* (Boston: Charles C. Little and James Brown, 1843), p. 24.

63. "Pollock's Course of Time," in *Poems and Prose Writings*, 2:350–51, 361.

64. Quoted in James Grant Wilson, *Bryant and His Friends: Some Reminiscences of the Knickerbocker Writers* (New York: Fords, Howard, and Hulbert, 1886), pp. 201–2.

65. Allston to Cogdell, 27 February 1832, in Flagg, p. 257.

66. Allston to McMurtrie, 2 March 1837, Pennsylvania Historical Society, Philadelphia, Pennsylvania.

67. Quoted in Flagg, p. 304.

68. Allston to Cogdell, 27 December 1825, Massachusetts Historical Society.

69. Stuart quoted by Walter Channing in "Reminiscences of Washington Allston," *Christian Register and Boston Observer*, 5 August 1843, p. 124.

70. "Exhibition of Pictures Painted by Washington Allston at Harding's Gallery, School Street," *North American Review* 50 (April 1840), p. 368.

71. "Washington Allston and Samuel Taylor Coleridge: A Remarkable Relationship," *Archives of American Art Journal* 19, no. 3 (1979), pp. 5–6.

72. Lockridge, *Coleridge the Moralist*, p. 76.

73. Allston, "Gloria Mundi," in *Lectures on Art and Poems*, pp. 317–18.

74. Ibid., p. 318.

Bibliography

Abrams, Ann Uhry. *The Valiant Hero: Benjamin West and Grand-Style History Painting.* New Directions in American Art. Washington, D.C.: Smithsonian Institution Press, 1985.

Adams, Charles Francis. *Richard Henry Dana.* 2 vols. Boston and New York: Houghton, Mifflin and Co., 1891.

Adams, Eric. *Francis Danby: Varieties of Poetic Landscape.* New Haven: Yale University Press, 1973.

Adams, Hannah. *The History of the Jews, from the Destruction of Jerusalem to the Present Time.* London: A. Macintosh, 1818.

Ahlstrom, Sydney E. *A Religious History of the American People.* New Haven: Yale University Press, 1972.

Albanese, Catherine L. *Sons of the Fathers: The Civil Religion of the American Revolution.* Philadelphia: Temple University Press, 1976.

Alberts, Robert C. *Benjamin West: A Biography.* Boston: Houghton Mifflin, 1978.

Albro, John A. *The Blessedness of Those Who Die in the Lord. A Sermon Occasioned by the Death of Washington Allston, Delivered in the Church of the Shepard Society, Cambridge, July 16, 1843.* Boston: Charles C. Little and James Brown, 1843.

Allston, Susan Lowndes. *Brookgreen Waccamaw in the South Carolina Low Country.* Charleston, S.C., 1956.

Allston, Washington. "Anibal Caracci." *Monthly Anthology* 8 (April 1810): 244.

————. Correspondence. Houghton Library, Harvard University, Cambridge, Massachusetts.

————. Correspondence. Pennsylvania Historical Society, Philadelphia.

————. Lectures on Art and Poems (1850), and Monaldi (1841). Reprint (2 vols. in 1). Gainesville, Florida: Scholars' Facsimiles and Reprints, 1967.

————. "Luca Giordano." *Monthly Anthology* 8 (April 1810): 242–43.

————. "Myrtilla." *Monthly Anthology* 8 (February 1810): 108–11.

————. "Note." *North American Review* 51 (October 1840): 518–20.

————. "Original Letters." *Monthly Anthology* 2 (August 1805):400–2; (September 1805):450–51; (December 1805): 633–36.

————. Papers. Dana Collection, Massachusetts Historical Society, Boston.

————. "Procrastination Is the Thief of Time." Pusey Library, Harvard University, Cambridge, Massachusetts.

"Allston's Monaldi." *Arcturus* 3 (December 1841): 49–51.

Anderson, Bernhard W. *Understanding the Old Testament.* 3d ed. Englewood Cliffs, New Jersey: Prentice-Hall, 1975.

Anderson, Patricia A. *Promoted to Glory: The Apotheosis of George Washington.* Northampton, Mass.: Smith College Museum of Art, 1980.

Andrews, Keith. *The Nazarenes: A Brotherhood of German Painters in Rome.* Oxford: Clarendon Press, 1964.

Arbuckle, James. *Mental Culture.* New York: D. Fanshaw, 1835.

Ashton, John. *English Caricature and Satire on Napoleon I.* 1888. Reprint. New York: Benjamin Blom, 1968.

Ashton, Thomas L. *Byron's Hebrew Melodies.* Austin: University of Texas Press, 1972.

"The Athenaeum Gallery and the Allston Collection." *Bulletin of the American Art-Union* (October 1850): 109–12.

Atherton, Herbert M. *Political Prints in the Age of Hogarth: A Study of the Ideographic Representation of Politics.* Oxford: Clarendon Press, 1974.

Bader, Alfred. *The Bible Through Dutch Eyes.* Milwaukee: Milwaukee Art Center, 1976.

Bailyn, Bernard. *The Ideological Origins of the American Revolution.* Cambridge: Belknap Press of Harvard University Press, 1967.

Baker, J. Wayne. *Heinrich Bullinger and the Covenant: The Other Reformed Tradition.* Athens, Ohio: University Press, 1980.

Bartlett, Irving H. *Daniel Webster.* New York: W. W. Norton, 1978.

Bartol, C. A. *Discourses on the Christian Spirit and Life.* Boston: Wm. Crosby and H. P. Nichols, 1850.

Bassham, Ben L. "The Anglo-Americans: American Painters in England and at Home, 1800–1820." Ph.D. dissertation. University of Wisconsin, 1972.

Beer, J. B. *Coleridge the Visionary.* London: Chatto and Windus, 1959.

Bercken, E. von der. "Unbekannte Werke des Jacopo Tintoretto in der Sammlung Italico Brass in Venedig." *Pantheon* 15 (January 1935): 24–30.

Bercovitch, Sacvan. *The American Jeremiad.* Madison: University of Wisconsin Press, 1978.

———. *The Puritan Origins of the American Self.* New Haven: Yale University Press, 1975.

Berens, John F. *Providence and Patriotism in Early America, 1640–1815.* Charlottesville: University of Virginia Press, 1978.

Billington, Ray Allen. *The Protestant Crusade, 1800–1860: A Study of the Origins of American Nativism.* 1938. Reprint. Chicago: Quadrangle Books, 1964.

"Biography of Daniel." *The Monitor, Designed to Improve the Taste, the Understanding and the Heart* 1 (January 1823): 13–18.

Blankert, Albert, et. al. *Gods, Saints and Heroes: Dutch Painting in the Age of Rembrandt.* Washington, D.C.: National Gallery, 1980.

Boase, T. S. R. "Macklin and Bowyer." *Journal of the Warburg and Courtauld Institutes* 26 (1963), 148–77.

Bode, John R. *The Protestant Clergy and Public Issues, 1812–1848.* Princeton: Princeton University Press, 1954.

Boller, Paul F., Jr. *George Washington and Religion.* Dallas: Southern Methodist University Press, 1963.

Bolton, C. K. *The Athenaeum Centenary: The Influence and the History of the Boston Athenaeum from 1807 to 1907.* Boston: Boston Athenaeum, 1907.

Boston Athenaeum. *The Anthology Society: Journal of the Proceedings of the Society which Conducts the Monthly Anthology and Boston Review.* Boston: Boston Athenaeum, 1910.

Bowyer, T. H. *A Bibliographical Examination of the Earliest Editions of the Letters of Junius.* Charlottesville: University of Virginia, 1957.

Boyett, Tanya. "Thomas Handasyd Perkins: An Essay on Material Culture." *Old Time New England* 70 (1980): 45–62.

Bradstreet, Anne. *The Works of Anne Bradstreet.* Edited by Jeannine Hensley. Cambridge: Belknap Press of Harvard University Press, 1967.

Broadley, A. M. *Napoleon in Caricature.* 2 vols. London and New York: John Lane, 1911.

Bromley, Robert Anthony. *A Philosophical and Critical History of the Fine Arts.* 2 vols. London: 1793–95.

Brooke, John. *King George III.* New York: McGraw Hill, 1972.

Brooks, Van Wyck. *The Flowering of New England, 1815–1865.* 1936. Reprint. New York: Houghton Mifflin Co., 1981.

Brownson, Orestes. *Babylon is Falling.* Boston: J. R. Butts, 1837.

Brumm, Ursula. *American Thought and Religious Typology.* New Brunswick, N.J.: Rutgers University Press, 1970.

Buckminister, Joseph Stevens. "On the Dangers and Duties of Men of Letters." *Monthly Anthology* 7 (September 1809): 145–58.

———. "Rappel des Juifs." *Monthly Anthology* 5 (March 1808): 147–48.

Butler, Frederick. *Complete History of the United States of Amerrica.* 2 vols. Hartford, Conn., 1821.

Calleo, David P. "Coleridge on Napoleon." *Yale French Studies* 26 (1960–61): 83–93.

Calvin, John. *Commentaries on the Book of Daniel.* Vol. 1. Translated and edited by Thomas Myers. Grand Rapids, Michigan: Wm. B. Eerdmans, 1948.

Cameron, Kenneth Walter, ed. *Research Keys to the American Renaissance: Source Indexes of the Christian Examiner, The North American Review, . . .* Hartford, Conn. Transcendental Books, 1967.

Campbell, Lily B. *Shakespeare's "Histories".* San Marino, Calif. Huntington Library, 1947.

Carpenter, Ralph E., Jr. *The Arts and Crafts of Newport Rhode Island, 1640–1820.* Newport: The Preservation Society of Newport County, 1954.

Channing, Edward T. *Lectures Read to Seniors in Harvard College.* Boston: Ticknor and Fields, 1856.

Channing, George Gibbs. *Early Recollections of Newport.* Newport, R.I.: 1868.

Channing, Walter. "Reminiscences of Washington Allston." *Christian Register and Boston Observer,* 5 August 1843, p. 124.

Channing, William Ellery. *Analysis of the Character of Napoleon Bonaparte.* Boston, 1828.

———. "Loose Paragraphs." *Monthly Anthology* 1 (February 1804): 176–77.

———. *Remarks on the Rev. Dr. Worcester's Letter to the Reverend William E. Channing, on the Subject of Unitarianism in a Late Panoplist.* Boston, 1815.

———. *Remarks on the Rev. Dr. Worcester's Second Letter to Mr. Channing, on American Unitarianism.* Boston, 1815.

———. "Scraps from a Correspondent." *Monthly Anthology* 1 (December 1803): 59–62.

———. *A Sermon, Delivered in Boston, September 18, 1814.* Boston, 1814.

———. *A Sermon Preached in Boston, April 5, 1810, the Day of the Public Fast.* Boston, 1810.

Channing, William Henry, ed. *Memoir of William Ellery Channing, with Extracts from His Correspondence and Manuscripts.* 3 vols. Boston: Wm. Crosby and H. P. Nichols, 1848.

Cheever, G. B. Review of *Lectures on the Sacred Poetry of the Hebrews,* by Robert Lowth. *North American Review* 31 (October 1830): 337–79.

Cherry, Conrad. *God's New Israel: Religious Interpretations of American Destiny.* Englewood Cliffs, N.J.: Prentice Hall, 1971.

Christianson, Paul. *Reformers and Babylon: English Apocalyptic Visions from the Reformation to the Eve of the Civil War.* Toronto: University of Toronto Press, 1978.

Clarke, Sarah. "Our First Great Painter and His Works." *Atlantic Monthly* XV (February 1865): 129–40.

Coburn, Kathleen, and Winer, Bart, eds. *The Collected Works of Samuel Taylor Coleridge.* Vol. 4, *The Friend.* 2 parts. Edited by Barbara E. Rooke. Bollingen Series, 75. Princeton: Princeton University Press, 1969.

———. *The Collected Works of Samuel Taylor Coleridge.* Vol. 6, *The Lay Sermons.* Edited by R. H. White. Bollingen Series, 75. Princeton: Princeton University Press, 1972.

Colbert, Charles. " 'Each Little Hillock Hath a Tongue'—Phrenology and the Art of Hiram Powrs." *Art Bulletin* LXVIII (June 1986): 281–300.

Coleridge, Samuel Taylor. *Aids to Reflection.* Edited by Henry Nelson Coleridge. Introduction by James Marsh. 4th ed. London: William Pickering, 1839.

———. *Collected Letters of Samuel Taylor Coleridge.* Edited by Earl Leslie Griggs. 6 vols. Oxford: Clarendon Press, 1956–71.

———. *Specimens of the Table Talk of the Late Samuel Taylor Coleridge.* 2 vols. New York: Harper and Brothers, 1835.

Collins, William Wilkie, ed. *Memoirs of the Life of William Colllins.* 2 vols. London: Longman, 1848.

Connecticut Historical Society. "Joseph Steward and the Hartford Museum." *Bulletin* 18 (January–April 1953): 1–16.

Cooper, Helen A., ed. *John Trumbull: The Hand and Spirit of a Painter.* New Haven: Yale University Art Gallery, 1982.

Crawford, Alexander Wellington. *The Philosophy of F. H. Jacobi.* Cornell Studies in Philosophy, no. 6. New York: MacMillan, 1905.

Crawford, John Stephens. "The Classical Orator in Nineteenth Century Sculpture." *American Art Journal* 6 (November 1974): 56–72.

Curti, Merle. *The Growth of American Thought,* 3d. ed. New York: Harper and Row, 1964.

Dahl, Curtis. "The American School of Catastrophe." *American Quarterly* 11 (Fall 1959): 380–90.

Daiches, David. "The Influence of the Bible on English Literature." In *The Jews: Their Role in Civilization,* pp. 388–407. Edited by Louis Finkelstein, 4th ed. New York: Schocken Books, 1971.

Dana, Daniel. *A Discourse Delivered in Newburyport, July 4, 1814, in Commemoration of American Independence, and the Deliverance of Europe.* Newburyport, Mass: 1814.

Dana, Henry Wadsworth Longfellow. "Allston at Harvard 1796–1800; Allston in Cambridgeport 1830–1843." *Cambridge Historical Society Publications,* no. 29, *Proceedings for the Year 1943.* Cambridge, Mass: 1948, pp. 13–67.

Dana, Richard Henry. *Poems and Prose Writings.* 2 vols. 1849. Reprint. Upper Saddle River, N.J.: Literature House/Gregg Pres, 1970.

Dana, Richard Henry, Jr. *Preface to Lectures on Art, and Poems,* by Washington Allston. 1850. Reprint. Gainesville, Florida: Scholars' Facsimiles and Reprints, 1967.

Davidson, Abraham A. *The Eccentrics and Other American Visionary Painters.* New York: Dutton Paperback, 1978.

Davidson, James West. *The Logic of Millennial Thought: Eighteenth-Century New England.* New Haven: Yale University Press, 1977.

Davis, David Brion. "Some Themes of Counter-Subversion: An Analysis of Anti-Masonic, Anti-Catholic, and Anti-Mormon Literature." *Mississippi Valley Historical Review* 47 (September 1960): 205–24.

Dawley, Power Mills. *The Story of the General Theological Seminary: A Sesquicentenniel History, 1817–1967.* New York: Oxford University Press, 1969.

Dean, Winton. *Handel's Dramatic Oratories and Masques.* London: Oxford University Press, 1959.

Dearborn, H. A. S. "Allston's Feast of Belshazzar." *Knickerbocker* 24 (September 1844): 205–17.

Dickson, Harold E. "Artists as Showmen." *American Art Journal* 5 (May 1973): 4–17.

Dillenberger, Jane, and Taylor, Joshua C. *The Hand and the Spirit: Religious Art in America 1700–1900.* Berkeley, Calif.: University Art Museum, 1972.

Dillenberger, John. *Benjamin West: The Context of His Life's Work with Particular Attention to Painting with Religious Subject Matter.* San Antonio, Tex.: Trinity University Press, 1977.

———. *The Visual Arts and Christianity in America: The Colonial Period Through the Nineteenth Century.* Studies in the Humanities Series, No. 5. Chico, Calif.: Scholars Press, 1984.

Dodwell, C. R. *Painting in Europe: 800 to 1200.* The Pelican History of Art. Edited by Nikolaus Pevsner. Baltimore: Penguin Books, 1971.

Douglas, Ann. *The Feminization of American Culture.* New York: Alfred A. Knopf, 1977.

Duffy, John F., ed. *Coleridge's American Disciples: The Selected Correspondence of James Marsh.* Amherst: University of Massachusetts Press, 1973.

Dunlap, William. *Diary of William Dunlap.* 3 vols. New York: New York Historical Society, 1931.

———. *A History of the Rise and Progress of the Arts of Design in the United States.* Edited by Rita Weiss. 2 vols. 1834. Reprint. New York: Dover Publications, 1969.

Dunstan, A. C. "The German Influence on Coleridge." *Modern Language Review* 18 (April 1923): 183–201.

Durand, Asher B. Papers. New York Public Library, New York City.

Dwight, Timothy. *A Sermon Delivered in Boston, Sept. 16, 1813, before the American Board of Commissioners for Foreign Missions.* Boston, 1813.

Eitner, Lorenz, ed. *Neoclassicism and Romanticism, 1750–1850.* 2 vols. Sources and Documents in the History of Art Series. Edited by H. W. Janson. Englewood Cliffs, N. J.: Prentice Hall, 1970.

Elliott, Emory, ed. *Puritan Influences in American Literature.* Urbana: University of Illinois Press, 1979.

Elson, Ruth Miller. *Guardians of Tradition: American Schoolbooks of the Nineteenth Century.* Lincoln: University of Nebraska Press, 1964.

Emerson, Ralph Waldo. *The Journals and Miscellaneous Notebooks of Ralph Waldo Emerson.* Vol. 5, *1835–1838.* Edited by Merton M. Sealts, Jr. Cambridge: The Belknap Press of Harvard University Press, 1956.

Engell, James. *The Creative Imagination: Enlightenment to Romanticism.* Cambridge: Harvard University Press, 1981.

Erdman, David V. *Blake: Prophet Against Empire.* Rev. ed. Garden City, N.Y.: Doubleday Anchor Book, 1969.

Essick, Robert, and La Belle, Jenijoy, eds. *Night Thoughts, or The Complaint and The Consolation,* by Edward Young. Illustrated by William Blake. New York: Dover Publications, 1975.

Evans, Dorinda. *Benjamin West and His American Students.* Washington, D.C.: Smithsonian Institution, 1980.

Everett, Alexander H. *The Conduct of the Administration.* Stimpson and Clapp, 1832.

———. *A Discourse on the Progress and Limits of Social Improvement; Including a General Survey of the History of Civilization.* Boston: Charles Bowen, 1834.

———. "Exhibition of Pictures at the Boston Athenaeum." *North American Review* 31 (October 1830): 309–37.

Everett, C. W., ed. *The Letters of Junius.* London: Faber and Gwyer, 1927.

Everett, Edward. *Bulletin of the New England Art-Union,* no. 1 (1852), p. 3.

"Exhibition of Pictures at the Boston Athenaeum." *North American Review* 25 (July 1827): 227–30.

Feaver, William. *The Art of John Martin.* Oxford: Clarendon Press, 1975.

Felton, Craig, and Jordan, William B., eds. *Jusepe de Ribera, lo Spagnoletto: 1591–1652.*

Fort Worth, Tex.: Kimbell Art Museum, 1982.

"Fine Arts." *The New Monthly Magazine, and Universal Register,* 1 June 1819, pp. 452–53.

Fischer, David Hackett. *The Revolution of American Conservatism: The Federalist Party in the Era of Jeffersonian Democracy.* New York: Harper and Row, 1967.

Flagg, Jared B. *The Life and Letters of Washington Allston.* 1892. Reprint. New York: Benjamin Blom, 1969.

Fletcher, Angus. *Allegory: The Theory of a Symbolic Mode.* Ithaca, N.Y.: Cornell University Press, 1964.

Flexner, James Thomas. *America's Old Masters.* Rev. ed. Garden City, N.Y.: Doubleday, 1980.

Flint, James. *A Discourse Delivered . . . on the Anniversary Election, May 31, 1815.* Boston: Russel, Cutler and Co., 1815.

Foster, Charles I. *An Errand of Mercy: The Evangelical United Front, 1790–1837.* Chapel Hill: University of North Carolina Press, 1960.

Freeman, James. *A Discourse on the Russian Victories, Given in King's Chapel, March 25, 1813.* Introuction by Henry Wilder Foote. Cambridge, Mass.: John Wilson and Son, 1881.

Fruchtman, Jack, Jr. "Politics and the Apocalypse: The Republic and the Millennium in Late Eighteenth-Century English Political Thought." In *Studies in Eighteenth-Century Culture,* Vol. X, pp. 153–64. Edited by Harry C. Payne. Madison: University of Wisconsin Press, 1981.

Fuller, Margaret. *Papers of Literature and Art.* New York: Wiley and Putnam, 1846.

Gallaway, Francis. *Reason, Rule, and Revolt in English Classicism.* 1940. Reprint. New York: Octagon Books, 1965.

Gear, Josephine. *Masters or Servants? A Study of Selected English Painters and their Patrons of the Late Eighteenth and Early Nineteenth Centuries.* New York: Garland Publishing, 1977.

Gerdts, William H. "Allston's 'Belshazzar's Feast'." *Art in America* 61 (March–April 1973): 59–66.

———. "Belshazzar's Feast II: 'That is his shroud'." *Art in America* 61 (May–June 1973): 58–65.

———. "Washington Allston and the German Romantic Classicists in Rome." *Art Quarterly* 32 (Summer 1969): 167–96.

Gerdts, William H., and Stebbins, Theodore E., Jr. "A Man of Genius": The Art of Washington Allston (1779–1843). Boston: Museum of Fine Arts, 1979.

Geertz, Clifford. "Art as a Cultural System." *MLN [Modern Language Notes]* 91 (1976): 1473–99.

———. *The Interpretation of Cultures.* New York: Basic Books, 1973.

Gilmore, Michael T. *The Middle Way: Puritanism and Ideology in American Fiction.* New Brunswick, N.J.: Rutgers University Press, 1977.

Glanz, Dawn. *How the West was Drawn: American Art and the Settling of the Frontier.* Studies in the Fine Arts: Iconography, No. 6. Ann Arbor, Mich.: UMI Research Press, 1982.

Glazer, Nathan. *American Judaism.* 2d ed. Chicago: University of Chicago Press, 1972.

Goethals, Martha Gregor T. "A Comparative Study in the Theory and Work of Washington Allston, Thomas Cole, and Horatio Greenough." Ph.D. dissertation, Harvard University, 1966.

Goldsmith, Oliver. *The Captivity: An Oratorio.* New York: G. Schirmer, 1890.

Gordenstein, Arnold Selig. "Washington Allston and the Psychology of Federalism." Ph.D. dissertation, Harvard University, 1968.

Graham, Walter James. *Tory Criticism in "The Quarterly Review," 1809–1853.* New York: Columbia University Press, 1921.

Graves, Algernon. *The British Institution, 1806–1867: A Complete Dictionary of Contributors and their Work from the Foundation of the Institution.* London: George Bell and Sons, 1908.

———. *The Royal Academy of Arts: A Complete Dictionary of Contributors and their Work from its Foundation to 1904.* 8 vols. London: Henry Graves and Co., 1906.

Greenewald, Gerard M. *Shakespeare's Attitude Towards the Catholic Church in "King John."* Washington, D.C.: Catholic University of America, 1938.

Greenough, Henry. "Allston's Feast of Belshazzar—No. 2." *Boston Post,* 25 July 1844, p. 1.

———. "Remarks on Allston's Belshazzar." *Boston Post,* 10 June 1844, p. 1.

Gribbin, William. *The Churches Militant: The War of 1812 and American Religion.* New Haven: Yale University Press, 1973.

Groves, Joseph A. *Tha Alstons and Allstons of North and South Carolina.* Atlanta: Franklin Printing and Publishing Co., 1901.

Gunn, Giles, ed. *The Bible and American Arts and Letters*. Society of Biblical Literature: The Bible in American Culture Series. Edited by Edwin S. Gaustad and Walter Harrelson. Philadelphia: Fortress Press and Chico, Calif.: Scholars Press, 1983.

Hall, Peter Dobkin. *The Organization of American Culture, 1700–1900: Private Institutions, Elites, and the Origins of American Nationality*. New York: New York University Press, 1982.

Handel, Georg Friedrich. *Belshazzar. An Oratorio*. London: J. Watts, 1745.

———. *Belshazzar. An Oratorio Composed in the Year 1744*. London: Sacred Harmonic Society, 1885.

Handlin, Oscar. *Boston's Immigrants: A Study in Acculturation*. Rev. ed. Cambridge: Belknap Press of Harvard University Press, 1969.

Harap, Louis. *The Image of the Jew in American Literature: From Early Republic to Mass Immigration*. Philadelphia: The Jewish Publication Society of America, 1974.

Harding, Chester. *My Egotistigraphy*. Cambridge, Mass.: John Wilson and Son, 1866.

Haroutunian, Joseph. *Piety Versus Moralism: The Passing of the New England Theology*. New York: Henry Holt, 1932.

Harper, Robert Goodloe. *Speech of Robert Goodloe Harper, Esq. at the Celebration of the Recent Triumphs of the Cause of Mankind, in Germany*. New Haven, 1814.

Harris, Neil. *The Artist in American Society: The Formative Years, 1790–1860*. New York: Simon and Schuster: A Clarion Book, 1970.

Harris, R. W. *Political Ideas: 1760–1792*. London: Victor Gollancz, 1963.

Harrison, J. F. C. *The Second Coming: Popular Millenarianism, 1780–1850*. New Brunswick, N.J.: Rutgers University Press, 1979.

Hatch, Nathan. *The Sacred Cause of Liberty: Republican Thought and the Millennium in Revolutionary New England*. New Haven: Yale University Press, 1977.

Hatch, Nathon O., and Noll, Mark A., eds. *The Bible in America: Essays in Cultural History*. New York: Oxford University Press, 1982.

Heckscher, William S. *Art and Literature: Studies in Relationship*. Durham, N.C.: Duke University Press, 1985.

Henkel, Arthur and Schöne, Albrecht, eds. *Emblemeta: Handbuch zur Sinnbildskunst des XVI and XVII Jahrhunderts*. Stuttgart: J. B. Metzlersche, Verlagsbuchhandlung, 1967.

Herder, Johann Gottfried. *Spirit of Hebrew Poetry*. Translated by James Marsh. 2 vols. Burlington, Vermont: Edward Smith, 1830.

Hill, Christopher. *The Century of Revolution: 1603–1714*. The Norton Library History of England. Edited by Christopher Brooke and Denis Mack Smith. New York: W. W. Norton, 1966.

Holmes, Abiel. *A Sermon Delivered at Cambridge, 30 September 1804. . . .* Cambridge, Mass.: University Press, 1804.

———. *A Sermon on the Freedom and Happiness of America; Preached at Cambridge, February 19, 1795. . . .* Boston: Samuel Hall, 1795.

———. *Two Discourses, on the Completion of the Second Century from the Landing of the Forefathers of New England at Plymouth, 22 December 1620, Delivered at Cambridge, 24 December 1820*. Cambridge: Hilliard and Metcalf, 1821.

Holmes, Oliver Wendell. "Exhibition of Pictures Painted by W. Allston at Harding's Gallery, School Street." *North American Review* 50 (April 1840): 358–81.

Holt, Elizabeth Gilmore. "Revivalist Themes in American Prints and Folksongs, 1830–50." In *American Printmaking before 1876: Fact, Fiction and Fantasy*, pp. 34–46. Papers presented at a symposium at the Library of Congress, June 12–13, 1972. Washington, D.C.: Library of Congress, 1975.

Honour, Hugh. *Romanticism*. New York: Harper and Row, 1979.

Hooker, Edward W. "Political Duties of Christians, as Exhibited in the Bible." *American Quarterly Observer* 1 (July 1833): 1–25.

Hopkins, Kenneth. *English Poetry*. London: Phoenix House, 1962.

Hovenkamp, Herbert. *Science and Religion in America, 1800–1860*. Philadelphia: University of Pennsylvania Press, 1978.

Howe, Daniel Walker. *The Political Culture of the American Whigs*. Chicago: University of Chicago Press, 1979.

———. *The Unitarian Conscience: Harvard Moral Philosophy, 1805–1861*. Cambridge: Harvard University Press, 1970.

Hughes, Thomas Smart. *Belshazzar's Feast*. Cambridge: J. Deighton and Sons, 1818.

Hunter, Doreen. "America's First Romantics: Richard Henry Dana, Sr. and Washington Allston." *New England Quarterly* 45 (March 1972):3–30.

Huntington, David Carew. *Art and the Excited Spirit: America in the Romantic Period*. Ann

Arbor: University of Michigan Museum of Art, 1972.

Hutchison, William R. *The Transcendentalist Ministers: Church Reform in the New England Renaissance.* New Haven: Yale University Press, 1959.

The Interpreter's Dictionary of the Bible. 4 vols. Nashville and New York: Abingdon Press, 1962.

Irving, Pierre. *The Life and Letters of Washington Irving.* 4 vols. 1862–64. Reprint. Detroit: Gale Research Co., 1967.

Irving, Washington. "Memoir of Washington Allston." In *The Complete Works of Washington Irving.* Edited by Richard Dilworth Rust. Vol. 2, *Miscellaneous Writings, 1803–1859*, pp. 173–78. Edited by Wayne R. Kame. Boston: Twayne Publishers, 1981.

Jacob, Margaret C. *The Newtonians and the English Revolution, 1689–1720.* Ithaca, N.Y.: Cornell University Press, 1976.

Jameson, Anna Brownell. *Studies, Stories, and Memoirs.* Boston: James R. Osgood, 1875.

Johns, Elizabeth. "Washington Allston: Method, Imagination, and Reality." *Winterthur Portfolio* 12 (1977): 1–18.

———. "Washington Allston and Samuel Taylor Coleridge: A Remarkable Relationship." *Archives of American Art Journal* 19, no. 3 (1979): 2–7.

———. "Washington Allston's "Dead Man Revived"." *Art Bulletin* 61 (March 1979): 79–99.

———. "Washington Allston's Later Career: Art About the Making of Art." *Arts Magazine* 54 (December 1979): 122–29.

———. "Washington Allston's Library." *American Art Journal* 7 (November 1975): 32–41.

———. Washington Allston's Theory of the Imagination." Ph.D. dissertation. Emory University, 1974.

Jones, M. G. *Hannah More.* Cambridge: Cambridge University Press, 1952.

Kasson, Joy S. *Artistic Voyagers: Europe and the American Imagination in the Works of Irving, Allston, Cole, Cooper, and Hawthorne.* Westport, Conn.: Greenwood Press, 1982.

Kerber, Linda K. *Federalists in Dissent: Imagery and Ideology in Jeffersonian America.* Ithaca, N.Y.: Cornell University Press, 1970.

Knapp, John. "Lines on the Death of David Tappan." *Monthly Anthology* 1 (February 1804): 181–82.

Knapp, Samuel Lorenzo. *Sketches of Public Characters.* New York: E. Bliss, 1830.

Kobler, Franz. *Napoleon and the Jews.* Jerusalem: Massada Press, 1975.

Koenigsberger, H. G., and Mosse, George L. *Europe in the Sixteenth Century.* A General History of Europe. Edited by Denis Hay. London: Longman Paperback, 1971.

Kohn, Hans. *The Idea of Nationalism: A Study in its Origins and Background.* Toronto: Collier Books, 1967.

Kraines, Oscar. "The Holmes Tradition." *Publication of the American Jewish Society* 42 (June 1953): 341–59.

Lavater, J. C. *Essays on Physiognomy; for the Promotion of the Knowledge and the Love of Mankind.* Translated by Thomas Holcroft. 3 vols. London: G. G. J. and J. Robinson, 1789.

Lee, Eliza Buckminster, ed. *Memoirs of Rev. Joseph Buckminster, D. D., and of His Son, Rev. Joseph Stevens Buckminster.* Boston: Wm. Crosby and H. P. Nichols, 1849.

Leslie, Charles Robert. *Autobiographical Recollections.* Edited by Tom Taylor. 2 vols. London: John Murray, 1860.

Lester, C. Edwards. *The Artists of America: A Series of Biographical Sketches of American Artists.* New York: Baker and Scribner, 1846.

Library Charging List. Harvard University Archives, Pusey Library, Cambridge, Mass.

Livermore, Shaw, Jr. *The Twilight of Federalism: The Disintegration of the Federalist Party, 1815–1830.* Princeton: Princeton University Press, 1962.

Lloyd, Phoebe. "Washington Allston: American Martyr?" *Art in America* 72 (March 1984): 145–55, 177.

Lockridge, Laurence S. *Coleridge the Moralist.* Ithaca, N.Y.: Cornell University Press, 1977.

London, Hannah R. *Miniatures of Early American Jews.* Rutland, Vermont: Charles E. Tuttle Co., 1970.

———. *Portraits of Jews by Gilbert Stuart and Other Early American Artists.* New York: William Edwin Rudge, 1927.

London *Times*, 6 April–30 June, 1814.

Longfellow, Henry Wadsworth. "The Jewish Cemetery at Newport," in *The New Oxford Book of American Verse.* Edited by Richard Ellman. New York: Oxford University Press, 1976.

Lovejoy, Arthur O. *Essays in the History of Ideas.* Baltimore: Johns Hopkins Press, 1948.

Lowth, Robert. *Lectures on the Sacred Poetry of the Hebrews.* Translated by G. Gregory. London: S. Chadwick, 1847.

Lunt, William Parsons. "Belshazzar's Feast." *Christian Examiner* 37 (July 1844): 49–57.

Lyons, Donald H. *A Brief History of St. Paul's Cathedral.* Boston: St. Paul's, n.d.

McFarland, Thomas. *Romanticism and the Forms of Ruin: Wordsworth, Coleridge and Modalities of Fragmentation.* Princeton: Princeton University Press, 1981.

McKenzie, Alexander. *Lectures on the History of the First Church in Cambridge.* Boston: Congregational Publishing Society, 1873.

McLanathan, Richard. *Gilbert Stuart.* The Library of American Art Series. Edited by Teresa Egan. New York: Harry N. Abrams, 1986.

McLoughlin, William G. *Revivals, Awakenings, and Reform: An Essay on Religion and Social Change in America, 1607–1977.* Chicago: University of Chicago Press, 1978.

Magoon, E. L. *Living Orators in America.* New York: Charles Scribner, 1851.

Mainwarning, Marion. *John Quincy Adams and Russia: A Sketch of Early Russian-American Relations as Recorded in the Papers of the Adams Family and Some of Their Contemporaries.* Quincy, Mass.: Patriot Ledger, 1965.

Marsden, George M. *The Evangelical Mind and the New School Presbyterian Experience.* New Haven: Yale University Press, 1970.

Marsh, James. *An Address Delivered in Burlington upon the Inauguration of the Author to the Office of President of the University of Vermont, November 28, 1826.* Burlington: E. and T. Mills, 1826.

Martin, Terence. *The Instructed Vision: Scottish Common Sense Philosophy and the Origins of American Fiction.* Bloomington: Indiana University Press, 1961.

Maser, Edward A., trans. and ed. *Baroque and Rococo Pictorial Imagery: The 1758–60 Hertel Edition of Ripa's "Iconologia".* Dover Pictorial Archive Series. New York: Dover Publications, 1971.

Mathews, Donald G. "The Second Great Awakening as an Organizing Process, 1780–1830: An Hypothesis." *American Quarterly* 21 (Spring 1969): 23–43.

Mead, Sidney. *Nathanial William Taylor, 1786–1858: A Connecticut Liberal.* Chicago: University of Chicago Press, 1942.

Meiss, Millard. "An Illuminated Inferno and Trecento Painting in Pisa." *Art Bulletin* 47 (March 1965): 21–34.

Meyer, D. H. *The Instructed Conscience: The Shaping of the American National Ethic.* Philadelphia: University of Pennsylvania Press, 1972.

Meyer, Jerry D. "Benjamin West's Chapel of Revealed Religion: A Study in Eighteenth-Century Protestant Religious Art." *Art Bulletin* 57 (June 1975): 247–65.

———. "Benjamin West's 'St. Stephan Altarpiece': A Study in Late Eighteenth-Century Protestant Church Patronage and English History Painting." *Burlington Magazine* 118 (September 1976): 634–43.

———. "The Religious Paintings of Benjamin West: A Study in Late Eighteenth and Early Nineteenth Century Moral Sentiment." Ph.D. dissertation. New York University, 1973.

Miller, John C. *The Federalist Era, 1789–1801.* The New American Nation Series. Edited by Henry Steele Commager and Richard B. Morris. New York: Harper Colophon Books, 1960.

Miller, Lillian B. *Patrons and Patriotism: The Encouragement of the Fine Arts in the United States, 1790–1860.* Chicago: University of Chicago Press, 1966.

Miller, Perry. "From the Covenant to the Revival." In *The Shaping of American Religion,* pp. 322–68. Edited by James Ward Smith and A. Leland Jamison. Princeton: Princeton University Press, 1961.

———. "The Garden of Eden and the Deacon's Meadow." *American Heritage* 7 (December 1955): 54–61, 102.

———. *The Life of the Mind in America: From the Revolution to the Civil War.* New York: Harcourt, Brace and World; Harvest Book, 1965.

Minter, David. "The Puritan Jeremiad as a Literary Form." In *The American Puritan Imagination: Essays in Revaluation,* pp. 45–55. Edited by Sacvan Bercovitch. Cambridge: Cambridge University Press, 1974.

More, Hannah. *The Works of Hannah More.* Vol. 1, *Sacred Dramas—Poems.* London: T. Cadell, Strand, 1830.

Morgan, Edmund S. *The Puritan Family: Religion and Domestic Relations in Seventeenth-Century New England.* Rev. ed. New York: Harper Torchbooks, 1966.

Morison, Samuel Eliot. *Harrison Gray Otis, 1765–1848: The Urbane Federalist.* Boston: Houghton Mifflin, 1969.

———. *Three Centuries of Harvard, 1636–1936.*

Cambridge: Harvard University Press, 1936.

Morris, David B. *The Religious Sublime: Christian Poetry and Critical Tradition in 18th Century England.* Lexington: University of Kentucky Press, 1972.

Morse, Edward Lind, ed. *Samuel F. B. Morse. His Letters and Journals.* 2 vols. Boston: Houghton Mifflin, 1914.

Morse, Jedidiah. "Correspondence." *Monthly Anthology* 2 (December 1805): 670–74.

Morse, Samuel F. B. *Foreign Conspiracy Against the United States.* 4th ed. New York: Van Nostrand and Dwight, 1836.

———. Papers. Library of Congress, Washington, D.C.

Mosse, George L. *The Culture of Western Europe: The Nineteenth and Twentieth Centuries.* Rand McNally History Series. Edited by Fred Harvey Harrington. New York: Rand McNally, 1961.

Mott, Frank Luther. *A History of American Magazines.* Vol. 1, *1741–1850.* Cambridge: Harvard University Press, 1938.

Nagel, Paul C. *This Sacred Trust: American Nationality, 1798–1898.* New York: Oxford University Press, 1971.

Nash, Gary B. "The American Clergy and the French Revolution." *The William and Mary Quarterly* 22 (July 1965): 392–412.

Nash, Roderick. *Wilderness and the American Mind.* Rev. ed. New Haven: Yale University Press, 1973.

National Gallery, London. *Venetian Seventeenth Century Painting.* London: National Gallery, 1979.

Neal, John. *American Writers: A Series of Papers Contributed to Blackwood's Magazine (1824–1825).* Edited by Fred Lewis Patee. Durham, N.C.: Duke University Press, 1937.

———. *Randolph, a Novel.* 2 vols. N.p., 1823.

Newton, Thomas. *Dissertations on the Prophecies.* Vol. 1. London: R. Baynes, et al. 1820.

Nisbet, Robert. *History of the Idea of Progress.* New York: Basic Books, 1980.

Novak, Barbara. *Nature and Culture: American Landscape and Painting, 1825–1875.* New York: Oxford University Press, 1980.

Nye, Russel Blaine. *The Cultural Life of the New Nation, 1776–1830.* The New American Nation Series. Edited by Henry Steele Commager and Richard B. Morris. New York: Harper Torchbooks, 1960.

Odell, George C. D. *Annals of the New York Stage.* 15 vols. New York: Columbia University Press, 1927–49.

Oliver, W. H. *Prophets and Millennialists: The Uses of Biblical Prophecy in England from the 1790s to the 1840s.* Oxford: Oxford University Press, 1978.

Opie, John. *Lectures on Painting Delivered at the Royal Academy.* London: Longman, et al., 1809.

"Original Letters. No. 3." *Monthly Anthology* 2 (October 1805): 502.

Paine, Thomas. *Age of Reason.* New York: Willey Book Co., n.d.

Paley, Morton D. *The Apocalyptic Sublime.* New Haven: Yale University Press, 1986.

Parry, Elwood C., III. "Thomas Cole and the Problem of Figure Painting." *American Art Journal* 4 (Spring 1972): 66–86.

Patterson, Frank Allen, ed. *The Works of John Milton.* 18 vols. New York: Columbia University Press, 1931–38.

Paulson, Ronald. *Hogarth: His Life, Art and Times.* 2 vols. New Haven: Yale University Press, 1971.

Peabody, Elizabeth Palmer. *Last Evening With Allston, and Other Papers.* Boston: D. Lothrop, 1886.

———. *Reminiscences of Rev. Wm. Ellery Channing.* Boston: Roberts Brothers, 1880.

Peck, George W. "Monaldi." *American Review: A Whig Journal* 7 (April 1848): 341–57.

Perkins, Charles C., and Dwight, John S. *History of the Handel and Haydn Society of Boston, Massachusetts.* Boston: Alfred Mudge and Son, 1883–93.

Perkins, Robert F., Jr., and Gavin, William J., III, eds. *The Boston Athenaeum Art Exhibition Index, 1827–1874.* Boston: Library of the Boston Athenaeum, 1980.

Philips, Adam, ed. *Charles Lamb: Selected Prose.* Harmondsworth, Middlesex, England: Penguin Books, 1985.

Pigler, Andor. *Barockthemen.* 2 vols. Budapest: Verlag der Ungarischen Akademie der Wissenschaften, 1956.

Piwonka, Ruth, and Blackburn, Roderic H. *A Remnant in the Wilderness: New York Dutch Scripture History Paintings of the Early Eighteenth Century.* Albany: Albany Institute of History and Art, 1980.

Podmaniczky, Christine Bauer. "Benjamin West's 'Daniel Interpreting to Belshazzar the Writing on the Wall.' " Unpublished manuscript. Berkshire Museum, Pittsfield, Mass.

Popkin, John Snelling. *A Discourse Delivered on the National Thanksgiving for Peace, April 13,*

1815. Newburyport, Mass.: W. B. Allen, 1815.

Praz, Mario. *The Romantic Agony.* Translated by Angus Davidson. 2d ed. 1951. Reprint. Oxford: Oxfored University Press, 1970.

Prown, Jules D. "The Sisters by Washington Allston." In *The Annual Report of the Fogg Art Museum,* pp. 45–48. Cambridge: Harvard University Press, 1956–57.

Quincy, Josiah. *The History of the Boston Athenaeum with Biographical Notices of the Deceased Founders.* Cambridge: Metcalf and Co., 1851.

Quincy, Josiah P., ed. "Letters of Miss Anna Cabot Lowell." *Massachusetts Historical Society, Proceedings* 18 (May 1904): 302–17.

Redway, Virginia Larkin. "Handel in Colonial and Post–Colonial America (to 1820)." *Musical Quarterly* 21 (1935): 190–207.

Remini, Robert V. *Andrew Jackson and the Course of Empire, 1767–1821.* New York: Harper and Row, 1977.

Review of *The Christian Examiner.* In *Spirit of the Pilgrims* 3 (October 1830): 544–45.

Review of *Discourses on the Christian Spirit,* by C. A. Bartol. *Literary World,* 17 November 1849, pp. 420–21.

Review of Ware's *Lectures* on Allston. *Literary World,* 16 October 1852, pp. 245–46.

Reynolds, David S. "From Doctrine to Narrative: The Rise of Pulpit Storytelling in America." *American Quarterly* 32 (Winter 1980): 479–98.

Richardson, E. P. *Washington Allston: A Study of the Romantic Artist in America.* Chicago: University of Chicago Press, 1948.

Richardson, Jonathan. *The Works of Jonathan Richardson.* London: T. and J. Egerton, 1792.

Robb, David M., Jr. "Benjamin West's 'The Death of the Earl of Chatham'." Paper presented at the Seventy-first Annual Meeting of the College Art Association, 1983.

Robbins, Caroline. *The Eighteenth-Century Commonwealthmen.* Cambridge: Harvard University Press, 1959.

Robinson, Henry Crabb. *Diary, Reminiscences, and Correspondence.* Edited by Thomas Sadler. 2d ed. 3 vols. London: Macmillan and Co., 1869.

Rollin, Charles. *The Ancient History of the Egyptians, Carthaginians, Assyrians, Babylonians, Medes and Persians, Macedonians and Grecians.* 6th ed. 8 vols. London: J. and F. Rivington, et al., 1774.

Rose, Anne C. *Transcendentalism as a Social Movement, 1830–1850.* New Haven: Yale University Press, 1981.

Rosenberg, Jakob. *Rembrandt: Life and Work.* Rev. ed. London: Phaidon press, 1964.

Roston, Murray. *Prophet and Poet: The Bible and the Growth of Romanticism.* Evanston, Ill.: Northwestern University Press, 1965.

Sabine, James. *The Relation the Present State of Religion Bears to the Expected Millennium.* Boston: Crocker and Brewster, 1823.

Sandeen, Ernest R. *The Roots of Fundamentalism: British and American Millenarianism, 1800–1930.* Chicago: University of Chicago Press, 1970.

Sands, Mollie. "Oliver Goldsmith and Music." *Music and Letters* 32 (April 1951): 147–53.

Sanford, Charles L. *The Quest for Paradise: Europe and the American Moral Imagination.* Urbana: University of Illinois Press, 1961.

Schapiro, Meyer. "The Beatus Apocalypse of Gerona." *Art News* 61 (January 1963): 36, 49–50.

Scharf, Frederic Alan. "Art and Life in Boston, 1837 to 1850: A Study of the Painter and Sculptor in American Society." Unpublished manuscript. Archives of American Art, Washington, D.C., n.d.

Schlesinger, Arthur M., Jr. *The Age of Jackson.* Boston: Little, Brown and Co., 1945.

Scott, Donald M. *From Office to Profession: The New England Ministry, 1750–1850.* Philadelphia: University of Pennsylvania Press, 1978.

Scott, Rev. W. A. *Daniel, a Model for Young Men.* New York: Robert Carter and Brothers, 1854.

Scult, Mel. *Millennial Expectations and Jewish Liberties: A Study of the Efforts to Convert the Jews in Britain, up to the Mid-Nineteenth Century.* Leiden: E. J. Brill, 1978.

Seaburg, Carl, and Paterson, Stanley. *Merchant Prince of Boston: Colonel T. H. Perkins, 1764–1854.* Cambridge: Harvard University Press, 1971.

Sellars, Charles Coleman. *Patience Wright: American Artist and Spy in George III's London.* Middletown, Conn. Wesleyan University Press, 1976.

Sellin, David. *American Art in the Making: Preparatory Studies for Masterpieces of American Painting, 1800–1900.* Washington, D.C.: Smithsonian Institution Press, 1976.

Silverman, Kenneth. *A Cultural History of the American Revolution.* New York: Thomas Y. Crowell, 1976.

Simpson, Lewis P. *The Man of Letters in New*

England and the South: Essays on the History of the Literary Vocation in America. Baton Rouge: Louisiana State University Press, 1973.

————, ed. *The Federalist Literary Mind: Selections from the Monthly Anthology and Boston Review, 1803–1811.* Baton Rouge: Louisiana State University Press, 1962.

Sisson, Daniel. *The American Revolution of 1800.* New York: Alfred A. Knopf, 1974.

Smith, Timothy L. "Righteousness and Hope: Christian Holiness and the Millennial Vision in America, 1800–1900." *American Quarterly* 31 (Spring 1979): 21–45.

Smolden, W. L., ed. *The Play of Daniel: A Medieval Liturgical Drama.* London: The Faith Press, 1960.

Smylie, James H. "Protestant Clergy, the First Amendment and Beginnings of a Constitutional Debate, in 1781–91." In *The Religion of the Republic,* pp. 116–53. Edited by Elwyn A. Smith. Philadelphia: Fortress Press, 1971.

Somkin, Fred. *Unquiet Eagle: Memory and Desire in the Idea of American Freedom, 1815–1860.* Ithaca, N.Y.: Cornell University Press, 1967.

Spear, Thomas T. *Description of the Grand Historical Picture of Belshazzar's Feast by Washington Allston. . . .* Boston: Eastburn's Press, 1846.

Staley, Allen. "West's 'Death on the Pale Horse'." *Bulletin of the Detroit Institute of Arts* 58 (1980): 137–49.

Stauffer, Vernon. *New England and the Bavarian Illuminati.* New York: Columbia University Press, 1918.

Stewart, Dugald. *Philosophical Essays.* 2d ed. Edinburgh, 1816.

Story, Ronald. "Class and Culture in Boston: The Athenaeum, 1807–1860." *American Quarterly* 27 (May 1975): 190–99.

————. *The Forging of an Aristocracy: Harvard and the Boston Upper Class, 1800–1870.* Middletown, Conn.: Wesleyan University Press, 1980.

Story, William Wetmore. "Athenaeum Gallery—Allston's Belshazzar." *Harbinger* 5 July 1845, pp. 55–58.

Strauch, Carl F. "Emerson's Phi Beta Kappa Poem." *New England Quarterly* 23 (March 1950): 65–90.

Strazdes, Diana. "Washington Allston's Early Career, 1796–1811." Ph.D. dissertation, Yale University, 1982.

Strong, Roy. *Recreating the Past: British History*

and the Victorian Painter. New York: The Pierpont Morgan Library, 1978.

Sumner, Charles. "The Scholar, the Jurist, the Artist, the Philanthropist. An Oration before the Phi Beta Kappa Society of Harvard University, at their Anniversary, August 27, 1846." In *The Works of Charles Sumner,* vol. 1, pp. 241–302. Boston: Lee and Shepard, 1874.

Swan, Mabel Munson. *The Athenaeum Gallery, 1827–1873: The Boston Athenaeum as an Early Patron of Art.* Boston: Boston Athenaeum, 1940.

Sweetser, M. F. *Allston.* Boston: Houghton, Osgood and Co., 1879.

Tappan, David. *Lectures on Jewish Antiquities.* Boston: W. Hilliard and E. Lincoln, 1807.

Thayer, William Roscoe, ed. "Journal of Benjamin Waterhouse." *Cambridge Historical Society Publications,* no. 4, *Proceedings,* January 26–October 26, 1909, pp. 22–37.

Thomas, Milton Halsey, ed. *Elias Boudinot's Journey to Boston in 1809.* Princeton: Princeton University Library, 1955.

Thompson, E. P. *The Making of the English Working Class.* New York: Vintage Books, 1963.

Thornton, John Wingate, ed. *The Pulpit of the American Revolution or, the Political Sermons of the Period of 1776.* 2d ed. Boston: D. Lothrop and Co., 1876.

Tietze, Hans. *Tintoretto.* New York: Phaidon Press, 1948.

Tomkins, J. M. S. *The Popular Novel in England, 1770–1800.* 1932. Reprint. Lincoln: University of Nebraska Press, 1961.

Troyen, Carol. *The Boston Tradition: American Paintings from the Museum of Fine Art, Boston.* New York: The American Federation of Arts, 1980.

Tuchman, Barbara W. *Bible and Sword: England and Palestine from the Bronze Age to Balfour.* New York: New York University Press, 1956.

Tuckerman, Henry. *Artist-Life: Or Sketches of American Painters.* New York: D. Appleton, 1847.

Tudor, William, Jr. "An Address Delivered to the Phi Beta Kappa Society, at their Anniversary Meeting in Cambridge." *North American Review* 2 (November 1815): 13–32.

————. "Institution for the Fine Arts." *North American Review* 2 (January 1816): 153–64.

————. *Letters on the Eastern States.* 2d ed. Boston: Wells and Lilly, 1821.

————. Review of *A General History of New England from the Discovery to 1680,* by Rev.

William Hubbard. *North American Review* 2 (January 1816): 221–30.

Tuveson, Ernest Lee. *Redeemer Nation: The Idea of America's Millennial Role.* Chicago: University of Chicago Press, 1968.

Tyack, David B. *George Ticknor and the Boston Brahmins.* Cambridge: Harvard University Press, 1967.

Vaughan, William. *German Romanticism and English Art.* New Haven: Yale University Press, 1979.

Verplanck, Gulian C. *Discourses and Addresses on Subjects of American History, Arts, and Literature.* New York: J. and J. Harper, 1833.

———. *Essays on the Nature and Uses of the Various Evidences of Revealed Religion.* New York: Charles Wiley, 1824.

———. Papers, New York Historical Society, New York, N.Y.

———, ed. *Shakespeare's Plays: With His Life.* Vol. 1, *Histories.* New York: Harper and Bros., 1847.

von Erffa, Helmut, and Staley, Allen. *The Paintings of Benjamin West.* New Haven: Yale University Press, 1986.

Walch, Peter S. "Charles Rollin and Early Neoclassicism." *Art Bulletin* 49 (June 1967): 123–26.

———. "French Eighteenth-Century Oil Sketches from an English Collection." *New Mexico Studies in the Fine Arts* 5 (1980).

Wallach, Alan. "Thomas Cole and the Aristocracy." *Arts Magazine* 56 (November 1981): 94–106.

Walter, Arthur Maynard. Introduction to "Original Letters." *Monthly Anthology* 2 (August 1805): 399–400.

Walzer, Michael. *The Revolution of the Saints: A Study in the Origin of Radical Politics.* New York: Athenaeum, 1968.

Ward, John William. *Andrew Jackson: Symbol for an Age.* New York: Oxford University Press, 1962.

Ware, William. *Lectures on the Works and Genius of Washington Allston.* Boston: Phillips, Sampson and Co., 1852.

Washington Monument Association Report, Boston, December 15, 1818. By John Lowell, Chairman. Boston Public Library, Boston.

Waterhouse, Benjamin. *An Essay on Junius and His Letters; Embracing a Sketch of William Pitt, Earl of Chatham.* Boston: Gray and Brown, 1831.

Wecter, Dixon. *The Hero in America: A Chronicle of Hero Worship.* Ann Arbor: University of Michigan Press, 1963.

Welsh, John R. "An Anglo-American Friendship: Allston and Coleridge." *Journal of American Studies* 5 (April 1971): 81–91.

White, Morton. *Science and Sentiment in America: Philosophical Thought from Jonathan Edwards to John Dewey.* New York: Oxford University Press, 1972.

Willey, Basil. *Nineteenth Century Studies: Coleridge to Matthew Arnold.* New York: Columbia University Press, 1949.

———. *The Seventeenth Century Background.* Garden City, N.Y.: Doubleday Anchor Books, 1953.

Williams, George H. *Wilderness and Paradise in Christian Thought.* New York: Harper and Brothers, 1962.

Wilson, James Grant. *Bryant and His Friends: Some Reminiscences of the Knickerbocker Writers.* New York: Fords, Howard, and Hulbert, 1886.

Winston, George P. "Washington Allston and the Objective Correlative." *Bucknell Review* 11 (December 1962): 95–108.

Winthrop, Robert Charles, Jr. *Memoir of the Honorable David Sears.* Cambridge, Mass.: John Wilson, 1886.

Wolf, Bryan Jay. *Romantic Re-Vision: Culture and Consciousness in Nineteenth-Century American Painting and Literature.* Chicago: The University of Chicago Press, 1982.

Woodring, Carl. *Politics in English Poetry.* Cambridge: Harvard University Press, 1970.

Worcester, Samuel. *A Letter to the Rev. William E. Channing, on the Subject of His Letter to the Rev. Samuel E. Thatcher, Relating to the Review in the Panoplist of American Unitarianism.* Boston, 1815.

———. *A Second Letter to the Rev. William E. Channing, on the Subject of Unitarianism.* Boston: 1815.

Wright, Conrad. *The Beginnings of Unitarianism in America.* Boston: Starr King Press, 1955.

Ziff, Larzer. *Literary Democracy: The Declaration of Cultural Independence in America.* New York: Viking Press, 1981.

List of Illustrations

Titles are of works in oil by Washington Allston unless otherwise noted.

Color Plates

Figures

Photographic Credits

The Berkshire Museum, Pittsfield, Massachusetts: pl. V, fig. 13.

Boston University Libraries, Massachusetts: fig. 37.

The British Museum, London: figs. 14, 26, 31.

Carolina Art Association, Gibbes Art Gallery, Charleston, South Carolina, figs. 19–20.

The Corcoran Gallery of Art, Washington, D.C.: fig. 4.

Courtauld Institute of Art, London: fig. 23.

The Detroit Institute of Arts, Michigan: pl. I, fig. 1.

Dover Publications, New York: fig. 10.

Fogg Art Museum, Harvard University, Cambridge, Massachusetts: pl. VIII, figs. 28–29.

Frick Art Reference Library, New York: fig. 7.

The Huntington Library, San Marino, California: fig. 25.

Massachusetts Historical Society, Boston: fig. 21.

Mead Art Museum, Amherst College, Massachusetts: fig. 35.

Museum of Fine Arts, Boston, Massachusetts: pls. IV, VI, VII, figs. 3, 15, 24, 27.

National Gallery, London: fig. 9.

National Museum of American Art, Smithsonian Institution, Washington, D.C.: fig. 5.

National Park Service, Longfellow National Historic Site, Cambridge, Massachusetts: figs. 16–18.

The New York Public Library, New York: fig. 12.

Pennsylvania Academy of the Fine Arts, Philadelphia: figs. 22, 33.

The Pierpont Morgan Library, New York, N.Y.: figs. 6, 11.

Princeton University Library, New Jersey: figs. 30, 32, 38.

Wadsworth Atheneum, Hartford, Connecticut: figs. 2, 8, 39.

William A. Farnsworth Library and Art Museum, Rockland, Maine: pl. III, fig. 36.

Yale University Art Gallery, New Haven, Connecticut: pl. II, fig. 34.

Index

226